'This book is an excellent example of how our attitude towards food and drink has developed over the years in Ireland. It shines a light on the past as well as looking to the future, showcasing the ways we can, as a culture, move beyond sustenance and embrace our varied food and drink heritage on this island.'

– Dr JP McMahon,
Chef, writer and restaurateur

'I really enjoyed Brian's book on the development and constantly changing nature of the Irish food and drink sector, particularly the references to our local South Kildare cafés which in many cases have quickly become centre points in their communities, as well as providers of top class local produce.'

– Martin Heydon TD,
Minister of State at the Department of Agriculture, Food and the Marine

Beyond Sustenance

Reimagining Ireland

Volume 119

Edited by Dr Eamon Maher,
Technological University Dublin – Tallaght Campus

PETER LANG

Oxford • Bern • Berlin • Bruxelles • New York • Wien

Beyond Sustenance

An Exploration of Food and Drink Culture in Ireland

Brian J. Murphy

PETER LANG

Oxford • Bern • Berlin • Bruxelles • New York • Wien

Bibliographic information published by Die Deutsche Nationalbibliothek. Die Deutsche Nationalbibliothek lists this publication in the Deutsche Nationalbibliografie; detailed bibliographic data is available on the Internet at http://dnb.d-nb.de.

A catalogue record for this book is available from the British Library.

Library of Congress Cataloging-in-Publication Data

Names: Murphy, Brian J, 1967- author.
Title: Beyond sfooustenance : an exploration of food and drink culture in Ireland / Brian J Murphy.
Description: New York : Peter Lang, [2023] | Series: Reimagining Ireland,
   16629094 ; vol. 119 | Includes bibliographical references and index. |
Identifiers: LCCN 2022032209 (print) | LCCN 2022032210 (ebook) | ISBN
   9781800799561 (paperback) | ISBN 9781800799578 (ebook) | ISBN 9781800799585
   (epub)
Subjects: LCSH: Gastronomy--Ireland--History. | Food habits--Ireland. | Drinking
customs--Ireland. | Ireland--Social life and customs.
Classification: LCC TX641 .M87 2023 (print) | LCC TX641 (ebook) | DDC
641.01/3--dc23/eng/20220930
LC record available at https://lccn.loc.gov/2022032209
LC ebook record available at https://lccn.loc.gov/2022032210

Cover image designed by Brian J Murphy.
Cover design by Peter Lang Ltd.

ISSN 1662-9094
ISBN 978-1-80079-956-1 (print)
ISBN 978-1-80079-957-8 (ePDF)
ISBN 978-1-80079-958-5 (ePub)

© Peter Lang Group AG 2023

Published by Peter Lang Ltd, International Academic Publishers, Oxford, United Kingdom
oxford@peterlang.com, www.peterlang.com

Brian J. Murphy has asserted his right under the Copyright, Designs and Patents Act, 1988, to be identified as Author of this Work.

This publication has been peer reviewed.

Contents

Images

Preface

By Máirtín Mac Con Iomaire

The Irish language saying *is túisce deoch ná scéal*, literally meaning 'a drink precedes a story', incapsulates a number of long-standing Irish traditions and cultural practices. Visit any Irish home and the first act of the host is often to put on the kettle or more recently, to warm up the Nespresso machine or open a bottle of wine. Hospitality has been central to Irish culture for millennia and those who shirked their obligations to the stranger or the visitor faced potential mockery or vilification. This same age-old tradition of hospitality ensures that a ham sandwich, some cheese and crackers, or at least a plate of biscuits are soon provided to visitors so that people would not consider the tea alone 'too wet'! The Mrs Doyle character in *Father Ted* is the epitome of this phenomenon, albeit bringing it to its comic extreme.

Irish poets (*filí*) and bards were both highly respected and feared by Gaelic chieftains who would provide them with lavish feasts. The Brehon Laws outlined the various obligations of guests and hosts in Ancient Ireland. The *briugu* or hospitaler, the wealthy land and stock owners, were the legal representatives of the institution of hospitality, which may have been the means for a non-noble to advance socially. The late eleventh- / early twelfth-century Middle Irish tale *Aislinge Meic Con Glinne* tells of a young scholar who was inhospitably welcomed by the monks of Cork, and how he took revenge on their chief Abbot, Manchín, through satire. Within the Christian tradition, there was always the possibility that a stranger or visitor seeking lodgings or alms might be Our Lord. The poorest in society were often the most generous, as Sigerson Clifford noted in his poem / song *The Ballad of the Tinker's Wife*:

> The tree tied house of planter is colder than east wind;
>
> The hall door of the gombeen has no welcome for our kind;
>
> The farmstead of the grabber is as cold as a stone;

But the little homes of Kerry will give us half their own.

Hospitality was expected, but also implied reciprocity. The sharing of food and drink brings people closer, but also infers bonds of obligation. The sight of many 'dead men' or stale pints of Guinness at the end of the night at an Irish wedding confirms that we would still prefer to buy a round of drinks that we know may never be consumed, then be perceived as shirking our reciprocal responsibilities. One of the most powerful weapons in the armour of medieval Ireland was that of 'fasting to disdain' where the aggrieved party would sit down outside the house of those who caused the perceived slight and refuse food and drink publicly, thus drawing attention to the contentious matter. This tradition of hunger strikes has been adopted in the modern era by numerous groups ranging from Irish suffragettes, revolutionaries, political prisoners, victims of clerical child sex abuse and more recently, asylum seekers in direct provision.

This book by Dr Brian Murphy is aptly titled, as it clearly illustrates how the food and drink culture of Ireland goes far beyond mere sustenance. Food and drink are powerful signifiers of culture and class, and a person's choices reveal their views, beliefs, assumptions, prejudices, and personalities. Food, as noted by anthropologist Arjun Appadurai, is a 'highly condensed social fact'[1] while Michael Dietler, another anthropologist, considers alcohol 'as a special class of food with psychoactive effects'.[2] We eat and drink to celebrate special occasions; we often consider food and drink as a reward, and we turn to them at times, for comfort and relief, whether alone or in company. This has never been truer than during the seismic shift that has occurred in Irish society from a food and beverage perspective in the last half century. This is a time with which both the author and I are well-familiar, having both passed our own half centuries. Rural electrification was completed during this period. Dining out in restaurants moved from

---

1   Arjun Appadurai, 'Gastro‑politics in Hindu South Asia', *American Ethnologist*, 8 (3), p. 494. Available at: <https://doi.org/10.1525/ae.1981.8.3.02a00050> (Accessed 7 July 2022).

2   Michael Dietler, 'Feasting and fasting', in Timothy Insoll, ed., *Oxford Handbook on the Archaeology of Ritual and Religion* (Oxford: Oxford University Press, 2012), p. 181.

being an occasional treat for special occasions to a regular past-time. Wine was predominantly Liebfraumilch ordered by colour (Black Tower, Green Label, or Blue Nun), whereas today Irish citizens have become prolific imbibers of both New World and Old World wines, and more recently of organic, biodynamic and natural wines. The nature of how we shop, prepare food, cook, dine and transmit these cultural and social traditions to the next generations has also been radically transformed.

I recall hearing the retired Senator Joe O'Toole describe how his childhood experience working behind the counter in the family public house in the town of Dingle, in County Kerry, where he had been exposed to all shades of society had prepared him for a life in politics. This similarly holds true for the insight that Brian Murphy brings to this publication based on his own youthful exposure in his father's butcher's shop, followed by his experiences in luxury hotels, private catering companies, wine bars and his subsequent thirty-year grounding in food and beverage education. One of the true riches of this collection is the short personal introductions to each chapter, which work as a form of autoethnography to the benefit of contextualising the publication as a whole.

In the last thirty years particularly, there has been a dramatic transformation of Ireland's relationship with food and drink. We gradually entered the experience economy, where we stopped dining out and began enjoying 'meal experiences'. In the early years of the new millennium, Irish people began to spend more on food consumed outside of the home than within the home. Increased employment, in particular for women, led to a rise in convenient foods and home replacement meal kits. Pre-prepared sandwiches and wraps became a huge industry. Kebabs, sushi, Chinese and Indian takeaways began competing with the longer established Italian fish and chip shops.

The roots of change in Irish society stem back further still to a number of landmark decisions, be it Donogh O'Malley's speech announcing free universal secondary education in 1966, or Ireland's entry to the European Economic Community in 1973. These decisions, among others, meant that the young highly educated professionals who emigrated during the 1980s had very different prospects compared to their relations who may have emigrated in the 1950s. Many of these same young professionals returned

in the early 1990s with both increased self-confidence and the lived experience of continental and world cuisines, having worked abroad and
travelled more widely than any previous generation of Irish people. Sport
proved to be another significant factor in transforming the Irish psyche.
The success of the Irish soccer team in the European Championships in
1988 and in the World Cup in 1990 rekindled national pride and self-worth.
For many, it was the first time that they could proudly wave the tricolour
without sectarian connotations. This was psychologically liberating. All
these factors contributed to the phenomenon known as the 'Celtic Tiger'.
The signing of the Good Friday Agreement, and subsequent relative peace
on the island of Ireland for the last twenty-five years, was an unimaginable
dream at times during the height of the Troubles. Even in the current era
of Brexit, there is cross border 'all-island' cooperation taking place within
agriculture and tourism, and the whiskey industry. This is hugely positive.

In a world where the zeitgeist is all about local, regional, and traditional, we increasingly embrace what we have on our doorstep. We also
respect and celebrate the cultural nuances within the traditions of each
of the provinces or individual counties. This is in essence the '*terroir*' or
'campanilismo' that our European neighbours have long practiced. For far
too long, postcolonial shame had engendered inferiority about all things
Irish – including food and drink. Although we always exported much of
our food, we are exporting as well as consuming premium products now-
adays. We have learned to market them as such and to charge for them
accordingly. This book discusses the phenomenon of '*terroir*' and of 'third
place' and indeed 'fourth spaces' using a range of locations from butcher
shops and Irish pubs to whiskey distilleries, and in so doing, highlights the
importance of authenticity and of storytelling.

Drawing on the author's own rich vein of publications and those of
the rising generation of food and drink scholars, this book provides a thoroughly up-to-date and cutting-edge picture of Irish food and drink culture in the post-pandemic period. The key theme is local, but the depth
of the research is global. There are lessons drawn from distillers in France
and Scotland, from shoemakers in Puerto Rico, wine marketing boards in
Australia, but also the wisdom and further exploration of the concept of
Irish terroir, first developed by the late Tomás Clancy. The Traditional Irish

Butcher Shop chapter notes that 'to make use of a truly successful Fourth Space strategy, one must not be driven solely by the desire for monetary success. The true passion of the individual artisan operator must shine through.' These sentiments mirror and reinforce the keynote lecture given by Professor Finbarr Bradley at the 2022 Dublin Gastronomy Symposium, whose left-brain message was to follow one's passion and be authentic, and that financial success would be one of the outcomes of staying true to one's core beliefs.

There is a strong beverage studies slant to this book, which is not unexpected from a scholar who completed a beverage-based doctorate. The role of place and story, which underpinned Murphy's PhD, is also further developed. Many of the chapters originated in conference papers at either the Association of Franco-Irish Studies (AFIS) or the Dublin Gastronomy Symposium (DGS). They have all been thoroughly updated and are newly contextualised with the autoethnographic introductions. They are joined by new scholarship around the rise of coffee-shops and social gastronomy. Recent doctoral research by Tara McConnell has explored the social significance of 'Claret' in Ireland during the long eighteenth century. Further research on food and drink in Irish poetry and songs discusses punch, tea, toddy, *scailtín*, and negus – a hot drink of port, sugar, lemon and spice. History shows that the phenomenon of distilleries emerging 'phoenix-like' out of the ashes of a once prominent sector in Ireland is actually a modern-day renaissance. In 1823, Ireland had no less than eighty-six distilleries in operation. Up until recently, it has been dominated by a single player. Research on the history of whiskey and its antecedents by Fionnán O'Connor has led to innovation in the industry and to changes within European legislation. Postgraduate Masters and Doctoral studies in the beverage area in Ireland is gaining momentum, with Brian Murphy and colleagues in Technological University Dublin at its core. This fine publication will be a valuable resource for all such scholars and for students of Irish Studies in particular and general readers alike. Drink, as mentioned at the beginning of this Preface, often precedes a story. The story of food and drink culture in Ireland, however, is fully enriched by this collection which goes far beyond sustenance. Our ancestors were famous for *deoch an dorais*, the literal 'drink for the door' or the parting glass. My parting thought is to wish this book and its author the success it deserves, and to advise its readers to 'drink deep and be silent' and to savour each chapter's gentle nuances like an Irish pot-still whiskey or a high-end coffee experience. *Bain sult as!*

Acknowledgements

Over the course of this project's development, I have incurred debts to a great many individuals. Apart from those mentioned here, there are countless others who have listened patiently while I ran ideas by them and who helped steer my opinion on many of the issues mentioned in this book. The following people have had an important influence in terms of both contribution and encouragement: Dr Patricia Medcalf, Raymond Keaney, Paul Linehan and of course my ever-tolerant wife and proofreader Gráinne and our three children Lorcán, Seanán and Sadhbh. My relationship with my publisher, Peter Lang, has always been a congenial and productive one, thanks in no small part to the sterling efforts of Tony Mason (Senior Commissioning Editor). Special mention must also go to Dr Máirtín Mac Con Iomaire who kindly wrote the Preface to this work. As a powerhouse of gastronomic studies, Máirtín has always been encouraging and generous with his time. Finally, I would like to pay special thanks and tribute to Dr Eamon Maher, Director of the National Centre for Franco-Irish Studies and General Editor of the Reimagining Ireland book series. As a great many of his colleagues already know, Eamon's vast and impeccable academic record speaks for itself. However, I would like to thank him, in particular, for all he has done to encourage my own academic journey over the last fifteen years. Eamon has that very rare quality of quietly encouraging research enthusiasm and output among people who don't yet recognise that they have something of value to contribute to the academic community. On their behalf, and on mine, I say thank you for your unwavering support and encouragement down through the years.

Introduction

Food and drink have always been important in shaping how we engage with society. From the earliest of times, humans have gathered in social groups to cook, to eat and to drink. While it is true that the rules of social engagement vary from culture to culture, the fundamental premise remains the same: food and drink provide sustenance and stability. When it was plentiful, ancient humans stayed close to their food sources and when it became scarce, nomadic hunter gatherers moved on to seek out other reliable sources of supply. This book stems from a lifetime of personal engagement with food and drink. My father gave me my first food job, helping in the family butcher shop at an age so young that I can't quite remember when exactly I started. We lived over that shop for much of my early childhood. That place was core to my formative years. I spent many years working the counter on Saturdays, weekdays after school and for long spells during the summer months. People often talk about the concept of smell bringing back food memories. For me, the unique aroma of a butcher shop serves as my own Proustian madeleine. That blend of fresh meat, blood and sawdust is the most evocative. No matter where I am in the world, it always reminds me of home, of my family and, in particular, of my father. This upbringing shaped a career choice that would keep me close to food and drink all my life. Following a degree in Hotel Management, my initial work years were spent in the food and beverage sector and for the past thirty years I have been teaching in food and drink–related areas.

Food and drink are important to Ireland. According to Bord Bia, Irish food, drink and horticulture exports were valued at 13 billion euro in 2020. The agri-food sector accounts for 175,000 jobs and our food and drink products are sold to 180 markets worldwide.[3] It is the mercantile

---

3   Irish Food and Drink.com. Available at: <https://www.irishfoodanddrink.com/about-us/> (Accessed 1 September 2021).

nature of food and drink consumption and exchange that drives much of the world's economy. This has led to a considerable educational focus over the years on areas such as food science, food and drink services, the hospitality industry and more recently the sustainable aspects of food and drink. There are now a great many third-level courses devoted to the science or the management of food and drink and yet relatively few are focused on food and drink culture. The area of food studies scholarship is at an early stage in academia and in truth hasn't always been considered worthy of academic consideration. Historically, food and drink were more aligned to the satisfaction of the lower senses. Many well-known writers including Warren Belasco, Ken Albala and Máirtín Mac Con Iomaire have written extensively about the fact that food studies are only now gaining recognition as a valid area of academic interest. My own food and drink journey mimics that progression.

For much of my life, I was focused on the material aspects of the food and drink world, through the medium of hospitality and service. I had a clear sense of its tangibility and its ability to quench a thirst or sate a hunger. Having worked in a succession of hotels, wine bars, pubs and restaurants, I found myself drawn to the real sense of community that is quite unique to that industry. I enjoyed being part of that 'tribe'. When I moved into education, even then I was primarily invested in the mechanics of food and drink operations, the language of professional service, and the business of food and drink. This changed around fifteen years ago when I embarked on a PhD that would ultimately lead me to consider food and drink in different ways. This monograph reflects the new lens that opened for me around the cultural significance of food and drink, its role in social discourse and its relevance beyond pure sustenance. I began to see food and drink as an expression of gastronomic identity, a tool for commensal living and a semiotic medium. Many of the chapters reference the breadth of research that is now emerging in the food and drink studies area and demonstrate that food and drink can be viewed in ways that transcend traditional interpretations.

This work is a blend of revised material that has already been published and new writing, all of which have a food and drink focus. Two years ago I was approached by the editor of *Reimagining Ireland* who suggested that bringing them together in a single study would serve a worthwhile purpose and show how the area of food and drink studies has evolved in the last few decades. The organisation of the book reflects the idea that food and drink can be viewed through a variety of ever-decreasing conical lenses: from a national or international perspective to a regional or local view, and finally at an individual product level. The book is divided into four thematic areas. The first section explores ideas beyond the notion of food and drink as typically seen on our plate or in our glass. It looks at food and drink from an international viewpoint and asks why country of origin matters. It considers how food and drink can be viewed through a more cultural lens and how perceptions of both commodities have changed in Ireland recently. The second section zones in on the individual food and drink places that contribute to the broader perspective examined in the first section. Using the examples of the Irish Pub, the Irish butcher shop and the Irish distillery, it examines how and why certain food and beverage sites reflect and contribute to our nation's gastronomic identity. It also examines the place of beverage studies in academia and whether the area has progressed sufficiently to be considered a part of an Irish Studies agenda. The third part of the book narrows the focus further by turning its attention to the products that are consumed within some of the places identified in section two. Wine, whiskey and cognac are used as vehicles to examine how historical importance and place-anchored identity can influence how products are perceived and ways in which we can learn from that. The final section then turns the spotlight on contemporary food and drink culture by examining more recent gastronomic phenomena and how they are impacting on our relationship with food and drink. Using history as a backdrop, it explores the phenomenon of an emerging coffee culture and how social gastronomy has now become an essential part of our food scape.

The recent global pandemic has changed how many of us view both our external and our internal worlds. It is yet unclear as to how we will emerge from the crisis and the level of damage that will ultimately pertain in the sector. Food and drink have played a central role during the worst of the Covid crisis as we have been forced to retreat into ever-decreasing circles of place. We have changed how we engage with food and drink in so many ways. A new vernacular has emerged. We got used to being greeted at the door with the request to see a 'Covid pass' if we would like to dine or drink inside. We sat where we used to stand. Old men no longer congregated at rural bar counters and the prohibition on 'vertical drinking'[4] became the norm. 'Cocooning', a word often used pre-pandemic to reflect people's desire to eat and drink more at home, has changed its meaning beyond all recognition. We have reluctantly embraced other terms such as 'wet pubs' or the idea of having a 'meaningful Christmas'. Our food and drink places have also changed. Food trucks have broken through into the epicurean mainstream and nearly all restaurants 'pivoted' to offer takeaway home dining experiences. The sense of community that restaurants and bars bring to our lives has been foregrounded and the pandemic has dramatically emphasised the importance of such places. A report from Loughborough University, mentioned in a later chapter, explores the role of rural pubs in combating loneliness among our older generations.[5] As many of us moved through various forms of restriction, we increasingly relied on the injection of normality that a Deliveroo or Just Eats driver provided on a Friday or Saturday night as we attempted to recreate some semblance of a normal social life. The prospect of a virtual pint with a friend over Zoom is a poor substitute for meeting up physically for a drink. The idea of dark kitchens, where places of food preparation are no longer tied to physical restaurants, fills many gastronomy lovers with dread. In 2021 YouTube sensation Jimmy Donaldson launched the Mr Beast virtual burger restaurant brand. This franchise operates a delivery only service with no physical restaurant spaces of its own. Recent figures indicate that Mr Beast is now available in 600 locations throughout forty-five US States.[6]

Despite such dramatic changes, food and drink engagement has always been and will continue to be about places and products, and this book

---

4   Barry Egan, 'I can't see much vertical drinking before Christmas', *The Sunday Independent*, 15 August 2021, p. 11.

5   Thomas Thurnell-Read, 'Open arms: The role of pubs in tackling loneliness', Loughborough University. Available at: <https://hdl.handle.net/2134/13663715. vi> (Accessed 28 August 2021), p. 25.

6   Seren Morris, 'Mr Beast Burger locations—Where to get the dream burger', Newsweek.com, 27 April 2021. Available at: <https://www.newsweek.com/mrbe ast-burger-locationswhere-get-dream-burger-1586667> (Accessed 8 August 2021).

reflects this. Where our food comes from matters, but so too does where that food is consumed. The etymology of the word 'company' comes from the Latin term *companio*, meaning quite literally 'bread fellow ' from the Latin *com*, meaning 'with, together' and *panis*, 'bread'. The commensal experience of breaking bread with others in a place that dedicates itself to relaxation and convivial atmosphere is as important as the food we eat. Perhaps the Covid 19 crisis has reminded us that food and drink experiences are not just about the flavours on the plate or the liquid in the glass, which is precisely what this book seeks to illustrate.

The title of the book suggests that food and drink have more to offer than sustenance and an ability to sate or to quench. It suggests that foods and drinks are to do with places as well as products, stories as well as service and the vast array of related menus, recipes, cocktail lists and wines cards can be interpreted in many ways. Gastronomy refers to the art and science of good eating, and the topics and themes within this book consider the broader societal impact and cultural significance of food from that gastronomic perspective.

It is important to note that the ability to engage with food in this way has been the privilege of select groups in most cultures. Down through the centuries much of what we now term 'food and drink engagement' has driven an economic wedge through any notions of an egalitarian society. As societies become wealthy, they increase their interaction with certain foods and drinks. French cultural theorist Pierre Bourdieu examined the theme of class in his important opus, *Distinction*.[7] Bourdieu emphasised the relationship between cultural and social capital and the food and drinks that we consume. Food and drink play a crucial role in terms of our cultural identity, social history, food sovereignty and independence and these all form a key part of our gastronomic understanding. However, we must recognise that global food poverty has always been one of the world's most difficult problems to solve, and remains so: 'Today, the UN World Food Programme's live Hunger Map aggregates 957 million people across 93

7   Pierre Bourdieu, *Distinction: A Social Critique of the Judgements of Taste*, translated by Richard Niece (Abingdon, Oxon: Routledge Classics, 2010).

countries who do not have enough to eat.'[8] While this book endeavours to analyse the cultural impact of food and drink, it also recognises that for much of the world's population, and a great many people in our own country, food is only about sustenance and thoughts of cultural impacts are of little or no importance when a family can't put adequate food on the table.

Potential solutions to these problems are complex, and hunger and poverty are just two of the enormous global challenges that our world must deal with. They can be joined by global health problems caused by diet and indeed the existential climate change challenges that our planet now faces. There are a great many global attempts to address these challenges and food is at the heart of many of these efforts. The recent work of the Eat Lancet Commission is a case in point. It brought together a thirty-seven strong multidisciplinary team of internationally recognised scientific experts from sixteen countries to address the challenge presented by our global food system and the need for a healthy diet and a sustainable food production model. The commission culminated in a major report entitled *Our Food in the Anthropocene: Healthy Diets from Sustainable Food Systems*.[9] The recommendations in this report and others like it around the necessity for a more plant-based diet continue to reverberate among a food and drink community that is trying to strike a balance between food and drink production efficiencies and the environmental impacts of that production. The development and implementation of the UN Sustainability Development Goals is perhaps one of the most recognisable global efforts to solve our planet's many problems and according to Johan Rockström each of its ambitious seventeen goals can be interpreted through a food lens.[10] COP 27 in

8   Gernot Laganda, '2021 is going to be a bad year for world hunger', United Nations News. Available at: <https://www.un.org/en/food-systems-summit/news/2021-going-be-bad-year-world-hunger> (Accessed 6 September 2021).

9   Walter et al., 'Food in the anthropocene: The EAT–Lancet Commission on healthy diets from sustainable food systems', *The Lancet*, 393 (10170), 2019, pp. 447–492. Available at: <https://www.sciencedirect.com/science/article/pii/S0140673618317884> (Accessed 23 February 2022).

10   Johan Rockström is Executive Director of Stockholm Resilience Centre, and Chairman of the EAT Advisory Board. Together with Pavan Sukhdev, Founder

Glasgow,[11] the European Green Deal,[12] and Ireland's our own recently launched Climate Action Plan[13] and Food Vision 2030 Strategy[14] are all policy attempts to address the problems of sustainability and food again plays a crucial role in each. While this book recognises that food and drink solutions are integral to solving all these issues, they are not challenges addressed in this work. As can be seen in the chapter entitled 'Beverage Spaces in Strange Places', food and drink studies can be explored through many different academic lenses. Areas such as diet and health, or the politics of food production and sustainability are extensively covered in a great many other works. The role that Ireland's food and drink culture might play in such global challenges is certainly one that warrants exploration but also one that needs extensive interrogation beyond the scope of this current work.

This book also provides a business focus in that it endeavours to consider how ideas around place can be harnessed to help offer competitor advantage in some instances. The association between high quality epicurean fare and a sense of place-integrity is ubiquitous and yet it can prove difficult to express this, and to develop strategies that can promote it to

---

and CEO of Gist Advisory he presented a State of The Union style address. EAT Stockholm Food Forum, June 2016 where he outlined how food was integral to each of the UN's SDG goals. Available at: <https://www.youtube.com/watch?v=tah8 QlhQLeQ> (Accessed 13 February 2022).

11   The UK hosted the 26th UN Climate Change Conference of the Parties (COP26) in Glasgow on 31 October–13 November 2021. Available at: <https://ukcop26.org/> (Accessed 13 February 2022).

12   On the 11 December 2019 The European Commission announced the Europe would be the first carbon neutral content by 2015. Available at: <https://ec.europa. eu/info/strategy/priorities-2019-2024/european-green-deal_en> (Accessed 10 February 2022).

13   In the 2 November 2021 the government publish its Climate Action Plan 2021 which provides a detailed plan for taking decisive action to achieve a 51% reduction in overall greenhouse gas emissions by 2030 and setting us on a path to reach net-zero emissions by no later than 2050, as committed to in the Programme for Government and set out in the Climate Act 2021. Available at: <https://www.gov. ie/en/publication/6223e-climate-action-plan-2021/> (Accessed 1 February 2022).

14   *Food Vision 2030*. Available at: <https://www.gov.ie/en/publication/c73a3-food-vision-2030-a-world-leader-in-sustainable-food-systems/> (Accessed 1 February 2022).

a food audience. One concept that comes close is the French wine term *terroir*. The word is a loaded one in modern gastronomic parlance. Some believe it relates purely to the soil of a region, others incorporate into their definition factors such as micro-climate, vineyard aspect and production methods. The *Oxford Companion to Wine* describes it as 'the much-discussed term for the total natural environment of any viticultural site. No precise English equivalent exists for this quintessentially French term and concept'.[15] Although originally only associated with oenology, in more recent years the concept has moved from a narrow and predominantly scientific explanation to a broader, more cultural definition. This latter interpretation is now solidly ensconced in the rhetoric of gastronomy. Contemporary chefs often describe their culinary ethos as being *terroir*-driven. In Ireland, we have seen the emergence of renowned *terroir*-based restaurants such as Aniar in Galway. According to Demossier, the concept has 'more recently attracted the attentions of American anthropologists who have examined the validity of *terroir* as a social construction'.[16] One such author is Amy Trubek who insists that 'culture, in the form of a group's identity, traditions and heritage in relation to place, must also be part of the equation'.[17] As such, the essence of *terroir* is perhaps less tangible than our traditional understanding of place and presents a challenge when we are trying to communicate with millennial audiences. The current study addresses this challenge by introducing the concept of Fourth Space which is used at stages throughout the book to help understand how food and drink places communicate with their audiences.

The Fourth Space model originated from research that explored the importance of place and story in French wine culture and how it might

15   Jancis Robinson and Julia Harding (eds), *The Oxford Companion to Wine* (Oxford: Oxford University Press, 2015), p.737.
16   Marion Demossier, 'Beyond Terroir: Territorial construction, hegemonic discourses, and French wine culture', *Journal of Royal Anthropological Institute*, 17, 2011, p. 686.
17   Amy Trubek, *The Taste of Place: A Cultural Journey into Terroir* (Oakland: University of California Press, 2008), p. 91.

be used to bolster the identity of French products.[18] The model recognises that French gastronomy underpins a great deal of our food and drink engagement and suggests several defined traits that allow food and drink sites communicate their sense of *terroir*. Traditionally we have defined the home as our First Place, the working environment as our Second Place and places where we relax such as the café or the bar as Third Places. Indeed, authors such as Ray Oldenburg, Perry Share, Gwen Scarborough and others have been keen to identify Third Place attributes that can be found in various food and beverage incarnations like French Cafés, Irish Pubs and others. The discussions within the covers of this collection consider the separate but related idea of Fourth Space. The use of the term 'space' reflects the fact that the concept of place can also increasingly be viewed as virtual. The recent launch of the Metaverse is a case in point, and digitally native audiences may in future relate to the idea of place in very different ways. Fourth Spaces have Third Place attributes as described by Oldenburg and others, but they have many other qualities as the table below shows. The model is based on five key strands and allows us to look at a variety of different food and drink sites, be they places of entertainment, tourism centres or simply places of respite where we can engage in the commensal experience of eating and drinking.

---

18   Brian Murphy, *Changing Identities in a Homogenised World: The Role of Place and Story in Modern Perceptions of French Wine Culture* (PhD thesis, 2013). Institute of Technology Tallaght, Dublin, Ireland.

The Fourth Space Model

Strand 1	Strand 2	Strand 3	Strand 4	Strand 5
A Fourth space creates a gastronomic identity by:	A Fourth space provides a sense of place/ regionality by:	A Fourth Space exploits new technology by:	A Fourth Space attaches cultural economy by:	A Fourth Space leverages the past by:
Incorporating a third-place function	Emphasising place of origin/ regionality	Using technology to bridge the place and story gap	Providing authentic links to a product's culture	Emphasising the importance of past related place anchors
Conveying the story of place	Avoiding fauxthenticity	Facilitating elements of 'Tourism without Travel'	Conflating with other cultural activities	Becoming rooted in real stories
Acting as a cultural ambassador to tourists	Providing an educational medium/ enable decodification	Providing personal interactions before and after the touristic experience	Striving for cultural capital while avoiding exploitation	Considering the role of 'invented traditions'
Providing authentic people engagement	Allowing for a food and drink place link	Targeting millennial audiences		Exploiting host country links

The first strand, creating a gastronomic identity, not only includes the Third Place concept but also introduces ideas such as enhancing communication of the place story, acting as a cultural ambassador and providing for authentic people engagement. The second strand relates directly to a food and beverage site's sense of place that is created by an emphasis on regionality, a place education element and direct links between food, drink and place. Our third strand deals with the increasing role that technology plays in the lives of food and drink consumers while the fourth provides for a location's cultural economy by highlighting authentic links with a place or product's culture, conflating the food or drink activity with other cultural pursuits and considering the role of cultural capital. The final strand concerns the issue of legacy and emphasises the importance of history in helping a food or drink site communicate an integrity of somewhereness to modern audiences. Some of the cases explored in later chapters, the traditional butcher shop, the whiskey distillery and the independent café, suggest how food and beverage sites might be influenced by some or all these Fourth Space principles. The paradigm proposes ways to communicate a sense of place to increasingly technologically aware food and drink audiences. The key to this successful communication lies in the potential of our Fourth Space model to incorporate the less tangible elements of culture, history, family and story that act as synecdoche for all manner of authentic food products and regions.

Food and drink sites possess a cultural uniqueness that is sometimes not as visible as it should be to the gastronomy lover. Communicating this will become increasingly important, as food and drink production globally becomes ever more intensive, homogenised and frequently bereft of place-integrity. My argument is that food and drink places and products of the future will need to incorporate Fourth Space elements into their provision to make themselves more relevant to contemporary audiences. Such audiences are seeking more complex interactions when compared to the traditional food and drink user's needs. They seek experiential engagement, an overall sense of well-being and knowledge enhancement. They want to embrace a broader definition of *terroir* that moves beyond the physical product and allows the audience access to the true story of a place, its culture, its traditions and, most importantly, its people. The Fourth Space elements as described here suggest one way to explore how food and drink places and products interact with the people who consume and experience them. The exact specifics of how some or all these individual strands might be woven into a single entity depend on the type of food and drink place or product in question. The flexibility necessary for such as approach is clearly demonstrated in future chapters. The Fourth Space, as a single entity, is built on five different strands but, there are separate elements of the approach that might be segued into different gastronomic realities. Food and drink audience demands are changing and those products and places that don't at least consider elements beyond a physical understanding of product attributes may find themselves at a disadvantage in attracting consumers in this increasingly competitive and crowded marketplace.

The book therefore brings together several Irish food and drink themes and explores how they relate to our past, present and, sometimes even, future lives. While it is true that some of these themes have been explored by others, it offers new interpretations of ways to engage with the food and beverage studies area. The content of the work is in no way exhaustive, but the hope is that it acts as a focal point for academic discourse around the theme of food and drink culture in Ireland. It is clear from many of the chapters that there is already innovative food and drink studies research underway both in Ireland and further afield. This work will add to an existing canon that moves beyond sustenance into a deeper understanding of how the foods we eat and drinks we imbibe impact on our lives.

The book also reflects a lifetime of personal engagement with Irish food and drink. The chapter on Irish butcher shops is clearly a part of this but so too are others and many chapters are prefaced by a brief personal anecdote that helps contextualise the ideas presented within. The themes that are explored, while positioned in an academic context, also stem from real life. Rather than shy away from that fact, it is embraced and some of what is written can be considered autoethnographic. I mentioned earlier in this introduction that the progression of food and drink into the academic arena very much mimics my own career. In the same way the themes discussed reflect a lifetime lived within that career and the small anecdotal pieces dotted throughout the work demonstrate this.

PART I

Beyond the Plate, Beyond the Glass

CHAPTER I

From Country of Origin to Irish *Terroir*: A Positioning of Place

Tomás Clancy, now sadly deceased, was one of Ireland's great wine writers. I had the pleasure of meeting Tomás a number of times and he was always encouraging and supportive of any food and drink research projects he came across. I always admired his work because his weekly columns in the *Sunday Business Post Magazine* often moved beyond descriptive wine writing into a more historical and cultural discussion of the gastronomic world. Tomás also had a blog entitled *An Irish AC (Appellation Contrôlée) Proposal* where he argued that as a nation, Ireland needs to emphasise recognised regional difference in terms of our food and drink output. The term Irish *Terroir* in the title and content of this chapter reflects some of Tomás's ideas and there are references throughout the book to his work.

One of the key themes within this book is the concept of place. How we interpret and react to that concept is important. When we think about food and drink in our everyday lives, initial impressions and assumptions are often governed by Country of Origin at a national level. We hear phrases like 'I usually prefer a French wine', 'Italian food is my favourite' or 'Irish beef is best'. This chapter examines how the influence of a food or a drink's national identity is perceived in a world that has become increasingly globalised. As such, it plays a crucial role in how consumers form relationships with products. Later chapters deal with more specific interpretations of place but at a macro-level, consumers pay clear attention to Country of Origin (CoO) when they are choosing to consume a food or a drink item. It's also often one of the first determining factors in our purchase decisions, particularly when people are unsure in terms of their food and drink knowledge. Much has been written on the concept of CoO and the early part of this chapter explores how it can influence how products are perceived. There are other aspects of place that are specific to gastronomic products. These include issues such as history, authenticity, provenance and security. Later in the chapter their impact on place and its relationship, in particular, with wine, both in France and in the New World is examined. In the final part of the chapter the Irish consumer's relationship with place is explored. Using the example of beer, a beverage long associated with Ireland, the concept of Irish *terroir* is introduced. It is our relationship with this specifically Irish *terroir* that has the potential to assist in understanding our own cultural relationship with the food and drink products we consume.

It is generally understood, through empirical observations and experiment, that CoO has a considerable influence on the consumer's perception of any product's quality. Bilkey and Nes refer to an interesting case to illustrate this point.[19] They recount the story of a Puerto Rican shoe manufacturer and his efforts to make his shoes more attractive in the marketplace. They show how, having made his shoes in Puerto Rico, the shoemaker went to the trouble of sending the shoes to New York City and back. He would then advertise the shoes as having been imported from New York. Though the shoe quality hadn't changed, people's perception of that product had, because they were influenced by the country of origin. There are similar food examples much closer to home. In recent years substantial media debate has been devoted to the subject of Ireland's food labelling laws. There has been a lot of criticism regarding the lack of origin labelling on Irish meat products like chicken. Ireland imported 305 million euro worth of poultry in 2018[20] but retailers can sometimes be quite reluctant to identify the actual country of origin of their products. Confusion is often more pronounced when dealing with a product that has been processed in Ireland and therefore labelled 'made in Ireland'. A recent case that made the headlines concerned a processed chicken product that was labelled as

19   Warren Bilkey and Eric Nes, 'Country of origin effects on product evaluations', *Journal of International Business Studies*, Spring/Summer 1982, p. 89.

20   Central Statistics Office, 'Ireland trade in goods 2018'. Available at: <https://www.cso.ie/en/releasesandpublications/ep/p-ti/irelandstradeingoods2018/meatexportsandimports2018/> (Accessed 10 September 2021).

'Made in Wicklow'.[21] On further investigation it was discovered that the chicken in the product was not of Irish origin. Under EU labelling laws such cases are quite common. According to the Food Safety Authority of Ireland (FSAI), processed meat products fall under 'general labelling rules' and 'aren't required to give the origin of the meat within the final sliced product'.[22] Though perfectly safe, as with Bilkey and Nes's shoe example, it is the emotional response to the perceived country of origin that appears to be the determining factor in the client's decision to purchase.

Key authors who have emerged since the mid-1960s have attempted to put some shape on CoO theory. While an overall image of the country of origin construct has been slowly emerging, there will always be debate regarding CoO influence. One of the more influential articles on the topic refers to a study carried out by Akira Nagashima on Japanese and US attitudes towards foreign products.[23] Nagashima assessed how Japanese businessmen perceived products made in France and it is interesting to note that he suggested that French products were characterised by Japanese businessmen as exclusive, handmade and luxurious. When participants were asked to list the products that first come to mind when you see certain 'made in' names, wine invariably features in products associated with France. This confirms the depth of recognised association between wine and France among different cultures as far back as 1970. This perception was somewhat mirrored in a later study into Chinese wine consumption which highlighted that consumers in China also recognised France's intrinsic relationship with quality wine. The study established that Chinese consumers had little or no knowledge of wines coming from any other country.[24] In a separate study it was established that CoO is a very important factor when

---

21   Cónal Thomas, 'The Real Veal: Here's how to tell if your meat is Irish or not', *The Journal* [online]. Available at: <https://www.thejournal.ie/the-real-veal-heres-how-to-tell-if-your-meat-is-irish-or-not-4477943-Feb2019/> (Accessed 12 September 2021).

22   Ibid.

23   Akira Nagashima, 'A comparison of Japanese and U.S. attitudes towards foreign products', *Journal of Marketing*, 34, 1970, pp. 68–74.

24   Fang Liu and Jamie Murphy, 'A qualitative study of Chinese wine consumption and purchasing, implications for Australian wines', *International Journal of Wine Business Research*, 19 (2), 2007.

the Chinese consumer evaluates wine and can even prove more important than brand, particularly when choosing a wine for a gift or evaluating wine at special occasions.[25] These findings are further endorsed by Balestrini and Gamble in their study into the country of origin effects in China.[26] It is important to note here that China is of particular interest to the French wine sector when it comes to perceptions regarding place, as it is a country that is relatively new to wine consumption and presents enormous market potential in the future.

Consumer behaviour tends to be favourably influenced when the products being purchased come from a country that enjoys a favourable image. However, it is also true that country of origin effects can be negative and thus adversely affect a consumer's willingness to purchase. Following the publication of cartoon images of the prophet Mohammad in the Danish media, Danish products were actively removed from the shelves of Middle Eastern stores.[27] There are other examples of similar reactions. Francophobia is defined by Amine as a consistent hostility towards government, culture, history or peoples of France.[28] In 2003 nationwide boycotts of French cheese and wine occurred across the USA following France's refusal to back the US in the Iraq war.[29] The negative images associated with France as a country of origin even led to the decision by American congress to rename the 'French fries' sold in government cafeterias 'freedom fries'.[30] These rather extreme examples illustrate that Country of Origin is important to consumers in terms of their food and drink purchase decisions. Certain

25   Xiaoling Hu, Li Leeva, Charlene Xie and Jun Zhou, 'The effects of country of origin on Chinese consumers' wine purchasing behaviour', *Journal of Technology Management in China*, 3 (3), 2008, p. 302.
26   Pierre Balestrini and Paul Gamble, 'Country of origin effects on Chinese wine consumers', *British Food Journal*, 108 (6), 2006, p. 407.
27   Roth, K. P. and Diamantopoulos, 'Advancing the country image construct', *Journal of Business Research*, 62 (7), 2009, pp. 726–740.
28   Lyn Suzanne Amine, 'Country of origin animosity and consumer response: Marketing implications of anti-Americanism and Francophobia', *International Business Review*, 17, 2008, p. 402.
29   Gillian Drummond, 'New Yorkers shun French restaurants', *Caterer and Hotelkeeper*, 15 May 2003, p. 11.
30   *The New York Times*, 'Au revoir freedom fries', 4 August 2006, p. 16.

countries according to Amine have involved themselves in 'country image management' to combat negative CoO perceptions in global markets.[31] Amine offers the example of France as well as Turkey, India and Kazakhstan who, the author says, are all currently pursuing nation branding strategies. Much of the research, however, tends to focus on how the country of origin of individual products can be used by marketing strategists to develop appropriate plans that make these products attractive to consumers in different countries. In the late 1990s, Jaffe and Lampert suggested that many CoO studies carried out were to some degree static in assessing the effect on consumer's perceptions of a products origin.[32] They argued that we need to consider that Country of Origin image changes over time in relation to the product's particular life cycle: hence the CoO is a dynamic rather than a static construct. This, they suggest, has important implications for marketing strategies in the future. While the depth of CoO research available is generally impressive, clarity on the area is difficult to establish. Johansson refers to such empirical ambiguity when he quotes arguments for and against the influence of CoO regarding consumers' perceptions of the product.[33] He presents three arguments in the negative, illustrating the lack of importance that can be attached to CoO. Firstly, he says that as consumers get more information about product attributes, the importance of CoO lessens. Secondly, as products manufactured in countries display better quality overall, the differentiation presented due to CoO becomes less important. Finally, with the advent of the global village concept, national borders tend to become less and less important, thus reducing CoO influence. Johansson uses these arguments, and the fact that it is difficult to defend against them, as a platform from which to develop his own theoretical framework which he calls 'An Integrative Framework'. This model explains the Country of Origin process and centres on a consumer's propensity to use a 'made in' label. When the consumer's propensity to use such a label is high it is expected that the label can influence the customer

31   Amine, 'Country of origin animosity and consumer response', p. 418.
32   Eugene Jaffe and Schlomo Lampert, 'A dynamic approach to country of origin of effect', *European Journal of Marketing*, 32 (1/2), 1998, pp. 61–78.
33   J. Johnny Johansson, 'Determinants and effects of the use of made in labels', *International Marketing Review*, 6 (1), 1988, pp. 47–58.

in cognition terms either by inference or proxy, by affect, in establishing whether they like the country in question or to help determine the social acceptability of the country of origin through the made in label. Johansson's view is mirrored to some extent by Parameswaran and Pisharodi in that they insist that the potential for using country of origin image as a marketing tool is limited by a lack of understanding caused in part by 'variations in definition, conceptualisation of components and measurement'.[34] They suggest that as further research is carried out CoO image can begin to be viewed as a multifaceted construct. These facets can then be clearly interpreted and put to good use by marketing specialists. The authors stress that while there is some evidence that plays down the importance of the CoO construct, a product's country image can be a definite advantage in terms of enhanced sales. They cite Papadopoulos who posits that if the McDonald's brand name is worth millions, as is widely acknowledged, then what must Germany's brand image be worth?[35] They are keen to point out the importance of the CoO construct and its useful role for multinational marketers. They emphasise that one of the reasons many marketers don't use country of image constructs is that CoO is 'culture laden'. Many managers are not trained or comfortable dealing with cultural issues. In addition, the relationship between a brand and its CoO can be more distant than its relationship with the firm, store or advertising associated with it. It is important to note that when it comes to CoO and gastronomy, the relationship between the brand and the CoO is often very well defined and clear. A classic example of this would include the *Piat d'Or* wine brand which dominated UK wine sales in the 1980s and early 1990s. The *Les Français adorent le Piat d'Or* campaigns propelled it to that position through clever marketing that emphasised the wine as inherently French despite the typical French consumer's lack of interest in that same product. This confirms the view of Han and Terpstra who stressed in their findings that CoO stimuli

---

34   Ravi Parameswaran and Rammohan Pisharodi, 'Facets of country of origin image: An empirical assessment', *Journal of Advertising*, 23 (1), 1994, p. 43.
35   Ibid., p. 44.

were found to have more powerful effects than brand name when it came to consumer perceptions of quality.[36]

One problem with the consumer's attitude to French wine stems from the impression that it can be hard to understand. Difficult terminology and a general lack of clarity are often associated with French wine labels. Terms such as *Appellation Contrôlée, Grand Cru* and others, along with limited identification of grape varieties, can discourage unfamiliar customers. There can also be undertones of snobbery associated with understanding French wine and the caricature of the superior French sommelier is familiar to many. The New world has deliberately opted for an opposite marketing strategy. Wine Australia, the organisation responsible for promoting Australian wines, took a taste centric approach to selling their wine making it very accessible and understandable to the average customer. They presented buyers with upfront, fruit-driven, flavoursome drinks that subsequently led to an attractive image of Australia as a wine-producing country. A BBC four documentary identified Hazel Murphy as the woman charged with the task of promoting unknown, and in some cases ridiculed, Australian wine in the UK during the 1980s. In the programme she referred to that exact premise.[37] Her strategy was to move away from an emphasis on complicated geographical detail and to focus purely on the liquid in the glass. According to wine writer Robert Joseph, the way Hazel promoted Australian wine differed in that she encouraged winemakers to go out and physically pour the wine for the customers to taste. Over the space of less than a decade, Hazel Murphy and her team poured Australian wine for over 250,000 people in venues ranging from food and wine exhibitions to agricultural shows and sporting events.[38] Providing such ready access to wine tasting for the public was relatively rare in those days. According to

36   Min C. Han and Vern Terpstra, 'Country of origin effects from uni-national and bi-national products', *Journal of International Business Studies*,19 (2), 1987, pp. 235–255.

37   *Chateau Chunder: When Australian Wine Changed the World*, BBC4 Television (2012). Available at: <https://www.bbc.co.uk/programmes/po111zzq> (Accessed 15 March 2020).

38   Do I like It.com (2013). Available at: <http://www.doilikeit.com/about/who-are-we/> (Accessed 23 January 2013).

Joseph, the French, Italian and Spanish wine makers did not pour their wines, as they did not really trust their customers. Murphy achieved success by allowing consumers to experience the wine's taste despite their general lack of wine knowledge. Because the style of Australian wine was and is very much based on simple upfront varietal fruit flavours, once experienced, the wine proved appealing. Because it was recognised by Country of Origin rather than by a more specific region, the strategy of getting out there and pouring Australian wine led to the clear association between these newly emerged accessible fruit-driven wines and their place.

Paul Chao and Pola Gupta developed an interesting multiple cue notion which suggested that there are a variety of ways that CoO effects on consumer demand can be moderated.[39] Additional attributes such as warranties, store prestige, price and material contents of the product can be used to mitigate against the influence of CoO. This idea raises interesting questions in relation to food and wine culture. It suggests that the consumer's impressions of the CoO can be altered by other multiple cue factors. A consumer who believes French food and wine to be complex and difficult can change those beliefs through mitigation. Chao and Gupta used the example of a car warranty which doesn't apply in a food context but their approach may offer credence to the theory that positive food reviews, wine labelling regulation and recommendations can do a lot to influence consumer behaviour. Manske and Cordua reviewed ten months of wine sales in Houston, USA, exploring whether sommeliers can affect wine sales in a restaurant. They concluded that employing a wine steward had a very significant positive effect on increasing wine sales.[40] The influence of the sommelier within the service setting has a similar effect to that of the warranty and prestige referred to by Chao and Gupta. In a practical restaurant setting, the sommelier might encourage a customer to try a wine from a particular country despite the customer's initial negative opinion

---

39 Paul Chao and Pola Gupta, 'Information search and efficiency of consumer choices of new cars, country of origin effects', *International Marketing Review*, 12 (6), 1995, pp. 47–59.

40 Melissa Manske and Glenn Cordua, 'Understanding the sommelier effect', *International Journal of Contemporary Hospitality Management*, 17 (7), 2005, pp. 569–576.

of that CoO. Chaney carried out a comparative analysis of wine reviews and established that New Zealand wines received a lot of print coverage, much more so than their market share might merit.[41] This, Chaney suggests, encourages consumers to indulge in what she refers to as experimental or promiscuous purchases. Again, with reference to Chao's moderating factors of warranty and prestige, print inches and recommendations can have a similar moderating effect on consumers who might not like a wine's CoO. Bilkey and Nes also refer to what they term 'risk relievers'. These are greater perceived risks that might be associated with lesser developed countries regarding quality concerns.[42] They argue that 'risk relievers' might include guarantees by third parties, independent tests and a myriad of other factors and that these can reduce risk perceptions based around CoO.

Food and wine have a unique co-dependent gastronomic relationship. In many situations the choice of wine consumption is based on the choice of food consumption or vice-versa. Although similar circumstances arise with other product groups, it is particularly evident when linking wine and food together. One of the key cues used when matching appropriate wines to food revolves around CoO. There is a natural tendency for consumers to match, for example, French wines with French food, Italian wines with Italian foods and Spanish wines with Spanish food. Traditionally, German wines were considered quite difficult to match with food. For many years they had a reputation for being too sweet to form appropriate matches and sales suffered as a result. This reputation was largely driven by the proliferation of cheap branded medium sweet German offerings that dominated marketplaces in the 1980s. More recently, there has been a better understanding of how many dry and off dry German wines suit certain foods. Fielden suggests that, historically, German wine was meant as a social drink not usually taken with food.[43] This led to Germans producing a drier product since the 1980s to specifically target the food/wine

---

41   Isabella M. Chaney, 'A comparative analysis of wine reviews', *British Food Journal*, 102 (7), 2000, pp. 472–480.

42   Warren Bilkey and Eric Nes, 'Country of origin effects on product evaluations', *Journal of International Business Studies*, Spring/Summer 1982, p. 93.

43   Christopher Fielden, *Exploring the World of Wines and Spirits* (London: Wine and Spirit Education Trust 2005), p. 85.

market. It could be argued that, in the Irish and UK market, part of the reason why New World wines have thrived over the last decade is exactly because these countries are not associated with the cuisine of any one place and offer a plurality of culinary influences.

French food and wine are agricultural products and are in many ways similar to other agricultural outputs but it is the influence of the *Appellation d'Origine Contrôlée* (AOC) system that makes them unique. In 2010, because of EU reforms introduced in 2008, this term was superseded by *Appellation d'Origine Protégée* (AOP) but many continue to use the term AOC.[44] If a food or a wine has been awarded an AOC/AOP, then it will have undergone certain rigorous tests. Every *appellation contrôlée* area in France is regulated by the government body known as the *Institut national de l'origine et de la qualité* (INAO). To achieve AOC/AOP status, food and drink producers must adhere to certain rules and regulations as determined by a designated *Cahier de Charges*. These govern such things as grape varieties permitted, location of production etc. Demossier suggests that the 'AOC system helped fix the mythical image of an historical *terroir* producing a wine with a taste unchanged since time immemorial.'[45] Implementation of the AOC/AOP system, therefore, suggests that a food or wine from one defined area or AOC/AOP with entitlement to one classification is a very different product, often with a different target market, to a food or wine from another classification. Because of strict regulations, these gastronomic products may be perceived as reflecting, through taste, the different *terroir* they are associated with. Amy Trubek offers us a good example of this when she quotes James Wilson in her book *The Taste of Place*. Wilson used champagne as an example to illustrate the influence of *terroir*:

> In his discussion of champagne and the region where this sparkling wine is made, he argues that the presence of chalk in the soil is what makes French champagne distinctive. Describing the taste of *terroir* you experience when you sip Dom Pérignon,

---

44   Jancis Robinson and Julia Harding, *The Oxford Companion to Wine* (Oxford: Oxford University Press, 2015), p. 28.

45   Demossier, 'Beyond Terroir', p. 690.

he writes 'Somehow, the chalk of Champagne soils imparts an *élan* to 'true' champagne that is not duplicated elsewhere in the world'[46]

The *élan* referred to by Wilson is an esoteric description of a quality inherent in true champagne that links this sparkling wine to its regional place. Whether such a quality is detectable is to some degree a moot point. Wilson and other connoisseurs are of the belief that it does and for them a true reflection of *terroir* is evident in the taste of Dom Pérignon.

The influence of AOC/AOP is a very important consideration when we are dealing with how a food or a wine relates to its place. Two products can be very different in terms of quality and indeed price. This difference may impact on how marketing approaches can be developed for these individual products. Felzenstein, Hibbert and Vong suggest that if geographic origin offers a quality differentiation, then the producer has an attribute to his/her product that can't be readily replicated.[47] The unique quality that is imparted by the influence of *terroir* and then verified by the awarding of AOC/AOP status is one of the things that differentiates French food and drink from other agri-products. It should be noted that the definition of *terroir* has been expanding in recent years and scholars like Trubek have suggested that culture must also play a part. Other chapters in this book will explore these broader definitions of *terroir* in this regard and attempt to consider ways in which such broader definitions might be communicated to audiences.

Irish people have a unique relationship with place and identity. Forged over many years, our history dictates that as a nation we have a strong affinity with the land. Perhaps the origins of such feelings lie in our colonial past, the dominance of agriculture in our economic make up or the poverty, death and destruction of the famine. Whatever the origin, we have arrived at a situation where land and property have become national obsessions. References to links with place in Ireland's cultural heritage have also always

46   Amy Trubek, *The Taste of Place: A Cultural Journey into Terroir* (London: University of California Press, 2008), pp. 67–68.

47   Christian Felzensztein, Sally Hubbert and Gertrude Vong, 'Is the country of origin the fifth element in the marketing mix of import wine? A critical review of the literature', *Journal of Food Products Marketing*, 10, 2004, p. 73.

methods. There has been a long held urban myth that Guinness is in fact made with water from the iconic River Liffey and that this is what makes Dublin Guinness taste so good. Though untrue it nonetheless furthers the argument that Guinness stout has a perceived *terroir*-based heritage.

> Even Queen Elisabeth and Prince Philip seemed to be taken by the Guinness myth-
> ology during their historic visit in June. The prince asked a question that is on the
> lips of tens of thousands of visitors 'Is it made from Liffey water?'[54]

Though not strictly regulated as with the AOC/AOP system in France, one might reasonably suggest that stout reflects its place and hence aspects of *terroir* apply. Place-allegiances associated with regional food and wine culture are also evident in the Irish stout market. Ireland has three main brands of stout: Guinness, Murphy's and Beamish and their production and consumption can be viewed along territorial lines. Murphy's and Beamish are produced and consumed in the southwest of the country, whereas Guinness is perceived by many as a Dublin/East Coast beverage. These types of territorial divisions are much more obvious in French gastronomic culture where populations are usually loyal to local foods and wines from their home regions.

An interesting example of the importance of place emerged from the 2008 announcement of the closure of the historic Beamish and Crawford Brewery in Cork, Ireland and the upset that accompanied the announce-ment. Beer had been brewed on the site by Beamish since 1792. At the time, the very survival of the stout, once its production had been moved from its historic place, was called into question; especially since a rival Cork brand Murphy's was already being brewed at the new site. It appears that the decision to move production of Beamish from its original historical site to the larger Murphy's Brewery in Cork, in fact, did little to damage its sales[55] but it remains to be seen whether the decision to close the historical

---

54   Kim Bielenberg, 'Guinness is good for tourism', *The Irish Independent*, 17 December
       2011. Available at: <http://www.independent.ie/lifestyle/guinness-is-good-for-
       tourism-2966533.html> (Accessed 23 January 2015).

55   Niamh Hennessy, 'Beamish acquisition boosts sales for Heineken Ireland', *The Irish
       Examiner*, 27 August 2009 [online]. Available at: <https://www.irishexaminer.
       com/business/arid-20099528.html> (Accessed 7 December 2015).

site impacts on national and international sales in the long term. Given that the product continues to be brewed in the Cork area, the breaking of the association between product and its historical place is unlikely to prove detrimental. The 2012 decision by Heineken Ireland to incorporate a brewery museum into the redevelopment of the Beamish brewery site[56] offers further indication of how important the brewery location is to the product's sense of place.

A second illustration of the importance of Irish *Terroir* in recent times was the, now abandoned, 2008 proposal to move Guinness production at the original and historic St James's Gate site on the Dublin quays and to establish a modern plant nearby. This decision was eventually over-turned due to the demise of Ireland's property market during the Celtic Tiger crash. According to Ciarán Hancock in an interview with then Diageo Chief Executive Pat Walsh:

> The cornerstone of that investment was the release of capital from surplus land at St James's Gate, which was ripe for development in inner city Dublin during the property bubble. 'We were prepared to reinvest that money in the fabric of the business' Walsh says. 'With the recession, those land prices evaporated. So, the whole raison d'être just dissolved and we had to retrench and see what's next.'[57]

One might speculate that Diageo recognised that the product-place connection with St James Gate was so strong that a full move away would ultimately damage product image and hence the market. In fact, this relationship between product and place even appears to have influenced the original 2008 choice for the location of Diageo's proposed new brewery. According to Hancock, Diageo was believed to have chosen Leixlip as the site for its newly proposed 550 million euro plant because of its historical links with the Guinness family. Both examples illustrate the important

56   Louise Roseingrave, 'Beamish Cork site plan gets €150m go-ahead', *Irish Times*, 6 January 2012 [online]. Available at: <http://www.irishtimes.com/> (Accessed 10 January 2015).

57   Ciaran Hancock, 'Diageo names Leixlip as site of new Guinness Brewery', *Irish Times*, 11 September 2008 [online]. Available at: <https://www.irishtimes.com/news/diageo-names-leixlip-as-site-of-new-guinness-brewery-> (Accessed 8 December 2020).

association between product and place and these relationships can prove very important in an Irish context where history, tradition and provenance offer key foundations in developing and maintaining beverage market share.

Conclusion

In attempting to come to an understanding of the importance of place in food and drink culture it has become clear that the term is multifaceted. It means so much more than simply where a food or a drink comes from. Once deciphered, a product's place has the potential to tell a story on two levels. Sometimes that story is obvious and can be communicated through visible cues such as packaging and labelling. More often this story is told subliminally through the communication of information regarding *terroir* and the influence of AOC/AOP. There is considerable academic research on how influential Country of Origin (CoO) can be. A food or wine's national identity is very important and people's perception of gastronomic culture is complex. Authors offer different opinions about the varying levels of influence that the CoO construct can wield. Many note that it is but one of several cues that customers use to determine how attractive a product might be. As we have seen, the influence of CoO can also be mitigated by other attributes such as restaurant reviews, scores, success at recognised competitions and even wine steward recommendations. It is reasonable to conclude that where a food or wine comes from has a considerable effect on consumer behaviour and must be of primary concern to anyone who wants to influence how gastronomic products are perceived. The concept of place is important for many different products that depend on aspects of identity to make them attractive to potential consumers. Based on the examples used throughout this chapter, it seems reasonable to contend that products can also have a very different relationship with place because of other inherent qualities. Understanding the importance of vintage, the regional food-wine relationship or the complexities involved in getting the place message across to consumers is crucial if we are to move to a fuller interpretation of the place concept. The important influence of systems like AOC/AOP and their relationship with *terroir* is fundamental. The unique concept of Irish *Terroir* helps illustrate the cultural affinity that the Irish traditionally have with place and important place-based relationships already exist in Ireland with beverage categories such as stout. When a product's identity is so clearly aligned to place, opportunities emerge within the food and drink sector and thus there are advantages to be gained by marking products out as distinct and anchored to defined regions in an increasingly international foodscape.

CHAPTER 2

A Hundred Thousand Welcomes: Food and Drink as Cultural Signifiers

In September 1998, after ten years working in London, my wife and I packed up our bags into a battered old Mazda 323 and returned to Ireland. The next seven years were an exciting period in terms of Ireland's food and drink scene and there was a real sense of change in the air. However, I, along with many others, also felt something was changing in terms of how we related to food and drink and our attitudes to the people who worked in the sector. These changes were well-reflected in the article mentioned below by Kathy Sheridan and I can remember that it caused quite a considerable stir at the time.

This chapter revolves around a very particular period in Ireland's gastronomic history. It explores the lead up to and subsequent consequences of the Celtic Tiger economic crash. It suggests that while the affluence experienced throughout the period in question led to the development of a gastronomic cultural field in Ireland, it was accompanied by a commensurate decline in our appreciation of hospitality and food and drink service.

Food and drink have always been important in Ireland. We have a worldwide reputation for the quality of our meat and dairy produce, and Ireland is synonymous with a wide range of iconic products such as whiskey and smoked salmon. Eugene O' Brien argues that a commodity such as Guinness even acts 'as a synecdoche of Ireland and has taken on a fetishistic association with the country'.[58] In addition to these associations, food and drink has also been historically associated with hospitality in Ireland.

---

58 Eugene O'Brien, 'Kicking Bishop Brennan Up the Arse': Negotiating Text and Contexts in Contemporary Irish Studies (Oxford: Peter Lang, 2009), p. 163.

This art of hospitality was considered to hold such esteem in early medieval times that the title of *Hospitaller* or *Briugu* was bestowed on wealthy men who had the ability to provide generous hospitality to their guests. According to Molloy, 'a chief *briugu* had similar status to a minor king or a chief poet'.[59] In more recent decades visitors from abroad have always noted Ireland as a place where the Irish welcome could be guaranteed. So successful was this association that we exported the culture of that *Céad Míle Fáilte* (a hundred thousand welcomes) across the world. People from Ireland were commonly believed to possess an inherent trait for true hospitality and service. Because of this, the Irish have flourished in all aspects of the hospitality and tourism industry internationally.

During the Celtic Tiger years, both Ireland's gastronomic culture and the story of Irish hospitality changed dramatically. Our distinctive service culture began to decline and Ireland was no longer perceived as the land of a hundred thousand welcomes. Over the same period attitudes to food and wine changed. This chapter argues that Ireland was revolutionised in culinary terms during the Celtic Tiger years and has, in fact, developed its own version of a gastronomic cultural field. However, these dramatic culinary changes also contributed to the denigration of Ireland's once strong reputation for hospitality.

In the 1970s and early 1980s, for many Irish people, eating outside the home in a formal dining environment was often reserved for very special occasions. Many of these occasions revolved around religious ceremonies such as communions, family meals in the local hotel, weddings, or funerals. Independent fine dining restaurants were relatively rare and often the preserve of the wealthier in society. Research by Máirtín Mac Con Iomaire confirms this view in an interview with Patrick Guilbaud, when he suggests that in 1980s Ireland eating out involved two extremes, fast food and fine dining, depending on whether one belonged to the wealthy minority or the poorer majority.

> In Ireland in the 80s going out to eat was very expensive, so the concept of going out to eat cheap food in a restaurant, people didn't know. Either you had a bit of money,

59   Cian Molloy, *The Story of the Irish Pub: An Intoxicating History of the Licensed Trade in Ireland* (Dublin: Liffey Press, 2002), p. 14.

and you went anywhere, or you had no money and didn't go anywhere. It was either McDonalds or Guilbauds.[60]

People were sometimes nervous of high-end hotels and haute cuisine restaurants, and the air of overt superiority they often sensed among the clientele and staff. Many of these restaurants were often considered out of the financial reach of many Irish people and the preserve of the well-to-do, perhaps a throwback to much earlier decades when a servile attitude prevailed among Ireland's working classes in deference to their aristocratic landlords. Dishes and food items now common in the middle-class lexicon were absent. For the majority, it was a time when coffee came from a jar as opposed to an espresso machine. Plates of food were considered good value if piled high. Service was considered good if extra portions were offered. The desire for a 'good feed' often surpassed the desire for a quality dining experience. Terms such as 'Nouvelle Cuisine' and 'Gastropub' had not yet arrived on our shores. In that same interview with well-known restaurateur Patrick Guilbaud, it was suggested that even the range of foods available in the main Dublin food markets was very limited at that time and consisted of only the most basic of ingredients.[61] As an Island nation, with little access to expensive air transport, foreign travel was rare among the masses, and exposure to the food and drink of foreign cultures even rarer. The image of the pre- celebrity era chef at the time was for the most part rooted in working class Ireland, a career associated with unsocial hours and difficult hot conditions, working a range of early morning, late and split shifts. As a society our perceptions of food were based more on physiological requirements rather than the social needs that would later become more prominent.

In the 1980s things began to change and we had the emergence of more modern purpose-built restaurants targeting the masses. Restaurants appeared on the Dublin scene such as Flanagan's, Gallagher's, Blake's of Stillorgan and later Roly's Bistro. These restaurants offered a more casual

60   Máirtín Mac Con Iomaire, *The Emergence, Development and Influence of French Haute Cuisine on Public Dining in Dublin Restaurants 1900–2000: An Oral History* (PhD thesis, Dublin Institute of Technology, 2009), p. 599.
61   Ibid., p. 598.

dining experience, one that greatly appealed to the clientele at the time. According to staff who worked in Blake's during this period, popular dishes of the day included Corn on the Cob, Egg Mayonnaise, Mixed Grills and Steaks with Banana splits or Black Forest Gateaux for dessert, all washed down with wines such as Black Tower, Piat d'Or or Mateus Rosé.[62] Eating out for purely social enjoyment was becoming more commonplace among middle-class Ireland, and attitudes to hospitality were changing. Ireland's food and drink culture was developing, and a conversation was emerging around food and wine both at home and in the media that would reflect the economic progress that was about to occur as Ireland moved from recession into the early Celtic Tiger years.

It is difficult to imagine now but there was a time when terms such as 'Barista', 'Americano' and 'Espresso' were unfamiliar. Dining terms such as 'early bird' and 'pre-theatre menus', 'first and second sittings', 'tasting menus', 'amuse bouche' and 'pre-starters' all became familiar during the Celtic Tiger period. Complex culinary terms and cooking methods that used to be the preserve of the professional chef or the elite diner were more widely understood. Depending on one's point of view, knowledge of this lexicon could be perceived as either pomposity or a sign of superior social status only afforded to those who were privy to the French menu descriptors that adorned the *à la carte* menus of the time. The development of a gastronomic cultural field during this period changed all that. For the first time the culinary terms and skills of the professional chef became democratised. Reality TV brought us behind the kitchen door and introduced us to the language of the professional where terms such as 'sous-chef', 'covers', 'chef de partie', 'sommelier', 'the pass' and others came into common usage. Frequent violent outbursts from celebrity chefs such as Gordon Ramsay on TV caught the public's imagination and encouraged further awareness of all things culinary. Up until now such language was kept hidden from the public. At the other end of the spectrum, we have had the rise in popularity of media cooks like Nigella Lawson who were chastised regularly for their choice of food language and accusations of the near sexualisation of the

---

62   Órla Fanthom, Phone Interview carried out by author with former employee of Blake's Restaurant 1982–1885, 6 March, 2012.

food world abounded with new terms such as 'gastroporn' coming to the fore. We had the emergence of open kitchens where diners could watch and listen to staff interact. Several high-end restaurants have subsequently taken this concept to new levels by placing a private customer table inside the kitchen so that willing diners can now experience the sounds, smells and techniques of the professionals up close while enjoying their meal experience. Michelin-starred restaurant Chapter One in Dublin introduced such a Chef's Table in 2009.[63] Its chef/owner Ross Lewis said in a radio interview at the time that customers who booked the Chef's Table often expressed surprise that the language and communication evident in the kitchen during service did not reflect the angry confrontational environment they were expecting.[64]

As Ireland's food and wine culture developed, dramatic changes also took place across the hospitality industry. The number of hotel rooms in Ireland rocketed from 26,400 in 1996 to 45,700 in 2005.[65] There were commensurate increases in employment opportunities in the hospitality and tourism sector. According to the *CERT Employment Survey 2000 in* 1996, there were 144,143 people employed in Ireland across the Hotel, Guesthouse, Restaurant and Licensed Premises sector; this rose to 184,140 in 2000.[66] A later more comprehensive Fáilte Ireland survey concluded that when the entire sector was considered, by 2005, 245,959 people were employed.[67] As the sector burgeoned, Ireland was rapidly coming of age in gastronomic terms. As we became more affluent, eating and drinking

63   Chapteronerestaurant.com. Available at: <http://www.chapteronerestaurant. com/chefstable.html> (Accessed 26 August 2021).

64   Ross Lewis, *CountryWide* RTÉ Radio interview [online] 2012. Available at: <http://www.rte.ie/radio1/podcast/podcast_countrywide.xml> (Accessed 4 October 2012).

65   Peter Bacon, 'Over-capacity in the Irish hotel industry and required elements of a recovery programme' (Peter Bacon and Associates, Wexford, 2009), p. 11.

66   CHL Consulting, *CERT Employment Survey of the Tourism Industry in Ireland 2000* (Dublin: CERT Limited, 2000), p. 6.

67   Fáilte Ireland, 'Tourism facts 2005', [online], p. 1. Available at: <http://www.failte ireland.ie/FailteIreland/media/WebsiteStructure/Documents/3_Research_Insig hts/3_General_SurveysReports/TourismIreland2005.pdf?ext=.pdf> (Accessed 28 September 2012).

outside the home became more common and we developed a newfound culinary confidence. We began to consider ourselves more sophisticated in our attitudes to hospitality and service. Along with our desire to accumulate economic capital during this period, a similar desire to accumulate social and cultural capital began to emerge and attitudes to those involved in the hospitality service sector changed. Our authentic Irish welcome started to come under serious threat.

Pierre Bourdieu emphasises the importance of different types of capital in his 1986 essay 'The Forms of Capital'. He believed that along with the more obvious desire for economic capital we should note that other forms of capital are every bit as necessary to account for the structure and functioning of society.[68] It is these Bourdieuian concepts of cultural and social capital that can be useful when we examine how food and drink can be viewed as cultural signifiers during the Celtic Tiger era. Of course, we cannot ignore economic capital and it is important to note that our food and drink culture has and always will be inextricably linked to economics in that it operates in the public sphere exclusively as a business. Restaurants, hotels, bars and wine stores all exist for profit. In fact, Peillon[69] discusses the tensions that exist between culture and economic capital in Ireland and suggests that the inimical relationship between the two is not something new in this country. He cites Hutchinson and Kane, both of whom suggest that in various spheres of 1970s Ireland, culture was seen to in some way impede economic progress. But it is Bourdieu who explains that both cultural and social capital also have the potential to be converted into money, even though this conversion is not as immediate as it is with economic capital. It could be argued that the gastronomic field is one most suited to analysis through this Bourdieuian lens of cultural and social capital.

A business lunch in a Michelin-starred restaurant can provide a useful example. Exposure to fine dining etiquette and using appropriate social

---

68   Pierre Bourdieu, 'The forms of capital', in J. Richardson (ed.), *Handbook of Theory and Research for the Sociology of Education* (New York: Greenwood Press, 1986), p. 242.

69   Michel Peillon, 'Culture, and state in Ireland's new economy' in Peadar Kirby, Luke Gibbons and Michael Cronin (eds), *Reinventing Ireland, Culture Society and the Global Economy* (London: Pluto Press, 2002), pp. 40–41.

norms while eating out is one of the key skills necessary to be achieve acceptance in such a situation. The required skills can be achieved in several ways. For some groups, such skills are acquired at home, while growing up, if a certain etiquette is observed. Alternatively, assuming appropriate access to resources, such social etiquette can be learned as adults over time due to frequent exposure to similar restaurant situations. In some instances, it may even be necessary for employers to formally train their staff in such skills, if such up-skilling is appropriate in their role. These skills might be described as a form of Bourdieu's cultural capital and although they do not directly convert into money, they have the potential to do so by helping to cement business and social relationships. During the Celtic Tiger period a gastronomic transformation took place among much of Irish society. In a relatively short period of time, they went from eating in the local pub, to brunches, lunches and dinners in up-market restaurants, wine bars and hotels. A gastronomic cultural field developed and with it emerged the necessity to accumulate cultural capital. A variety of factors encouraged the development of this field and the consequent requirement for people involved in that field to enhance their own cultural capital. Improved financial stability played a part but there were other things such as an increased exposure to gastronomy through cheaper travel with the arrival of budget carriers such as Ryan Air. The huge influx of a returning diaspora during the period also played a part. Another important factor involved the relatively new exposure to all things culinary in the media. TV programmes emerged, initially in the UK and then on terrestrial TV in Ireland, which extolled the skills and personalities of celebrity chefs. A range of magazines such as *Food and Wine* and *Wine Ireland* became popular. Newspapers began including extensive weekend supplements on food and wine, which provided information on current happenings in the gastronomic world. Farmers' markets, slow food and organic movements began to take hold. The number of restaurants awarded the prestigious Michelin star increased from just two in the early 1990s to a high of nine in 1998 with Ireland achieving two 2-star restaurants for the first time between 2001 and 2005. These indicators all pointed to the emergence of an Irish gastronomic cultural field and a newfound emphasis on cultural and social capital.

Priscilla Parkhurst Ferguson[70] uses Bourdieuian field theory to argue
that gastronomy first became a cultural field in nineteenth-century France
and although Ferguson later argues the uniqueness of France in this regard
it can be posited that Celtic Tiger Ireland, in some ways, mirrored this
development between the early 1990s and the present day. In her chapter
Parkhurst-Ferguson introduces five key structural factors that signalled
the transformation of gastronomy into a gastronomic field in nineteenth-
century France.[71] Celtic Tiger Ireland reflects many of these factors and
therefore constitutes its own, admittedly limited, version of a gastronomic
cultural field. Firstly, she suggested that in France at the time 'new social
and cultural conditions stimulated production, sustained broad social par-
ticipation and encouraged a general cultural enthusiasm for the product in
question'. Here in Ireland the increase in personal disposable income along
with the returning diaspora and increased foreign travel from the mid-1990s
until the end of the Celtic Tiger period led to the new social and cultural
conditions necessary for our version of a gastronomic field to emerge.
Parkhurst-Ferguson goes on to note that 'specific sites become dedicated
to cultural production and consumption'. By comparison, Ireland had the
increased popularity of various Irish institutions that became the focus of
gastronomic production and consumption. Examples included destination
fine dining restaurants, private cookery schools such as Ballymaloe House
and even new high-level culinary courses up to and including master's
degree levels in third-level colleges. Thirdly, Parkhurst-Ferguson suggests
that 'the institution of standards and models of authority ensure an acute
critical consciousness that focused and checked, yet also legitimated the
expression of cultural excitement'. In Ireland we had the introduction and
enforcement of various rules and regulations governing how our restaurants operate as well as awarding bodies and guides that allowed the food
and drink industry to become legitimised and standardised. At the same
time, particularly in the case of Michelin, a fervour was created around
the awarding of certain accolades. The author also suggested that 'subfields

70   Pricilla Parkhurst-Ferguson, 'A cultural field in the making: Gastronomy in 19th
     Century France', in Lawrence Schehr and Alan Weiss (eds), *French Food on the
     Table, on the Page and in French Culture* (New York: Routledge, 2001), pp. 5–45.
71   Ibid., p. 9.

generated by the continued expansion of the field assured the simultaneous concord and conflict of the parties involved'. One could argue that gastronomic subfields in the form of the previously mentioned farmers markets, artisan producer organisations, organic and slow food movements developed in Ireland and contributed to the continuing development of a cultural field. Finally, Parkhurst-Ferguson says that in nineteenth-century France 'networks of individuals and institutions forged links with adjacent fields and it is these links that are largely responsible for the social prestige of gastronomy'.[72] This final factor is particularly evident in Ireland more recently with strong links developing between gastronomy and other legitimate fields such a history, literature, health and even art through the development of disciplines such as food photography, food and wine journalism, and gastronomy-themed theatre.

If we accept that Celtic Tiger Ireland did contribute to the development of its own version of a gastronomic cultural field, how can this relate to our original premise that along with the arrival of a gastronomic culture our reputation for hospitality declined? Did we become so involved in our desire to become gastronomically aware that our attitudes to service changed? Kathy Sheridan wrote an article in 1999 entitled 'Frosty Fáilte' that underlined the cultural shift that was in motion regarding our attitudes to hospitality and service. She explains how the hospitable attitudes that prevailed among the Irish for so long had begun to disappear during the Celtic Tiger period. She offers the example of the Belgian tourists who found the Irish rude and off-hand. She discusses the American couple who discovered a 'very real lack of warmth and hospitality 'and the German and Danish visitors to a well-known Clare Pub 'who were asked to leave because they were lingering too long over the drinks that they had ordered and paid for'.[73] One might argue that such a shift in our collective attitude was inevitable given the economic growth that was experienced in Ireland over the Celtic Tiger years and the accompanying greed that followed. Sheridan suggested reasons why this situation had come about:

72   Ibid.
73   Kathy Sheridan, 'Frosty Fáilte', *The Irish Times*, 23 January 1999 [online]. Available at: <http://o-www.irishtimes.com.millennium.it-tallaght.ie/newspaper/weekend/1999/0123/99012300184.html> (Accessed 29 June 2012).

It's not that we hadn't been warned. The chat, the craic, the curiosity, were always what made us different. They even made us 'cool'. So cool in fact that we began to fancy ourselves as being above all that aul' stuff. Like an aging starlet, we fell for our own publicity: world conquerors of the music, film, (River) dance and literature stakes, churning out one bestseller after another, renowned every last one of us-for spouting Heaney, Yeats and bits of Ulysses at the drop of a hat, dreamily indifferent to the international stars fetching up at the airport, falling in love with us and craving a bit of property at Paris prices ... Sure what had we to learn from blow ins? And why should we bother with them at all.[74]

Bourdieu's concept of social capital might suggest that a mentality developed among some groups in Celtic Tiger Ireland that allowed them to believe they were superior because of their perceived association with 'cool Ireland'. And as Sheridan's article indicates this group felt that such collectively owned social capital enhanced and reaffirmed their status to such a degree that they need no longer bother with our long-standing national reputation for hospitality and friendliness. The emerging gastronomic class composed mainly of younger prosperous Irish men and women had begun forming themselves into social groups that now looked upon gastronomic experiences at all levels as being part of their lives in a way that they had not been for previous generations. In tandem with this cultural entitlement came a negative attitude to our traditional service culture and a view that this group of young Irish, no longer placed value on jobs within the hospitality sector. Irish attitudes to welcome and service changed perceptibly. This new social grouping was eating and drinking out much more than previous generations. Social expectation was often governed by what people experienced abroad or picked up through the media and through interaction with their own social groups. As a nation of gastronomes emerged, accompanying attitudes towards hospitality and service deteriorated. Just like our desire for Bourdieu's economic and cultural capital now social capital was being accumulated through gastronomic experiences such as eating in the latest Michelin-starred restaurant or drinking in trendiest bar.

At the end of 1998 Henry O Neill, then Chief Executive of the Restaurant Association of Ireland suggested the emergence of:

74   Ibid.

a new generation of restaurant owner catering to a demand born of a Celtic Tiger whose cubs have a greater disposable income, have travelled more widely and have watched more eccentric cookery programmes than their parents ever did. Into the stew pot add the concentration of people now living in the city, and returned emigrants, and you have a melting pot of spend happy eaters.[75]

There was a lot of discussion in the media during this period about the shortage of hospitality staff. Demands for reductions in the minimum wage were made time and again by representatives of the business community and commentary regarding the hospitality industry becoming a 'race to the bottom' in terms of pay and conditions was common. Frequent reference was also made to the fact that the Irish no longer wanted to work in restaurants and hotels. As a new gastronomic social group was emerging, staffing was becoming the greatest source of pressure in the hospitality industry. In a country that was nearing full employment many restaurateurs were looking abroad to recruit staff. The *CERT Employment Survey of the Tourism Sector* at the end of 1998 recorded a 16% increase in the number of restaurants in Ireland in the space of just two years with a commensurate employee shortfall estimated at 5,632. 'This acute skills shortage is put down variously to anti-social hours, low wages and burn out – all of which, in turn, contribute to the increasingly prevalent perception of the industry as a short term, transitory career option.'[76] One must qualify this with the fact that there was also an abundance of available employment in industries outside the hospitality sector during this period.

In March 2000 a restaurant proprietor whose restaurant had just closed due to an inability to attract suitable staff claimed 'that getting even untrained staff to serve lunch and dinner was proving difficult despite wages of £200 per week with the same in tips'.[77] The service sector was

---

75   Anon., 'The waiting game', *The Irish Times*, 29 December 1998 [online]. Available at: <https://www.irishtimes.com/culture/the-waiting-game-1.229340> (Accessed 26 June 2020).

76   Ibid.

77   Colm Keena, 'Shortage of staff closes successful Dublin restaurant', *The Irish Times*, 23 March 2000 [online]. Available at: <http://0-www.irishtimes.com.millennium. it-tallaght.ie/newspaper/finance/2000/0323/00032300136.html> (Accessed 25 June 2021).

now competing with other more attractive industries in the search for good employees and the service sector was losing. Two years after Sheridan's Frosty Fáilte article, the same journalist once more brought up the topic of hospitality and service in an article entitled 'Is smugness going to do for us in the end'.[78] Sheridan echoes the sentiments above by suggesting that Dublin in the new millennium had become vastly overpriced with an underperforming service staff:

> In the real world, a Dublin restaurateur can charge £14 (per head) for a few slivers of cheese after lunch. His peers in the hotel and restaurant business grow steadily more contemptuous of their patrons as they charge Paris prices for uninspiring food served by untrained students and offensively casual (and probably underpaid) staff. A confident professional at this level is a rare sight.[79]

She goes on to question where these attitudes regarding hospitality and service will ultimately lead Celtic Tiger Ireland. Later in her piece she asks:

> Is this hubris going to do for us in the end? As we rear our children to perceive university-based education as our success standard and continue to confuse service with servility, where are the front-line workers capable of providing a Cipriani-type service going to come from?[80]

The answer to Sheridan's question became very clear throughout the early noughties and the vacuum that existed in the space once occupied by our world-renowned service mentality was to be filled from a variety of Eastern European countries. Though many of these employees compe-tently filled the service roles that the Irish were no longer willing to do,

---

78   Kathy Sheridan, 'Is smugness going to do for us in the end?', *The Irish Times*, 23 January 1999 [online]. Available at: <http://o-www.irishtimes.com.millennium. it-tallaght.ie/newspaper/weekend/1999/0123/99012300184.html> (Accessed 29 June 2012).

79   Kathy Sheridan, 'It's all smiles as "Ireland of the welcomes" reopens for business', *The Irish Times*, 30 March 2000 [online]. Available at : <https://www.irishtimes. com/opinion/is-smugness-going-to-do-for-us-in-the-end-1.261345> (Accessed 15 December 2021).

80   Ibid.

it led to further inevitable claims that the Irish welcome could not be authentically offered by non-Irish personnel and thus a perception that such a welcome was again in decline.

Conclusion

It seems that towards the end of the Celtic Tiger period things had almost come full circle. A new type of gastronomic field had emerged in an Ireland populated by cuisine-savvy Celtic Tiger gastronomes who now knew their Pinot Noir from their Pinot Grigio, and who could converse in a language previously the preserve of the professional restaurateur. They eschewed careers that they associated with, as Sheridan rightly observed, servility rather than service. They could leave those jobs in hospitality and tourism to others, while basking in the idea of being fully fledged gastronomes. And perhaps the small price paid would be the denigration of Ireland's world-renowned reputation for hospitality. But no matter, because many believed we would never again need to trade on our reputation for hospitality and service due to the wealth of opportunity that existed elsewhere in Ireland's Tiger economy. And this is perhaps how Ireland's culinary story might have ended except that the Celtic Tiger that carried the nation forward into gastronomic accomplishment unfortunately keeled over and died in 2007.

For the Irish watching the tiger's demise, the culinary genie was out of the bottle and could not be put back. The country could not return to pre-Celtic Tiger Ireland to dine on corn on the cob and Black Tower wine. Celtic cubs could not unlearn the art of the gastronome. After an initial decline with the demise of the Celtic Tiger, it is interesting to note that wine sales in Ireland increased from 8.7 million cases at the height of the boom to 9 million cases in 2011.[81] That same year sales of gourmet coffee

---

81   The Irish Wine Association, *The Irish Wine Market 201*, [online]. Available at: <http://www.abfi.ie/Sectors/ABFI/ABFI.nsf/vPages/Sector_Association_-_Irish_Wine_Association~industry-profile/$file/ABFI_Wine%20Facts%20Brochure-WEB%202011.pdf> (Accessed 15 September 2012).

machines for use in the home also increased. Despite the deep recession that followed the Celtic Tiger boom, there has been an explosion in retail offers of 'Dine-In Meals for Two' in stores such as Tesco's and Marks and Spencer's. The Irish gastronome never went away. They merely retreated into the kitchen of their negatively leveraged home. They could be found on a high stool at their kitchen island on a Friday night matching wines from German discount stores to Dine at Home meal ranges while verbally admonishing the men and women who killed our Celtic Tiger.

And what of the decline in our reputation for hospitality? Just as the economic boom encouraged the acquisition of economic, cultural and social capital, the subsequent decline in Ireland's economic fortunes led to a renewed focus on sectors such as food, agriculture, hospitality and tourism. At the 2011 global economic forum in Farmleigh former President Bill Clinton was keen to highlight the potential for tourism development in Ireland and the potential for future employment in the area. At the very heart of plans for continued tourism growth must be our attitudes to hospitality and service and with a recent focus on tourism, a new era of hospitality is perhaps emerging. In 2009, ten years after her 'Frosty Fáilte' article Sheridan wrote an article entitled 'It's all smiles as "Ireland of the welcomes" reopens for business.'[82] In the article, she quotes Jim Deegan of Railtours, Ireland who reminds us: 'The Celtic Tiger was no friend to tourism; we became too busy … tourists were only getting in the way of ourselves … We started losing the welcome … now you see people going out of their way because they're appreciative again.'[83]

It seems that our worldwide reputation for hospitality was not wholly devoured by the Celtic Tiger and a new revived culture of service has emerged less driven by economic greed and more closely related to that long association with the *Céad Míle Fáilte* so ingrained in the Irish psyche down through the years. Today Ireland competes on the world stage in terms of our food quality and restaurant offering and it appears that a renewed post Celtic Tiger focus on hospitality and service continues to have benefits for a sector that has gone through so much change recently.

82   Sheridan, 'It's all smiles as "Ireland of the welcomes" reopens for business', 2000.
83   Ibid.

Influential Chief Editor of *Le Guide de Routarde* Pierre Josse said of post Celtic Tiger Ireland:

> Thirty years ago, when we first started the Irish edition, the food here was a disaster. It was very poor and there was no imagination. Now the level of food in Ireland is nothing short of tremendous. The food is gorgeous, it's now very reasonably priced and there is a very high level of service. All in all, I would say the Irish dining experience is now as good, if not better, than anywhere else in the world.[84]

Josse's comments emphasise one of the positive outcomes to emerge from the economic trauma of the Celtic Tiger years and signifies that Irish society has perhaps grown up in terms of its food and drink culture. Hopefully, this newfound gastronomic appreciation can, in future, thrive hand in hand with a more mature and enlightened attitude to our traditional reputation for hospitality. The 'Frosty Fáilte' attitude is, with any luck, now in terminal decline and Ireland will once again become known the world over for the quality of its *Céad Míle Failte*.

84 Nick Bramhill, 'Irish chefs best in world', *Sunday Independent*, 9 January 2011 [online]. Available at: <http://www.independent.ie/national-news/irish-chefs-best-in-world-2489465.html?service=Print> (Accessed 6 October 2012).

CHAPTER 3

Food, Wine, Art and Music

In 2014, I helped organise an Association of Franco-Irish Studies conference at the National Concert Hall in Dublin. The theme for the conference was 'France and Ireland: Celebrating Music, Words and Art' and it encouraged me to consider the relationship between gastronomy and the arts. To this day many are sceptical of linking food and drink to areas like music, but it is becoming increasingly clear that connections do exist. What follows considers how these once tenuous connections are becoming more mainstream, particularly when it comes to influencing food and drink taste experiences and how music can change our perceptions of both.

The preceding chapter dealt with the idea of establishing gastronomy as a cultural field. This chapter posits that food and drink have always been integrated into our cultural lives, through the traditional mediums of art and music. It suggests that there is a deeper relationship between these fields, one that moves beyond using gastronomy as a mere theme in music or art and rather considers that music or art can be a fundamental element of the cultural experience in question.

Food and wine have always been synonymous with the arts. At times, they have acted as subject, sometimes as muse and even as the art form itself. In recent years, western society has become exposed to endless streams of food related material through all forms of media. Formerly considered a subject that was the preserve of an aristocratic class, gastronomy has been democratised and has assumed a greater importance and visibility in many aspects of our everyday lives. As noted in the introduction to this book, food studies were historically viewed as less cerebral than other areas of study but recently gastronomy has become more associated with the upper senses. These senses include hearing and sight and are reputed to allow more considered objective contemplation. There are many contemporary examples of food and wine intersecting with the arts and displaying a symbiotic

relationship that is considerably more complex than the traditional dynamic that was the norm between subject and artist. Such developments
have allowed interactions between gastronomy and cultural areas such as
music and art to become increasingly discussed and documented and food
and drink are embedded elements in practically every cultural pursuit.

Gastronomy as Art

The old culinary proverb that one eats first with one's eyes is undoubtedly true and the contemporary focus on visual presentation has had a lot
to do with gastronomy being perceived as art. Both food and wine have
always had pedigree in terms of their perceived aesthetic quality. Even the
very first category of wine analysis – as dictated by the Wine and Spirit
Education Trust's systematic approach to tasting – concerns visual perception.[85] During that analysis, and before any other engagement, a wine
is visually described across a spectrum of colour, consistency and interaction with the glass in terms of viscosity. Nomenclature in third-level
catering courses also helps to emphasise the importance of the aesthetic.
Programmes that were for many years described as professional cookery
courses have, in recent years, changed into qualifications in the Culinary
Arts. The traditional lexicon associated with epicurean skills has changed
and a new vernacular now presents as something more cultural. It is now
the case that 'a coffee producer' is an incomplete description. Nespresso
recently began to celebrate its 'coffee artists'.[86] International fast food
chain Subway now uses the term 'sandwich artist' when referring to their
operative level employees.[87]

---

85   See <http://www.wsetglobal.com/qualifications/25.asp> (Accessed 3 April 2014).
86   Nespresso Campaign, 'Made with care-Coffee artists'. Available at: <https://www.
      nespresso.com/ie/en/commitments/coffee-farmers?> (Accessed 4 October 2021).
87   See <https://jobs.mysubwaycareer.eu/careers/sandwich-artist.htm> (Accessed 20
      September 2021).

It is also not uncommon to hear successful chefs described as artists. Their manifest anger in the heated chaos of a busy kitchen hints at the image of the proverbial tortured artist. Celebrity chefs frequently portray themselves as dark, introspective characters more concerned with the protection of their art than with the service industry in which they work. One might contrast the rebellious hair and rather intentionally menacing image of famous chef Marco Pierre-White, unshaven and brandishing a cleaver, with the more traditional image of the classic French head chef, resplendent in starched whites, neatly tied neckerchief and tall, rigid, white hat. Their most unique plates of food are described as signature dishes, a term derived from the signature artwork of painters whose individual style was easily recognised. In *The Virtues of the Table: How to Eat and Think*, Julian Baggini likens a meal in a Michelin-starred restaurant to an artistic performance and draws interesting comparisons between it and more accepted art forms. While admitting that many are sceptical of such comparisons, Baggini feels that the comparison is apposite, 'Some say a meal just comes and goes but all performances are experienced in time and once finished cannot be exactly replicated.'[88] Of course, a piece of visual art such as a painting has consistency of effect but perhaps a comparison between a 3-star meal and a live musical performance has more in common than one might initially think. No two such performances can ever be exactly replicated. They are artistically dependent on time and space. Baggini points out that some detractors insist that food has no 'cognitive content, no truths – moral or metaphysical – to take away or think about'.[89] It can be argued, as Baggini does, that many art examples don't possess those qualities either. However, on closer inspection one can find evidence of a more cognitive and even a metaphysical interpretation of both food and wine. There is now increasing analysis of how flavours and compounds found in both food and wine interact and affect the senses. For example, *The Flavour Thesaurus* offers an in-depth analysis of how certain food flavours interact. In summary, it says, 'What *The Flavour Thesauraus* does add up to, in the

88   Julian Baggini, *The Virtues of the Table: How to Eat and Think* (London: Granta Publications, 2014), p. 222.

89   Baggini, *The Virtues of the Table*, pp. 222–223.

end, is a patchwork of facts, connections, impressions and recollections, designed less to tell you exactly what to do than provide the spark for your own recipe or adaptation. It's there, in short, to get the juices flowing.'[90]

In recent years we have witnessed the often meticulous scrutiny of expensive wines by recognised experts. Flavour and structure are analysed in tremendous detail, debated, discussed and broken down in terms of complexity and effect. High end wines have even been compared at times to the human condition. The well-known winemaker Paul Pontallier of Château Margaux, who sadly passed away in 2016, suggested that 'wine is not just fermented juice, it can be philosophical, it is so close to ourselves, its life expectancy is more or less ours'.[91] Pontallier's words suggest that wine is akin to a living thing: it matures over time, the bottle acts as a vessel that has captured a moment in space and time because of a strict association with an individual *terroir*. Opening a bottle of wine allows it to breathe, to escape from its confines and to rest. Some connoisseurs are even more fervent in their analysis, going so far as to bestow a vinous personality on a wine, referring to it as brash, upfront or pretentious. While frequently dismissed as frivolous, these examples show that, for some people, food and wine possess substantial cognitive depths that a great many would consider of value both in terms of appreciation and of related discussion. The personification of wine has no doubt been bolstered by prominent culinary personalities who feature more and more in our everyday consumption of modern media. Simple interpretations of wine no longer suffice. Complex and lavish descriptions by media wine experts as well as frequent descriptions in dedicated magazines such as *Decanter* have contributed to the acceptance among some of wine as a topic for more metaphysical analysis.

There are many contemporary cases of food and wine intersecting with the art world and displaying a symbiotic relationship that is considerably more complex than the traditional dynamic that has been the norm between subject and artist. Recent studies have cited some good examples which include Rirkrit Tirivanija who has cooked meals for gallery-goers as a form of installation art since the 1990s, Sonja Alhauser who is famous

90   Niki Segnit, *The Flavour Thesaurus* (London: Bloomsbury Press, 2010), p. 11.
91   'Wine – The Faith', *Wine*, Episode 2. BBC 4 Television, 23 February 2009.

for exploring the issue of eating as an aesthetic experience and Jana Sterbak whose work *Vanitas: Flesh dress for albino anorexic* explores the idea of food being tied into the perception of self.[92] Further illustration is provided by Kirsten Ditterich-Shilakes who explains how four selected wine-related artworks at San Francisco's Fine art and Asian Museum help portray four classic civilisations where wine, as it is known today began, namely Greece, France, China and Japan. She explores two artworks from the West, a Black-figure Greek Amphora from 510–500 BCE and a painting by John Sargent entitled *Le Verre de Porto,* and two wine-related works from the East, a Chinese Ritual Wine vessel from 1300–1050 BCE and a traditional Japanese Sake bottle created by Fujiwara Yu. In her view, all four works 'encapsulate the height of classic civilisations and artistic technical perfection in the West and the East and rise to the category of "iconic".[93] What is interesting about the author's use of these works is not how gastronomy was used as the subject matter but how Ditterich-Shilakes interprets the oenological aspect of these four wine vessels and how they reflect, among other things, a real sense of history, class and society. Her research illustrates how culturally important gastronomy has been down through the ages. She shows that food and wine in art have the potential to move beyond their mere utilitarian function. The ancient Greeks gave us Dionysus, the god of wine. Both he and his mythical entourage feature heavily in Greek literature and art. According to John Varianno, 'he and his circle of maenads, nymphs, satyrs and sileni were among the most colourful and frequently represented figures in all classical art and literature'.[94] There is also clear evidence of wine having the ability to intersect with other cultural forms. Varriano raises the cultural profile of gastronomy by suggesting that

92 Charles Spence, Mayu U. Shankar and Heston Blumenthal, '"Sound bites": Auditory contributions to the perception and consumption of food and drink', in Francesca Bacci and David Melcher (eds), *Art and the Senses* (New York: Oxford University Press, 2011), p. 209.

93 Kirsten Ditterich-Shilakes, 'Muse in a stem glass: Art, wine and philosophy', in Fritz Allhoff (ed.), *Wine and Philosophy: A Symposium on Thinking and Drinking* (Oxford: Blackwell Publishing, 2008), pp. 44–62.

94 John Varriano, *Wine: A Cultural History* (London: Reaktion Books Ltd, 2010), pp. 24–25.

when a respected contemporary philosopher compares a Chablis to a Jane Austen
novel, a Collioure to a sculpture by Maillol and a rare American varietal to 'the sound
of a deep organ note beneath the choir of summer perfumes', he is only following a
rhetorical practice that began with Homer's 'wine-dark sea'.[95]

More than any other beverage, wine harbours attributes that appear
to allow it to intersect with broader cultural areas. A case in point is the
extraordinary vineyard of Château La Coste, near Aix-en-Provence which
offers an interesting amalgamation of wine and the arts. Owned by Irish
property tycoon Paddy McKillen, and run by his sister Mara, the winery
is a wonderland of cutting-edge building design populated by renowned
works of modern art. Many famous artists and architects have contributed
to its development. International architect and creator of the Guggenheim
Museum in Bilbao, Frank Gehry, designed the music pavilion in the grounds
of the Château. In August 2014 La Coste hosted a series of piano performances in the pavilion dedicated to the works of Chopin and Liszt
among many others.[96] The works of other well-known artists are carefully
distributed around the grounds of the Château and indeed in some cases
McKillen's Irish heritage is clear in his support of Irish designers and materials. According to *The Sunday Times*, 'Paddy McKillen can now medi-
tate on his problems in a purpose-built chapel. Made from 8000 pieces
of Waterford Crystal and slabs of Kilkenny black stone, the chapel was
designed by John Rocca in his Dublin studio and then transported in 26
panels to McKillen's vineyard in Provence, France.'[97] It would be simplistic
to interpret the La Coste example as a simple vineyard with beautiful
buildings. David Aylward introduced the concept of attaching a cultural
economy[98] to a food or drink product. He suggests that a product, such as
wine, through its association with defined cultural elements, can come to
be perceived as something more than its original incarnation as a pleasant

95   Ibid., p. 7. This reference relates to philosopher Roger Scruton.
96   Available at: <http://www.musiquesechanges.com/academie/nos-concerts#soir
      ees> (Accessed 2 February 2015).
97   Gabrielle Monaghan, 'McKillen retreats to crystal palace', *The Sunday Times*, 12
      January 2014, p. 3.
98   David Aylward, 'Towards a cultural economy paradigm for the Australian wine in-
      dustry', *Prometheus*, 26 (4), 2008, pp. 373–385.

alcoholic drink. Thus, in the case of Château La Coste, wine and the arts have been combined to form a new cultural entity that has the potential to be appreciated in its own right. Neither the wine nor its surroundings can be viewed separately. There are few food products that can match wine in terms of blatant associations with another cultural form. Although not impossible it is more difficult to imagine such an association between art and, for example, beer, bread or cheese. Throughout a 6000-year oenological history, this ancient beverage has threaded its way through many aspects of cultural life and so its association with other cultural domains seems somehow natural. More recently wine has even started to blend seamlessly with another stalwart of cultural appreciation, the world of music.

Wine and Music: A Special Bond

Steve Charters and Simone Pettigrew have agreed that wine consumption is an aesthetic experience[99] and although they have accepted that many philosophical writers have long dismissed any relationship between food, drink and aesthetics, they conclude in their own research that 'informants generally saw similarities between the consumption of wine and the consumption of aesthetic products – notably music'.[100] In particular, the authors refer to the similarity between wine and music in terms of common evaluative criteria that can be used across a range of aesthetic products. Using the suggestions of Beardsley,[101] these criteria included concepts of balance/unity, complexity and intensity. All of these are terms that sit well when applied to a high-end wine and they are likely to underpin any discussions that one might overhear at a professional wine tasting. The very nature of such a tasting can, in a sense, reflect a similar appreciation of music. To the knowledgeable taster, wine can be made up of highs and

---

99   Steve Charters and Simone Pettigrew, 'Is wine consumption an aesthetic experience', *Journal of Wine Research*, 16 (2), 2005, pp. 121–136.
100 Ibid., p. 133.
101 Ibid., p. 134.

lows. They talk negatively of an over emphasis on individual elements such as acidity or tannin. They discuss the lack of depth, structure and cohesion in a wine. They consider a wine to be at its best when all elements are balanced and working in unison, keen for no one element to dominate the 'show' at the expense of the other individual participants. The affinity with assessment of an orchestral performance cannot be ignored.

Wine writers have often compared wine to individual pieces of music and there has been considerable research looking at this relationship. There are obvious commercial applications here and there have been examples where music has played an important role in determining a customer's purchase decision. One such example involved researchers from the Music Research Group at the University of Leicester who discovered that playing background French music in a wine store had subliminally encouraged customers to purchase French wine.[102] Other research examined the effect of background music on the taste of wine and found that 'auditory stimuli can in fact influence flavour perception'.[103] Both sets of findings are not all that surprising when one considers a more everyday example of an Italian-themed restaurant playing authentic Italian music in order to enhance and complement the style of décor service and the food and wine being offered. Playing a completely different style of music would potentially inhibit the experience of the diner.

One winemaker taking this idea very seriously suggests that different styles of music can make the same wine taste differently by causing what is referred to as a cross-modal influence. Clark Smith is a winemaker and the author of *Postmodern Winemaking*.[104] He suggests that music can strongly influence the way a wine might taste. When even the most ardent sceptics can accept that glassware, tableware, ambient temperature and décor can influence an overall meal experience, is it really such a leap to suggest that

---

102   Leon Jaroff, 'Days of Wine and Muzak', *Time Magazine* [online], V 150, 22 (1997). Available at: <https://content.time.com/time/subscriber/article/0,33009,987 433,00.html> (Accessed 19 May 2022).

103   Adrian North, 'The effect of background music on the taste of wine', *British Journal of Psychology*, 103, 2012, p. 298.

104   Clark Smith, *Post Modern Wine Making* (California: University of California Press, 2014).

the auditory senses can also play a part in influencing how a particular wine's flavour is perceived? Unlike other research in the same area, Smith suggests that music not only enhances but actually changes how a wine tastes. A simple but admittedly unscientific experiment took place during a radio interview with Smith and helps to illustrate the point. The show's host was blindfolded and offered three wines to taste. The first was tasted while listening to a *Beach Boys* track, the second with a flamenco track and the third was tasted in conjunction with a *Metallica* track. The host then described each of the wines live on air. Of note even in this most informal of experiments was that all three blind wines were described very differently. They were in fact all the same.

Clark Smith offers actual album tracks on his website, ones that he judges best to accompany his wine selection.[105] He defines postmodern winemaking as 'the practical art of touching the human soul by rendering its grapes into liquid music'[106] and likens the intricacy involved in making wine to the complexity involved in achieving a good orchestral performance. He talks of the illusory nature of harmony. 'When an orchestra tunes up, there's lots of noise but not much harmony between the instruments. 'But then there's music', he says, 'which is perceived as sad or joyful. It carries emotion.'[107] That orchestral comparison is reminiscent of earlier discussion comparing wine appreciation to music appreciation. Individual elements included by the winemaker such as acidity, tannin or fruit intensity might be compared to sounds created by the combination of instruments in an orchestra. It is only through the skill and competence of the 'wine conductor' that these independent elements can achieve balance and unity thus allowing an accomplished performance to be appreciated by the audience. According to Smith, the following guidelines help achieve successful wine and music pairings.

---

105 See <http://postmodernwinemaking.com/wine-and-music> (Accessed 6 May 2021).

106 W. Blake Grey, 'Music to drink wine by: Vintner insists music can change wines flavours', *San Francisco Chronicle* [online]. Available at: <http://www.sfgate.com/wine/article/Music-to-drink-wine-by-Vintner-insists-music-can-3235602.php> (Accessed 24 April 2014).

107 See <http://www.wineanorak.com/clark_smith.htm> (Accessed 12 May 2014).

Red wines need either minor key or they need music that has negative emotion

Pinot noir generally likes romantic music

Polka music does not pair with any wine

Cabernets are more at home with angry music.[108]

Though something of a wine maverick, Clark Smith is not alone in his explorations of cross-modal relationships between wine and music. Work by Charles Spence and others has garnered a lot of publicity in the wine world. Spence is Professor of Experimental Psychology in Oxford[109] and has carried out research into the influence of contextual variables on multisensory flavour. Recently, he has been looking for cross-modal links between classical music and fine wine. His early studies found that participants did in fact match recognised wine aromas with classes of instruments and musical notes in a non-random way: 'It is clear that participants picked much lower pitched sounds as corresponding with the smell of smoke, musk, dark chocolate and cut hay while generally associating the fruitier aromas (apple, lemon, apricot, raspberry, pineapple and blackberry) with higher pitched notes instead.'[110]

Another study by Spence and his colleagues scientifically examined the relationship between four specifically chosen and significantly different wines and eight pieces of music as chosen by the London Symphony Orchestra. The results of these experiments suggested that there was significant agreement among participants that certain wines went well with pieces of music and that other wines did not blend as well. In fact, some wines

108   Blake Grey, 'Music to drink wine by: Vintner insists music can change wines flavours'.

109   Recently the subject of an RTÉ radio discussion on matching wine to music. Available at: <http://www.rte.ie/radio1/today-with-sean-o-rourke/programmes/2014/0416/609206-today-with-sean-o-rourke-wednesday-16-april-2014/?clipid=1535470> (Accessed 17 April 2020).

110   Charles Spence, Liana Richards, Emma Kjellin, Anna-Maria Huhnt, Victoria Daskal, Alexandra Scheybeler, Carlos Velasco and Ophelia Deroy, 'Looking for crossmodal correspondences between classical music and fine wine', *Flavour*, 2, 2013, p. 29 [online] Available at: <http://www.flavourjournal.com/content/2/1/29> (Accessed 2 May 2014).

were enhanced by the addition of certain types of music during the tasting. Spence is not unique in his scientific conclusions and Adrian North's 2012 study at Edinburgh University confirmed his view that 'auditory stimuli can influence flavour perception'.[111] Such conclusions have led Dave Williams, editor of *Wine and Spirit* magazine, to suggest that it is quite possible that diners in Michelin-starred restaurants might soon be presented with music lists to choose from to best match with their food and wine. The development of hyper directional speakers would in theory make this possible.[112] Such technology would allow individual tables within close proximity to each other to channel individual pieces of music according to requirements. This would quite feasibly enhance their fine dining experience.

Not all interactions between music and oenology have been positive. In 2012, an Australian wine competition commissioned a special piece of music to be played while the designated judges tasted certain wines. The competition in question was the Adelaide Review Hot 100 Wines Show. The organiser of the show, James Erskine, commissioned an original piece from composer Eugene Ughetti which was subsequently performed by one of South Australia's most renowned pianists, Gabriella Smart. The piece was played during the judging of individual wines entered into the category 'Wines produced without the addition of commercial yeasts or acids'. According to Erskine, the music was included because he wanted

> to provide an environment which forces the judges wherever they are from, to think, feel and taste in a South Australian mindset to better understand the emotional, or non-geophysical, terroir of South Australia that influences the wine styles we are tasting.[113]

The inclusion of the piece entitled *Terroir* was not to everyone's taste. While many people accept that music has the potential to influence how a particular wine might be perceived, some commentators felt that such an intrusion into the process would have an unfair impact on a judge's

111   North, 'The effect of background Music on the Taste of Wine', p. 298.
112   Spence et al., 'Looking for crossmodal correspondences', p. 217.
113   Christina Pickard, 'Judges treated to live music at wine competition', *Decanter* [online]. Available at: <http://www.decanter.com/news/wine-news/530467/jud ges-treated-to-live-music-at-wine-competition> (Accessed 14 January 2014).

objectivity. Guy Woodward, editor of *Decanter*, clearly wasn't a fan when he said that the idea was ridiculous, 'Music quite clearly affects people's moods –there are enough studies to show that. So, it follows that how an individual reacts to a certain type of music could put them in a certain frame of mind when judging the wines and could quite easily impact on their judgment.'[114]

Wine and Music: Closer to Home

While the work of Smith, Spence and North are good examples of how music and wine relationships are beginning to be explored at a scientific level, there are many other examples of how these two cultural entities interact closer to home. An Irish theatre piece helps to emphasise how music-wine linkages can enhance an entertainment experience. A play entitled *A Wine Goose Chase* is an innovative one-woman show that integrates wine tasting, Franco-Irish connections, music and theatre. The show is written and performed by Kildare woman Susan Boyle.[115] It is accompanied by several intermittent wine tastings which are linked to the performance. It is frequently enacted in a beverage setting such as a wine bar or pub. Boyle takes her audience on a vinous journey through the centuries, detailing the long and surprisingly tangible connections that have tied Ireland to the wines of France and other countries down through the ages. However, for many, the highlight of the show occurs at the end when the audience are asked to raise a final tasting glass in celebration of the many Irish wine connections and to raucously sing together that evocative Irish song *The Parting Glass*. The lyrics of the song itself reflect the warmth of the association between drink and music when each verse concludes with the line 'so fill to me the parting glass, goodnight and joy be with you all'.[116] There are other examples of music and wine enthusiasts

114   Ibid.
115   See <http://awinegoosechase.com/> (Accessed 18 January 2014).
116   Lyrics from the song made famous by The Clancy Brothers.

attempting to marry their two cultural loves. One final example is worth mentioning. It was offered by *Food and Wine's* wine editor Raymond Blake and by the recently deceased *Sunday Business Post's* wine writer Tomás Clancy. Both renowned oenophiles hosted a show called *Intermezzo* on RTE's Lyric FM which fused the two distinct artistic fields of classical music and wine culture. Examples of show descriptions include:

> The salubrious effects of a thimble of Domaine de la Romanée-Conti and Prokofiev's last great chess game are under discussion as Tomás Clancy and Raymond Blake find a seat in the foyer for an interval chat.

> Conversation in the lobby tonight alights on Kodaly's little-known influence on Steven Spielberg's *Close Encounters of the Third Kind* and the burnt orange notes of Liszt's favourite wine, Tokaji, as Tomás Clancy and Raymond Blake meet up for an interval jar.[117]

Both *A Wine Goose Chase* and *Intermezzo* are good examples of how gastronomic culture is intersecting with the music world. Unlike previous interactions, these examples portray gastronomy as an equal partner in the cultural relationship. Its traditional role was one of the subject or in some cases the libatious muse that encouraged art creation. Instead, it has become an integral part of the performance in the case of the play and is granted cultural parity through discussions in the *Intermezzo* example.

Conclusion

Food and wine have always been part of artistic and literary culture. The earliest Greek symposia provided a forum where 'men drank and talked, often about specified topics in a convivial setting removed from the constraints of everyday life'.[118] Not only was wine used as an essential libation to help loosen the tongues of symposiasts, but there are numerous

---

117　See <http://www.rte.ie/radio1/podcast/podcast_the-lyric-concert.xml> (Accessed 4 February 2014).
118　Varriano, *Wine*, p. 37.

examples showing the incorporation of food and wine culture into art-istic and literary representations of the time. Gastronomy itself has always been there on the periphery, sometimes as muse, sometimes as subject. More recently it has emerged as a cultural entity and consider-able epicurean-themed academic discourse continues to emerge. Though far from the mainstream, the developments discussed here suggest that gastronomy can engage with distant cultural cousins in many ways. The examples provided have shown how food, wine, art and even music can complement each other. Though many may still be sceptical, it should be noted that reputable researchers are beginning to examine how music can influence not only the enjoyment of gastronomic experiences but even the perceptions of taste. There may be a long way to travel before there can be widespread agreement with the views of maverick winemaker Clark Smith who suggests that Cabernet Sauvignon is a perfect match for heavy rock music. The public will remain somewhat dubious about statements such as 'red wines need either minor keys or they need music that has negative emotion. They don't like happy music ... Cabernets like angry music.'[119]

Sadly, the future of research into how food, wine, art and music relate to each other is most likely to be driven by commercial interests. It will be undertaken by corporations who are likely to be less interested in cultural appreciation and more interested in how relationships can be exploited. Their sole aim will be to harness the power of art, music, food and wine, good or bad, to subliminally influence how the consumer spends money. However, it is refreshing to think that the subject of gastronomy can be analysed and appreciated in different, more artistic and non-mercantile ways. When contemplating their interrelated pleasures, enthusiasts of both art and gastronomy may still indulge in their own scientific experimen-tation. The hypothesis of Charles Spence et al that 'Tchaikovsky's String Quartet No 1 in D major turned out to be a particularly good match for the Château Margaux 2004'[120] is one that gastronomes may happily choose to put to the test.

119   Spence et al., 'Looking for crossmodal correspondences'.
120   Ibid.

PART II

Places

CHAPTER 4

Drinking Spaces in Strange Places

In the mid-1990s, I had a job managing one of the corporate dining tents at the Wimbledon Tennis Championships. These were a series of corporate spaces where large companies would entertain favoured clients with copious quantities of Pimm's, smoked salmon and strawberries. I got chatting to the manager running the corporate tent next door and he very proudly informed me he was returning to college in September to train to become a lecturer in food and beverage studies. I had never even considered that this might be an option for me but by the following September I had enrolled in the same full-time Postgraduate Certificate in Further Education at the University of Greenwich. This was a turning point for me. I realised that I could apply my practical skills and qualifications to an academic purpose. The examples below try to capture where we are now in terms of how a very practical area like beverage can play a role in academia and how vocational food and drink skills don't necessarily have to be seen as 'other'.

Later chapters in this section will deal with clearly identifiable physical locations that act as sites of gastronomic experience. This chapter examines place from a somewhat different perspective. It explores whether beverage as an academic discipline has a place in Irish Studies, whether that place is justified and how it might develop in the future.

The everyday task of drinking is something that appears remarkably simple and is part of normal activity for those of us lucky enough to live in a bountiful society. Like food, it is a necessary sustenance without which the human body cannot survive. And yet, down through the centuries the drinks we consume and the way in which we consume them have become cultural signifiers that can tell us much about who we are. Many research areas have their origins in the more practical and applied aspects of life and food studies (which incorporates beverage studies) is perhaps the most pertinent example of this. Despite recently becoming a field of study, it still struggles at times to be considered worthy of serious academic endeavour. Warren Belasco suggests:

> Even now, with the rising interest in food studies, a serious analysis of family dinner rituals, cookbooks, or the appeal of fast food may still evoke surprise and even scorn. 'Do professors really study that?' your friends and family ask. 'If you're going to go around telling your colleagues you are a philosopher of food,' philosopher Lisa Heldke writes, 'you better be prepared to develop a thick skin – and start a wise-crack collection.'[121]

As an important subset of food studies, beverage scholars have also been developing their own distinct research field and this chapter posits that recent forays into the area have the potential to play an important role in an Irish Studies context. A context that has reached far into many other interdisciplinary areas including sport, food and tourism. The developing role of beverage studies presents an interesting example when viewed through a similar lens. Its history lies in the applied arts of service and hospitality.

Down through the years beverage as part of the dining experience became enhanced through the change from *service à la française* in the nineteenth century into service *à la russe*[122] which placed a focus on serving selected wines as opposed to guests choosing for themselves what to drink. In more recent times we have seen an increasing value placed upon cocktail, barista and sommelier skills with the global success of Netflix programmes such *Somm*, a proliferation of wine, spirit and coffee courses and opportunities for professionals and the public alike to undertake formal beverage qualifications. In tandem with the rise of food studies and the emergence of a gastronomic cultural field in Ireland as discussed in an earlier chapter, its lesser cousin beverage studies has started to emerge as an area worthy of academic study. There have also been considerable developments regarding

121   Warren Belasco, *Food: The Key Concepts* (New York: Berg, 2008), p. 1.
122   Prior to the nineteenth century the meal experience consisted of a large number of dishes and drinks presented together at the same time for guests to help themselves. This was known a *service à la française*. With the development of *service à la russe*, guests began to choose their dishes from a formalised menu and waiting staff had a bigger role in serving wines with foods of choice.

the formal recognition of beverage qualifications in third-level institutions with the development of degrees in areas such as Beverage Management, Wine Studies and Brewing and Distilling. From an Irish research perspective, there have been notable beverage research outputs across several academic platforms including the biennial Dublin Gastronomy Symposium, the Association of Franco-Irish Studies, the Beverage Research Network and the National Centre for Franco-Irish Studies, all of whom have endeavoured to include and promote Irish beverage studies as part of their research output through annual conferences, seminars, publications and events.

Despite the prevalence of beverage in daily life, prior to the intervention of the aforementioned groups, beverage studies have traditionally remained in the wings when it comes to interpreting its value through an Irish academic lens. Areas of Irish Studies are broad and often aligned to subjects like postcolonial studies, literature, language and history. This chapter argues for the consideration of beverage studies as part of the Irish Studies research agenda because of its importance as a backdrop to many cultural aspects of Irish life. Understanding beverage in Ireland means understanding its role in our history, the nature of beverage consumption spaces and their importance in Irish commensality. Beverages have much to tell us about human nature and how we interact with others. Our beverage identity has been exported around the world through products like Guinness, Irish whiskey, Baileys and the ubiquitous Irish pub, which has also become a strong vehicle of cultural export. This chapter is not confined to alcoholic beverages and considers the role of Ireland's emerging coffee culture, the rise of non-alcoholic products and their potential in shaping future generations of Irish people. The recent Covid 19 crisis has impacted on how we interact with drinking and our drinking spaces. In fact, this chapter was started on the 29th of June 2020, the first day that restaurants and pubs that serve food were allowed to reopen following the unprecedented COVID lockdown in the months prior to that. The restrictions imposed presented many with a vista of how our lives can be changed when the social spaces, that up to now have been the fabric of many of our lives, are suddenly removed. The significant consequences of this removal have been amplified during this period and the reimagining of our drinking spaces has had significant implications sociologically. Moreover, our relationship with our drinking spaces had already started to change pre-Covid and it is this changed landscape that begs strong consideration when considering the role of beverage in Irish Studies.

Setting a Context

The area of beverage studies can be divided into three main categories. Firstly, we have the practical, more applied aspect of beverage studies populated by an ontology of drinks understanding, ingredients, methods and hospitality skills dominated by extensive levels of product knowledge and skills among practitioners. This is a world populated by masters of wine, mixologists, sommeliers, restaurateurs, baristas and bar tenders. It is also an area that has been well serviced by further and higher education in Ireland in recent decades through a variety of practically focused programmes. Secondly, we have an area of academic discourse that deals primarily with beverage through the lens of business and science. This area explores topics such as the health impacts of beverage consumption, the societal effects of alcohol abuse and the economic consequences of the drinks industry. It is an area which frequently dominates political discourse and, in some cases, has led to a diminution of the importance of beverage culture in Irish society. The final category of beverage studies and the principal subject of this chapter concerns an area of academic study that explores other important aspects of the beverage world. This category deals with issues including gastronomic identity, communication of *terroir*, the language and lexicon of drinks and the semiotics of drinks products. It explores the sociological history of drinks and the role beverage spaces can play in cultural expression. All three beverage categories intersect at various points and are interdependent. They all have something to offer within a general cultural studies context, but it is the final one that most lends itself to an Irish Studies research agenda.

A Developing Literature

There have been considerable developments in beverage literature and although an exhaustive review is beyond the scope of this chapter there
are several important sources that should be identified. Early forays in
an Irish context focused on the wine world and both Renagh Holohan's
The Irish Chateaux[123] and T. P. Whelehan's *The Irish Wines of Bordeaux*[124]
demonstrated interest in the field. In 1998, Elisabeth Malcolm explored
the pub in both a cultural and historical context in an important chapter
entitled 'The Rise of the Irish Pub: A study in the disciplining of popular
culture' that featured in *Irish Popular Culture 1650–1850*.[125] In 1996, Kevin
Kearns published *Dublin Pub Life and Lore: An Oral History*[126] which
explored the pub's impact on Irish cultural life through the testimonies
of publicans and barmen. Cian Molloy's 2002 book *The Story of the Irish
Pub*[127] offered another key text exploring the history of the pub and the
families that were key to its evolution. Ted Murphy's important and substantial tome *A Kingdom of Wine*[128] was first published in 2005, with a
revised edition published in 2013, and it charts the drinking traditions,
wine making and wine trading history of the Irish from pre-Christian
times to the present day. There continued to be considerable interest in
the study of the Irish Pub and following sociologist Perry Share's early

123   Renagh Holohan, *The Irish Chateaux: In Search of the Wild Geese* (Dublin: Lilliput
      Press, 1989).
124   T. P. Whelehan, *The Irish Wines of Bordeaux* (Dublin: The Vine Press, 1990).
125   Elisabeth Malcolm, 'The rise of the Irish pub: A study in the disciplining of
      popular culture', in James S. Donnelly and Kerby A. Miller (eds), *Irish Popular
      Culture 1650–1850* (Dublin: Irish Academic Press,1998), pp. 50–75.
126   Kevin C. Kearns, *Dublin Pub Life and Lore: An Oral History* (Dublin: Gill
      Books, 1996).
127   Cian Molloy, *The Story of the Irish Pub: An Intoxicating History of the Licensed
      Trade in Ireland* (Dublin: The Liffey Press, 2002).
128   Ted Murphy, *A Kingdom of Wine: A Celebration of Ireland's Winegeese*
      (Cork: Onstream Publications, 2005).

incorporation of the 'Third Place' concept in the context of the Irish Pub,[129] 2008 saw the publication of Gwen Scarborough's PhD, *The Irish Pub as Third Place: A sociological exploration of people place and identity*.[130] That same year brought the beautifully photographed *The Irish Pub* by James Fennel and Turtle Bunbury, a substantial contribution that detailed some of Ireland's most historic public houses.[131] A year later came Bill Barich's *A Pint of Plain: Tradition, Change, and the Fate of the Irish Pub*[132] and then in 2010, Robert E. Connolly published *The Rise and Fall of the Irish Pub* which tracked the pubs journey from its early origins, into its heyday and then on to its recent decline.[133]

In terms of more technical books, the beverage education sector frequently relied on both UK and US texts. However, tourism organisations such as the Council for Education, Recruitment and Training (CERT) and industry bodies such as the Vintners Federation of Ireland (VFI) produced several useful trade manuals, texts and guides down through the years that helped with delivery on many beverage-related training courses. In 2013, James Murphy added two very important and comprehensive educational texts, *Principles and Practices of Bar and Beverage Management*,[134] and *Principles and Practices of Bar and Beverage Management: The Drinks Handbook*.[135] These books were an important contribution to the beverage

129   Perry Share, 'A genuine "third place"? Towards an understanding of the pub in contemporary Irish society' (Sociological Association Ireland Conference, Cavan, 2003). Available at: <https://www.academia.edu/805791/A_genuine_third_place_Towards_an_understanding_of_the_pub_in_contemporary_Irish_society> (Accessed 2 January 2014).

130   Gwen Scarborough, *The Irish Pub as a 'Third Place': A Sociological Exploration of People, Place and Identity* (PhD Thesis, Institute of Technology Sligo, 2008).

131   James Fennel and Turtle Bunbury, *The Irish Pub* (Thames and Hudson, 2008).

132   Bill Barich, *A Pint of Plain: Tradition, Change, and the Fate of the Irish Pub* (New York: Bloomsbury Publishing USA, 2009).

133   Robert E. Connolly, *The Rise and Fall of the Irish Pub* (Dublin: The Liffey Press, 2010).

134   James Murphy, *Principles and Practices of Bar and Beverage Management* (Oxford: Goodfellow Publisher, 2013).

135   James Murphy, *Principles and Practices of Bar and Beverage Management: The Drinks Handbook* (Oxford: Goodfellow Publisher, 2013).

education canon and provided a much needed Irish text for applied practitioners in the area. Ireland's pub culture again came to the fore in 2013, this time through a new medium with Alex Fegan's widely acclaimed film documentary *The Irish Pub*,[136] which was released to both cinema audiences and on DVD in 2013. It offered a unique historical and cultural insight into the role of the pub in Irish society. Among the many books published on Irish Whiskey and other drinks products, Fionnán O' Connor's 2015 book *A Glass Apart*[137] stands out as offering an erudite exploration of the historical importance of Irish Single Pot Still Whiskey, the origins of Irish whiskey in general and its important recent revival. Ireland's beverage culture crossed media boundaries once again with Susan Boyle's aforementioned show *A Wine Goose Chase*.[138] The one-woman performance integrates wine tasting, history, music and drama and has been running at various locations and food festivals throughout Ireland since the show's inception at the Aboslut Dublin Fringe Festival in 2012. Kevin Martin's 2016 publication *Have You no Homes to go to*[139] provided yet another excellent historical insight into the Irish Pub and its role in Irish society. Finally, well-known Irish historian Diarmuid Ferriter has also written extensively on the country's historical association with drink and both his book *Nation of Extremes: Pioneers in Twentieth-Century Ireland*[140] and the recent chapter, 'Drink and society in twentieth-century Ireland' in *Food and Drink in Ireland*[141] are important examples which examine and debate controversies and trends in relation to the consumption of alcoholic drink in twentieth-century Ireland and its role in stereotyping Irish identity.

---

136   Alex Fegan, *The Irish Pub* (Element Pictures Distribution, 2013).

137   Fionnán O' Connor, *A Glass Apart: Irish Single Pot Still Whiskey* (Mulgarve, Victoria: The Images Publishing Group, 2015).

138   Brian Murphy, 'A Wine Goose Chase reviewed', *Canadian Journal of Irish Studies*, 41, 2018, pp. 292–294. Available at: <https://www.jstor.org/stable/e26435216> (Accessed 23 September 2020).

139   Kevin Martin, *Have You No Homes to Go To* (Cork Collins Press, 2016).

140   Diarmuid Ferriter, *Nation of Extremes: Pioneers in Twentieth-century Ireland* (Dublin: Irish Academic Press, 1999).

141   Diarmuid Ferriter, 'Drink and society in twentieth-century Ireland', in Elisabeth Fitzpatrick and James Kelly (eds), *Food and Drink in Ireland* (Dublin: The Royal Irish Academy, 2016).

There are also many wine writers and journalists who have contributed to Ireland's unique beverage culture. Names like John Wilson, Mary Dowey, Ernie Whalley and Mairtin Moran immediately spring to mind, but special mention must be made of the recently deceased Tomás Clancy, wine correspondent with the *Sunday Business Post*; whose weekly articles frequently moved beyond wine writing and description and delved into the historical and cultural context of beverage and its engagement with Irish society. A keen supporter of beverage research in Ireland, Clancy was always available to lend an encouraging hand to those engaged in drinks research endeavours. In addition to the beverage literature mentioned above, there are a variety of research projects currently underway in Irish beverage studies areas. These projects are housed in several research centres that have been at the forefront in promoting beverage research in recent years.

The School of Culinary Arts and Food Technology

The School of Culinary Arts and Food Technology at Technological University Dublin (TU Dublin) has been at the heart of food and beverage education for over seventy-five years. Now based at the new TU Dublin City Campus in Grangegorman, the School has long been recognised as a centre of excellence with a wide array of courses specific to the drinks industry from higher certificate to honours degree level. In more recent years the School has developed an extensive beverage research agenda and currently has several postgraduate projects underway exploring diverse themes including formal wine writing in Ireland, historical whiskey mashbills, oral histories of rural publicans and the social meaning of claret in Georgian Ireland. There have already been substantial research outputs from these projects including conference organisation, presentations and publications. Tara McConnell has recently published a chapter entitled 'The Social Meaning of Claret in Eighteenth Century Ireland' in *The Irish Community in Bordeaux in the Eighteenth*

Century: Contributions and Contexts.[142] RTÉ's *Brainstorm*[143] is another important academic platform, and hosts Diarmuid Cawley's pieces, 'All you ever wanted to know about natural wines'[144] and 'A nose for wine: all you need to know about sommeliers'.[145] James McCauley has also been published on *Brainstorm* with titles including 'The death of the Irish rural publican'[146] and 'What's next for the Irish Pub?'[147]

The National Centre for Franco-Irish Studies

The National Centre for Franco-Irish Studies (NCFIS), under the direction of Dr Eamon Maher, is a research centre based in TU Dublin and provides another important Irish beverage research hub. Though historically focused on more traditional humanities research areas, it has recently encouraged and supported several gastronomic projects. Current

142 Tara McConnell, 'The social meaning of Claret in eighteenth century Ireland', in Charles C. Luddington (eds), *The Irish Community in Bordeaux in the Eighteenth Century: Contributions and Contexts* (New Haven, CT: Yale University Press).

143 RTÉ's *Brainstorm* is a partnership between RTÉ and Irish third-level institutions, University College Cork, NUI Galway, University of Limerick, DCU, Technological University Dublin and Maynooth University. The Irish Research Council and Teagasc are also promoters of the online platform.

144 Diarmuid Cawley, 'All you ever wanted to know about natural wines'. Available at: <https://www.rte.ie/brainstorm/2018/0814/985019-guide-to-natural-wines/> (Accessed 16 September 2020).

145 Diarmuid Cawley, 'A nose for wine: All you need to know about sommeliers'. Available at: <https://www.rte.ie/brainstorm/2019/0314/1036356-a-nose-for-wine-all-you-need-to-know-about-sommeliers/> (2019) (Accessed 16 September 2020).

146 James McCauley, 'The death of the Irish rural publican'. Available at: <https://www.rte.ie/brainstorm/2019/0418/1043366-the-death-of-the-irish-rural-publican/> (Accessed 16 October 2020).

147 James McCauley, 'What's next for the Irish pub?' Available at: <https://www.rte.ie/brainstorm/2020/0507/1136959-pubs-ireland-future-coronavirus/> (Accessed 17 October 2020).

postgraduate research themes being explored within the centre include cultural representations of the Irish Pub, the role of performance in beverage culture and the role of whiskey in shaping Irish identity. Over the last ten years the NCFIS has also supported other projects where beverage culture and Irish Studies have been foregrounded, including *Exploring the role of place and story in perceptions of French wine culture*'[148] and *Five Decades of Guinness Advertising in Ireland: Increments of Change.*[149] In addition, the Centre publishes the *Journal of Franco-Irish Studies*[150] and the sixth volume of this journal was entirely devoted to beverage culture.[151]

There have also been two biennial academic conferences in Ireland where beverage studies have found a willing platform in terms of both presentation and publication.

The Dublin Gastronomy Symposium

Since its inaugural conference in 2012, the Dublin Gastronomy Symposium (DGS) has provided a unique forum for beverage research. Chaired by Dr Máirtín Mac Con Iomaire from TU Dublin and heavily focused on food studies, each of its biennial conferences has also contained panels and papers on drinks. In addition, the DGS, in collaboration with the NCFIS, was core to the development of the Beverage Research Network which organised beverage culture research seminars in 2015, 2017 and 2019. The DGS also provides an extensive academic resource in the form of the DGS Arrow portal.[152] Prominent beverage

---

148   Brian Murphy, PhD Thesis (2013).

149   Patricia Medcalf PhD, Thesis (2017).

150   *The Journal of Franco-Irish Studies* is a peer reviewed postgraduate online journal that seeks to explore relevant intersections and shared experiences between France and Ireland.

151   *JOFIS* Volume 6. Available at: <https://arrow.tudublin.ie/jofis/> (Accessed 10 October 2020).

152   The DGS hosts an extensive resource of its papers on the TU Dublin Arrow platform. Available at: <https://arrow.tudublin.ie/dgs/> (Accessed 10 October 2020).

papers available on this online platform include 'The Power of Wine Language: Critics, Labels and Sexism',[153] Powerful Puzzles: Mapping the Symbiosis Between Two Great Signifiers of Irishness, The Writer and The Pub',[154] 'Claret: the preferred libation of Georgian Ireland's élite',[155] 'Shaken not Stirred – The Evolution of the Cocktail Shaker',[156] 'The Irish Whiskey Renaissance: A Revolution of Sorts?'[157] and 'Guinness and Food: Ingredients in an Unlikely Gastronomic Revolution'.[158]

The Association of Franco-Irish Studies (AFIS)

The Association of Franco Irish Studies (AFIS) is an international collaborative network of institutions and scholars. Formed in 2003 at the Institute of Technology Tallaght, the association hosts international conferences on the links between Irish Studies in France and Ireland. The association is currently chaired by Dr Sarah Balen from the Dun Laoghaire Institute of Art, Design and Technology and has published

153 Diarmuid Cawley, 'The power of wine language – Critics, Labels and Sexism'. Available at: <https://arrow.tudublin.ie/dgs/2018/may30/12/> (Accessed 7 October 2020).

154 Aoife Carrigy, 'Powerful puzzles: Mapping the symbiosis between two great signifiers of Irishness, The Writer and The Pub.' Available at: <https://arrow.tudublin.ie/dgs/2018/may30/11/> (Accessed 6 September 2020).

155 Tara McConnell, 'Claret: The preferred libation of Georgian Ireland's élite'. Available at: <https://arrow.tudublin.ie/dgs/2012/june612/3/> (Accessed 6 September 2020).

156 James Murphy, 'Shaken not stirred – The evolution of the cocktail shaker'. Available at: <https://arrow.tudublin.ie/dgs/2012/june612/4/> (Accessed 6 September 2020).

157 Sylvain Tondeur, 'The Irish whiskey renaissance: A revolution of sorts?' Available at: <https://arrow.tudublin.ie/dgs/2016/June1/7/> (Accessed 6 October 2020).

158 Patricia Medcalf, 'Guinness and food: Ingredients in an unlikely gastronomic revolution'. Food and Revolution. Dublin Gastronomy Symposium, Dublin, 1st June. Arrow@DIT. Available at: <https://arrow.dit.ie/cgi/viewcontent.cgi?article=1084&context=dgs> (Accessed 22 October 2020).

a wide range of conference proceedings both in Ireland and in France over its seventeen-year history. These books have included many beverage chapters including, 'Using a 17th century Benedictine monk to convert myth into history in an effort to sell more fizz', [159] 'The Role of Revolution and Rioting in French Wine's relationship with Place', [160] 'Cognac, Scotch and Irish: Lessons in Gastronomic Identity', [161] 'A New Phenomenon: Whiskey Tourism in Ireland', [162] 'Calling Time on Alcohol Advertising in Ireland' [163] and 'Irish Cultural Heritage through the Prism of Guinness's Ads in the 1980s'. [164] The association's fourteenth conference took place in TU Dublin in October 2021 and once again included a number of papers focused on beverage culture generally and the Irish Pub in particular. [165]

159   Brian Murphy, 'Using a 17th century Benedictine monk to convert myth into history in an effort to sell more fizz', in Sylvie Mikowski (ed.), *Histoire et Mémoire en France et en Irlande/History and Memory in France and Ireland* (Reims: Épure, 2011), pp. 291–308.

160   Brian Murphy, 'The role of revolution and rioting in French wine's relationship with place', in Yann Bévant, Anne Goarzin and Grace Neville (eds), *France, Ireland and Rebellion* (Rennes: Tir, 2011), pp. 149–167.

161   Brian Murphy, 'Cognac, Scotch and Irish: Lessons in gastronomic identity', in Frank Healy and Brigitte Bastiat (eds), *Voyages between France and Ireland: Culture, Tourism and Sport* (Oxford: Peter Lang, 2017), pp. 237–255.

162   Sylvain Tondeur, 'A new phenomenon: Whiskey tourism in Ireland', in Frank Healy and Brigitte Bastiat (eds), *Voyages between France and Ireland: Culture, Tourism and Sport* (Oxford: Peter Lang, 2017), pp. 257–274.

163   Patricia Medcalf, 'Calling time on alcohol advertising in Ireland', in Catherine Maignant, SylainTondeur and Déborah Vandewoude (eds), *Margins and Marginalities in Ireland and France: A Socio-Cultural Perspective* (Oxford: Peter Lang, 2020).

164   Patricia Medcalf, 'Irish cultural heritage through the prism of Guinness's ads in the 1980s', in Eamon Maher and Eugene O'Brien (eds), *Patrimoine/Cultural Heritage in France and Ireland* (Oxford: Peter Lang, 2018).

165   Patricia Medcalf and Brian Murphy, 'Doing it for themselves: The new reality when it comes to promoting pubs'; and Grainne Murphy, 'Learning from the UK experience: How the social entrepreneurship model can help save the rural Irish Pub.' Papers presented at the 14th Association of Franco Irish Studies Conference, TU Dublin Tallaght Campus, 28–29 October 2021.

The Reimagining Ireland Book Series

The *Reimagining Ireland* series began in 2003. Edited by Dr Eamon Maher, the series now boasts an impressive 106 volumes and covers a very wide range of diverse Irish Studies topics. The very first volume in the series was a monograph from cultural theorist Eugene O' Brien, which included a chapter entitled on 'Tá Siad ag Teacht: Guinness as a Signifier of Irish Cultural Transformation'. This important contribution undoubtedly encouraged further exploration of other beverage-related topics in the series. Some of the topics covered include: 'Appellation "Éire" Contrôlée: Historical Links Between France's Wine Heritage and Ireland',[166] 'The Irish Pub Abroad: Lessons in the Commodification of Gastronomic Culture',[167] 'Wine and Music: An Emerging Cultural Relationship',[168] 'Thinking Beyond the Bottle: Traditional French Wine versus New Media'[169] and 'Brew as much as possible during the proper season: Beer Consumption in Elite Households in Eighteenth-Century Ireland'.[170] By far the most prominent beverage example of the series is

---

166 Brian Murphy, 'Appellation "Éire" Contrôlée - Heritage links between France's wine heritage and Ireland', in Eamon Maher and Catherine Maignant (eds), *Franco-Irish Connections in Space and Time: Peregrinations and Ruminations* (Oxford: Peter Lang, 2012), pp. 117–132.

167 Brian Murphy, 'The Irish pub Abroad: Lessons in the commodification of gastronomic culture', in Máirtín Mac Con Iomaire and Eamon Maher (eds), *'Tickling the Palate': Gastronomy in Irish Literature and Culture* (Oxford: Peter Lang, 2014), pp. 191–205.

168 Brian Murphy, 'Wine and music: An emerging cultural relationship', in Una Hunt and Mary Pierce (eds), *France and Ireland: Notes and Narratives* (Oxford: Peter Lang, 2015), pp. 143–158.

169 Brian Murphy, 'Thinking beyond the Bottle: Traditional French wine versus new media', in Anne Goarzin (ed.), *New Critical Perspectives on Franco-Irish Relations* (Oxford: Peter Lang, 2015), pp. 159–180.

170 Tara Kellaghan, '"Brew as much as possible during the proper season": Beer consumption in elite households in eighteenth-century Ireland', in *'Tickling the Palate': Gastronomy in Irish Literature and Culture*, pp. 177–190.

Patricia Medcalf's monograph, *Advertising the Black Stuff in Ireland*,[171] which uses the story of Guinness to interpret Ireland's cultural history between the years 1959 to 1999. In a recent *Irish Times* review, John Fanning described Medcalf's contribution as 'ground-breaking'. Fanning's comments help highlight the important role beverage studies can play in understanding Ireland's cultural landscape. He says:

> I'm not suggesting that *Advertising the Black Stuff* should replace the collected works of Diarmuid Ferriter and Roy Foster, but it can augment what they have to say and hopefully it may inspire other academics to dip their toes into advertising's Aladdin's cave and add to our understanding of our collective times past and present.[172]

In addition to the material mentioned above, there have been other academic publications that are relevant in the field of Irish beverage studies. These include, 'The rise of whiskey tourism in Ireland: Developing a *terroir* engagement template', in the *Journal of Gastronomy and Tourism*,[173] 'In search of identity: an exploration of the relationship between Guinness's advertising and Ireland's social and economic evolution between 1959 and 1969',[174] and 'Advertising gastronomic identity in an epicurean world: the case for Irish Single Pot Still Whiskey',[175] in *The Irish Communications*

---

171   Patricia Medcalf, *Advertising the Black Stuff in Ireland 1959–1999: Increments of Change* (Oxford: Peter Lang, 2020).

172   John Fanning, 'Advertising the Black Stuff in Ireland 1959–1999: Through a Guinness glass brightly', in *The Irish Times*, 25 July 2020. Available at: <https://www.irishtimes.com/culture/books/advertising-the-black-stuff-in-ireland-1959–1999-through-a-guinness-glass-brightly-1.4306112> (Accessed 10 September 2020).

173   Brian Murphy, 'The rise of whiskey tourism in Ireland: Developing a terroir engagement template', in a special edition in the *Journal of Gastronomy and Tourism*, 3 (2), 2018, pp. 107–123. Available at: <https://www.cognizantcommunication.com/journal-titles/journal-of-gastronomy-and-tourism> (Accessed 23 September 2020).

174   Patricia Medcalf, 'In search of identity: An exploration of the relationship between Guinness's advertising and Ireland's social and economic evolution between 1959 and 1969', *Irish Communication Review*, 15 (1), p. 3. Available at: <https://arrow.dit.ie/cgi/viewcontent.cgi?article=1143&context=icr> (Accessed 17 September 2020).

175   Brian Murphy, 'Advertising gastronomic identity in an epicurean world: The case for Irish single pot still whiskey', *Irish Communication Review*, 15 (1),

Review.[176] Although not exhaustive, the publications identified above suggest that beverage research has played a considerable role in Irish academic discourse over recent years and helps bolster the argument for it to be considered as an important part of Irish cultural studies.

New Directions for Beverage Research

The physical spaces where beverage has been consumed have historically been quite limited and fixed by place and time. As such, beverage research tended to be centred on these spaces. For example, the Irish Pub provided a key focal point for consideration of issues such as gender, music, story and performance. It acted as a refuge for artists and writers alike who used its muse-like influence for inspiration and sometimes solace to cope with frequent rejection. Drinking within the home was another source of subject material for playwrights and poets. In more recent times both beverages and the places associated with their consumption have changed, but their ability to contribute to the discourse on Irish cultural life is no less diminished. The following examples help demonstrate that beverage research remains contemporary and relevant in an Ireland that has changed considerably in terms of its drinking culture over recent years and suggest that new drinks and new drinking spaces will continue to act as important cultural signifiers.

Article 7, 2016. Available at: <http://arrow.dit.ie/icr/vol15/iss1/7> (Accessed 18 September 2020).

176   <https://arrow.tudublin.ie/icr/vol15/iss1/> (Accessed 18 September 2020).

Image 1. The Coffee Cart in Penneys, Mary Street, Dublin.

The Coffee Cart in Penneys of Mary Street. Photo by Brian Murphy taken 22 December 2019.

Beverage Spaces and Irish Retail: Penneys Coffee Cart, Mary Street, Dublin

In 2018, Penneys unveiled their newest addition to the Irish retail market that 'basically guarantees we're never going to want to leave'.[177] The Primark Coffee Cart pictured above is positioned in the middle of the shopping aisles in Penneys' flagship store in Mary Street, Dublin. Although coffee shops have long been associated with large retail stores this somewhat

---

177   Kelley Ryan, Penneys newest addition basically guarantees we're never going to want to leave'. Available at: <https://www.her.ie/food/penneys-newest-addition-basically-guarantees-never-going-want-leave-439546> (Accessed 20 October 2020).

unique approach presents an incongruous picture of how beverage can be directly integrated into the on-floor shopping experience. Its introduction exemplifies Ireland's love affair with both coffee and retail and how this ancient beverage has become synonymous with every aspect of our lives. This seemingly inconsequential example can provide substantial material for the exploration of modern Irish society, its mercantile nature, our desire for instant gratification, for cheap food and drink and for fast fashion. Identifying such a drinking space in such a strange location demonstrates the important role coffee plays in Irish culture and the rich vein of investigation it potentially facilitates.

Beverage Spaces and Irish Corporate Culture: O' Barnaby's Pub, Fifth Floor Qualtrics, Dublin

There can be few more odd locations for a traditional Irish Pub than the fifth floor of the Dublin offices of Qualtrics, a billion-dollar market research firm based in the US. However, this was the location of O' Barnaby's Irish Pub, part of the staff facilities that Qualtrics made available to their young workforce, along with games rooms, coffee shops and relaxing breakout spaces.[178] According to Qualtrics EMEA chairman Dermot Costello, who sadly passed away in 2018, the pub 'opens on Thursday and Friday evenings for a few hours so staff can come, have a few drinks and catch up on the week'.[179] O' Barnaby's presents another example of an atypical new drinking space that might be used to explore

---

178 Killian Woods, 'Take a guided tour of … the billion-dollar tech firm with an Irish pub in its office'. Available at: <https://www.thejournal.ie/office-tour-qualtrics-dublin-3-3447734-Jun2017/> (Accessed 18 May 2020).

179 This is a quote from a 2017 video tour/interview that Dermot Costello did with the Journal.ie where he explained the working environment for the staff at Qualtrics Dublin offices.

Image 2. The Virgin Mary Bar, Capel Street, Dublin.

The Virgin Mary at 54 Capel Street, Dublin. Photo by Brian Murphy taken 6 July 2022.

Irish cultural themes such as authenticity, globalisation, cultural appropriation and how Irish society is viewed both from within and without.[180]

Beverage Spaces and the Pub with No Beer: The Virgin Mary, Capel Street, Dublin

A third example of a somewhat atypical Irish drinking space and how it might be of value in a cultural studies context is Dublin's first

180   O' Barnaby's Pub has recently been renamed Dermot's Pub in honour of Qualtrics Chairman, Dermot Costello, who passed away in 2018.

non-alcoholic pub located in Capel Street. The opening of the Virgin Mary pub, pictured above, in May 2019 caused something of a stir at the time with considerable media attention noting the unusual nature of such a concept in Irish cultural life. Rory Carroll, Irish correspondent with *The Guardian*, noted at the time:

> The Irish writer Brendan Behan made a famous declaration that he drank only on two occasions. 'When I'm thirsty and when I'm not.' Many compatriots adopted the quip as a defiant motto, an embrace of the stereotype of the boozy Irishman swaying on a bar stool. But the image needs updating because Dublin is about to get a pub with a twist: no alcohol.[181]

The Virgin Mary's opening in the capital marks a significant departure in terms of the nation's perceived relationship with drinking. It encourages further exploration in terms of cultural tropes, inherent Irish attitudes to alcohol or even religious interpretations considering the pub's name. One can imagine the furore regarding the name, if the pub had opened in previous years given the then dominance of the Catholic Church.

Beverage Spaces and Cycling Cafes: The Old Hardware, Narraghmore

Sport and fitness have become major pursuits in Ireland and while there have always been strong beverage links through GAA, rugby or golf clubs, some less obvious partnerships have developed as modern Ireland embraces a more active health and wellness culture. Cycling has become a feature in many people's lives and there are emerging examples of beverage spaces becoming core to the biking experience. Rural coffee shops and community cafés have become synonymous with the Irish cycling

---

181   Rory Carroll, '"Ireland is changing": Booze-free bar opens in Dublin', *The Guardian*, 8 May 2019. Available at: <https://www.theguardian.com/world/2019/may/08/ireland-is-changing-booze-free-bar-opens-in-dublin> (Accessed 18 May 2020).

Image 3. The Old Hardware Community Café, Narraghmore, Co. Kildare.

Photo of The Old Hardware Community Café a newly designated Cycle Café, Narraghmore, Co Kildare taken by Brian Murphy 11 October 2020.

community as long cycle routes are often informally structured around potential stop off points. A more formal engagement between such cafés and cycling enthusiasts is now under way with recent government allocations for the development of formal Cycling Cafés:

> Drive-through cinemas, 'cycle cafés', and outdoor seating and dining facilities are among the projects to be funded in a €2.8 million package to help rural communities adapt to the Covid 19 pandemic ... Funding will also go to supporting the establishment of cycle cafes – coffee stops for cyclists on greenways and other rural cycling routes.[182]

182   Marie O Halloran, 'Towns and villages to get €2.8m for 'cycle cafes' and outdoor cinemas', *The Irish Times*, 3 August 2020. Available at: <https://www.irishtimes.

The Old Hardware, Narraghmore, pictured above is an excellent example of a community café that has recently received Cycling Café status from Kildare County Council having met a range of required criteria. It provides a welcome respite for local cyclists on long journeys. Historically, we may have considered a pub crawl on a Saturday night, an inevitable consequence of Irish drinking culture; now a 50 km cycle on a Sunday morning through rural Ireland on a route peppered with designated cycle cafés is considered a normal part of life.

Conclusion

Ireland has a unique relationship with beverage. Though not always positive, it has nonetheless acted as a cultural backdrop for many aspects of our society. Just as food studies has become defined by a strong research agenda this chapter argues that the field of Irish beverage studies deserves similar consideration. It posits that drink studies can be considered a legitimate part of the Irish Studies research agenda and suggests that a new cohort of researcher is emerging in the field, one that comes from the more practical and applied side of the sector. Historians, sociologists and literature scholars will always have a keen interest in the topic but this new cohort has the potential to complement more traditional approaches by focusing on new emerging areas of beverage and beverage spaces. Products such as coffee, tea and non-alcoholic alternatives are increasingly being foregrounded and deserve considerable attention as new Irish generations engage with beverage and the places of its consumption in previously inconceivable ways. Earlier the chapter alluded to the fact that food studies is a relatively new academic phenomenon and was until recently somewhat looked down upon by more traditional academic communities.[183] Experience tells us that the same premise applies to beverage

---

com/news/politics/towns-and-villages-to-get-2-8m-for-cycle-cafes-and-outdoor-cinemas-1.4320134> (Accessed 21 August 2020).

183   Warren Belasco, *Food: The Key Concepts* (New York: Berg, 2008).

studies. Anybody working in the area will recognise the refrain, 'Sure isn't that only about pulling pints?' This chapter has hopefully demonstrated that, like food studies, there have been substantial advances in how beverage studies are perceived in Ireland, much of it due to the hard work of the research communities described above. It has argued that beverage studies, particularly in an Irish Studies context, deserves a similar academic fate but only time will tell whether the valued research contribution it makes will ultimately be recognised.

CHAPTER 5

The Rural Irish Pub: From Beating Heart to Beaten Down and Back Again

In the mid-1970s we moved from living over the family butcher shop in Inchicore to the rural surroundings of the Dublin Kildare border. Our nearest pub was the Hatch Bar on the banks of the Grand Canal in Hazelhatch, Co. Kildare. Though now closed, that pub was both my father's local and a very important part of our local community. Run by the Lee family, the pub provided the type of traditional bar that is sadly disappearing from Irish life. It was a place of refuge from the everyday, where locals and visitors were welcomed into what was essentially the front room of the Lee family home. One of my strongest and most treasured memories is of having a pint of Guinness alongside my father at that bar in the final years of his life. What follows laments the disappearance of rural pubs like the Hatch Bar in Co. Kildare but also offers hope by suggesting that there might still be ways to stem the decline of these important reservoirs of Irish heritage before it's too late.

Places in our lives tend be either central or peripheral and this chapter examines how the rural pub has moved from the former to the latter. It describes not only the reasons for that move but also possible ways in which it might be reversed and how the pub can once again play a key role in the social life of rural Ireland.

The concept of marginality, when applied to people and place, can have both positive and negative connotations. Society sometimes views those that exist on its margins in a positive light; as people to look up to, inspirational people like writers, artists and musicians. They are often considered outliers with more interesting perspectives than the mundane opinion of the masses. There are also others who exist on the margins due a consequence of misfortune. These groups might include the homeless or the poor who appear as outcasts in that same society. Just like people, marginal places can also be viewed positively and negatively. Positive marginal

Image 4. The Hatch Bar, Hazelhatch, Co Kildare.

Picture of The Hatch Bar, Hazelhatch, Kildare (now closed) taken 5 June 2002, courtesy of the National Inventory of Architectural Heritage. Available at: <https://www.buildingsofireland.ie/buildings-search/build ing/11207018/the-hatch-bar-hazelhatch-bridge-commons-ne-by-newcastle-ed-hazelhatch-dublin> (Accessed 24 March 2022).

places might include locations like the islands that surround our shores, religious or secular retreats and even increasingly popular locations where limited access to technology is considered a positive thing. But this chapter speaks to the more negative aspects of place marginality and explores how the Irish Pub has itself been pushed from a central role in rural life to the margins of that same society. The chapter posits that the appreciation of the pub's social value in Ireland has declined, explores reasons for that decline and ultimately proposes possible solutions that might help bring the Irish Pub back into the beating heart of rural life.

In 2018, Na Fianna, one of the most prominent GAA clubs in Ireland found themselves facing an impossible dilemma. They discovered that the proposed route for a new national infrastructure project was to encroach on key club facilities located at Mobhi Road, Dublin. This new project would by necessity cause a substantial threat to the very survival of the club over a long period of time. 'If this came to pass, Na Fianna was certain that there would be multiple negative consequences for the club, in both the medium- and long-term.'[1] The club's response was rapid and vocal. In addition to several organised protests and media mentions, they commissioned a report entitled *The Social Value of CLG Na Fianna*. This extensive 120-page report was compiled by Sandra Velthius of Whitebarn Consulting, accredited by Social Value International and was published in April 2019.

The report reached several important conclusions:

Na Fianna generated in the order of €50 million of social value in the club year.

For every €1 equivalent invested into Na Fianna, in the region of €15 of social value was created.

Conservatively extrapolating these results to all 91 clubs under the remit of the Dublin County Board, around €1 billion of social value is generated each year.[2]

The Na Fianna GAA example is useful in the context of the Irish Pub in that it proposed an innovative solution to the substantial disruption of its core activity. The importance of its sense of place in the local community was put under threat due to circumstances beyond its control. In a sense its primary social role was being ignored and pushed to the margins as government infrastructure policy took precedence. This chapter suggests that another of Ireland's traditional places, the rural pub, has also been 'marginalised'. Not by one clearly identifiable proposed infrastructure

---

1 Sandra Velthius, *The Social Value of CLG Na Fianna: A Demonstration Study*, undertaken by Whitebarn Consulting on behalf of the Dublin GAA County Board, April 2019. Available at: <http://clgnafianna.com/wp-content/uploads/2019/05/Na_Fianna_Social_Value_Report_Final_1May2019.pdf> (Accessed May 2019).

2 Ibid., p. 32.

project as in the case of Na Fianna but in a variety of both external and internal ways. Such marginalisation has caused a diminution of the central
role the pub's 'sense of place' plays in Irish rural life. As with the Na Fianna
example, this has not only had economic consequences, but also a range
of social consequences. However, unlike the Na Fianna example, to date,
there has been a limited emphasis on quantifying, in monetary terms, the
social value of the rural Irish Pub. A great amount of political rhetoric is
devoted to the demise of rural life and yet few solutions are offered. This
chapter acknowledges that communicating social consequences can be difficult, especially when social value discourse is increasingly governed by the
language of economics and terms such as cost benefit analysis, break even
and marginal contributions are common when discussing society's needs.
While it is true that the Na Fianna example relates to an urban environment, their experience can be applied to rural situations where the need
for solutions is often more pronounced. Somehow, we need to measure
and evaluate the long-term social impact of disrupting the places that were
once the 'beating heart' of local rural communities.

    Unlike the GAA, Irish Pubs are 'for profit' businesses and this also plays
a role in perception where the provision of social good gets blended with
the inherent drive for material gain. Perhaps unfairly at times the traditional
publican has frequently been perceived as one of the wealthier people in
rural Irish society. However, despite the obvious business benefit, in many
rural communities, the places they operate also play an important role that
moves beyond pure monetary gain. They fulfil what Ray Oldenburg, Perry
Share and others refer to as Third Place functions. According to Share:

> It is in this regard that the concept of 'third place' may be of use. (…) It provides us
> with a way to understand and value the type of activity that occurs in this social site
> and provides a possibility for critical response to the changes that may be taking place.
> For Oldenburg, echoing 'social capital' writers such as Putnam (1999) and Wilkinson
> (1999), involvement in informal public life has important psychological, social, and
> political implications. Such involvement is facilitated by the existence of third places.[3]

---

3   Perry Share, 'A genuine third place? Towards an understanding of the pub in con-
     temporary Irish Society', 30th SAI Annual Conference, Cavan, 26 April 2003.
     Available   at: <https://www.academia.edu/805791/A_genuine_third_place_

Traditional rural 'places' like the pub provide focal points for community activity and social interaction. Like the more recent development of the 'Men's Shed' movement these places provide a cure for rural isolation, they offer a place where local culture and traditions can be observed. They are living, breathing aspects of rural life. However, these places are quietly disappearing.

> Just prior to the pandemic, there were 7,137 licenced pubs throughout the country. That has dropped to 6,788. The 349 pubs that have closed were in 25 counties. Some 37 pubs shut in Cork, with the overall number declining from 910 to 873. In Dublin, 33 pubs closed, with the city and county now having 752 pubs, and in Kerry, the number dropped from 448 to 426. Donegal lost 33, decreasing from 367 to 334. By contrast, Co Monaghan, lost just two (99 to 97) and Co Sligo lost four going from 140 to 136.[4]

This is neither a recent phenomenon nor a consequence of the Covid 19 crisis. Figures from the Drinks Industry Group of Ireland (DIGI) show that there were 1,477 fewer pubs in operation in 2017 when compared with 2005.[5] Their place in Irish culture has been marginalised by a range of external and internal factors that have led to their current perilous predicament. That 'sense of place' once so prevalent in rural Irish life has been disrupted to such a degree that it has increasingly become the focal point of water cooler discussions on the demise of rural Ireland and potential ways in which it may be saved. This chapter argues for a similar approach to rural Ireland's places as was undertaken by Na Fianna. It suggests that the rural Irish pub sector might consider commissioning its own 'Social Value of the Rural Irish Pub Report' to help quantifiably highlight its plight. The detail of such an extensive report is beyond the

---

Towards_an_understanding_of_the_pub_in_contemporary_Irish_society>
(Accessed 20 March 2020).

4   Sean O Riordan, 'Last orders: Almost 350 pubs have closed since the start of the Covid 19 pandemic', *The Irish Examiner* [online], 17 October 2021. Available at: <https://www.irishexaminer.com/news/arid-40723155.html> (Accessed 4 November 2021).

5   Charlie Taylor, 'Last orders: Number of pubs in the republic continues to drop', The Irish Times.com, 22 August 2018. Available at: <https://www.irishtimes.com/business/agribusiness-and-food/last-orders-number-of-pubs-in-the-republic-continues-to-drop-1.3603452> (Accessed 19 January 2019).

scope of this research but this work can perhaps play a role in setting the scene for encouraging such a report to happen. The chapter identifies and analyses key marginalising factors that have played a significant role in the demise of the rural Irish pub. Some of these factors are external in nature and beyond the control of the rural publican. Others, as we shall see below, are more closely aligned to the publican's own actions and his or her difficulty in proactively engaging with potential opportunities may have had a substantial impact on the rural pub's demise.

The Irish Pub through a Tourism Lens

In Irish society the rural pub can be viewed in many ways. It is not only a purveyor of alcoholic drinks, but also as a place of local congregation, of music, of community. Its renowned muse-like qualities have provided considerable cultural inspiration down through the years and one finds many great Irish writers, artists and musicians who have referenced the Irish Pub, both in their work and in their personal life. Indeed, according to Scarborough, Share and others it forms an important aspect of Ireland's intangible cultural heritage, and as mentioned, has been identified in academic literature as a clear manifestation of Oldenburg's Third Place concept.[6] However, the Irish Pub also provides another key function. It has been extensively used in tourism promotion down through the years and many see a visit to the pub, be it rural or urban, as essential to the Irish touristic experience. As far back as 2012 The *Lonely Planet Guide* ranked going to the pub as 'the greatest experience a tourist can have in Ireland'.[7]

---

6   Gwen Scarborough, *The Irish Pub as a 'Third Place': A Sociological Exploration of People, Place and Identity* (PhD Thesis, Institute of Technology Sligo, 2008).

7   Anon., 'After rating thousands of Ireland's hotels, restaurants and galleries, Lonely Planet advises tourists: Go to the pub!' *The Daily Mail* [online], 12 January 2012. Available at: <https://www.dailymail.co.uk/news/article-2085612/Lonely-Planet-travel-guide-Ireland-advises-tourists-Go-pub.html> (Accessed 12 February 2019).

Furthermore, in its more recent description of things to do in Ireland the guide continues to emphasise the pub's touristic role:

> There's no better place to sample Irish culture and friendliness than in the pub. Despite all the distractions that the 21st century offers, the pub remains at the heart of Ireland's social life and joining the locals for a drink or three is a must for any visitor to the country.[8]

The links between the pub and Irish identity are strong and it has expanded its touristic role to include the promotion of our unique sense of place beyond Ireland's shores. As such, the Irish Pub abroad influences how people view both our cultural and our gastronomic identity. Such exposure can encourage people to engage with Irish culture and hopefully encourage future tourism visits. Many would argue, perhaps with some validity, that the Irish Pub, when viewed through a tourism lens, is also a somewhat contrived reflection of Irish culture.

Barbara O'Connor suggests that 'cultural and national identities are constructed from the representations which certain people both inside and outside our culture produce for us'.[9] She likens this to how personal identities are developed through interactions with others and goes on to explore tourist images of Ireland and the sense of identity which is engendered by such representations. It seems reasonable to explore how associations with 'place' might also be used to encourage relationships between food and drink products and consumers. O'Connor uses Irish tourism as an example, suggesting that several writers agree that there are a variety of tourism markers which represent how people abroad view Ireland. In many cases these images of what O'Connor refers to as 'paddy whackery' are what shape people's views of Irish identity.[10] The Irish pub abroad can also offer a certain representation of Irishness, although many argue that this representation is a contrived reflection of Irish culture. Honor Fagan

---

8   The Lonely Planet.com. Available at: <https://www.lonelyplanet.com/ireland/thi ngs-to-do/ireland-s-top-pubs> (Accessed 12 March 2019).

9   Barbara O' Connor, 'Myths and mirrors: Tourist images and national identity', in O' Barbara O Connor, and Michael Cronin (eds), *Tourism In Ireland: A Critical Analysis* (Cork: Cork University Press, 1993), p. 68.

10   Ibid., p. 70.

argues: 'What passes for Irish culture today – the musical dance show Riverdance, the supergroup U2, or the ubiquitous global Irish pub – does not spring from the eternal wells of the Irish soul. Rather these phenomena are, to a large extent, manufactured by the global cultural industry.'[11] There is much validity in what Fagan says but one might counter her argument by citing examples that show the importance of the modern Irish pub in framing, outside of Ireland, people's view of certain aspects of Irish culture. One recent example of this was the extensive coverage of the visit of Eric and Donald Trump Jr to three rural pubs in Doonbeg, Co Clare at the height of their father's presidency. Media coverage of their father's Irish trip was for a time dominated by the Trump sons' pub crawl and the images that were published around the world very much reflected Ireland's pub culture.[12] In a similar way, international coverage of President Obama's 2011 trip to Ireland featured his visit to Hayes' pub in Moneygall.[13] Queen Elisabeth and Prince Philip's visit that same year to the Gravity Bar in the Guinness Storehouse, pictured below, was also of note among the international media. Even former Taoiseach Bertie Ahern's long association with Fagan's pub, in Drumcondra, Dublin, offers us a unique example of how modern Irish culture is inextricably linked to the Irish Pub[14] and thus provides the perfect vehicle to help communicate our sense of place. Grace Neville is keen to offer some words of caution regarding the portrayal of Ireland in such a fashion when she says, 'In all this we are in danger of believing our own hype, of crossing to the other side of the

11 Honor Fagan, 'Globalisation and culture: Placing Ireland', *Annals AAPSS*, 581, 2002, p. 137.
12 Clodagh Kilcoyne, 'With free beers Trump brothers thank devoted Irish village', Reuters.com. 2019. Available at: <https://www.reuters.com/news/picture/with-free-beers-trump-brothers-thank-dev-idUSKCN1T62X2> (Accessed 5 June 2019).
13 Cathal Dervan, 'Guinness cash in on Obama's Moneygall visit', Irishcentral.com, 2011. Available at: <http://www.irishcentral.com/news/Guinness-cash-in-on-Obamas-Moneygall-vist--122495959.html> (Accessed 14 June 2018).
14 Harry McGee, 'Bertie Ahern and the long winding road to rehabilitation', *The Irish Times* [online], 5 December 2015. Available at: <https://www.irishtimes.com/news/politics/bertie-ahern-and-the-long-winding-road-to-rehabilitation-1.2455075> (Accessed 14 July 2022).

Image 5.   Queen Elisabeth and Prince Philip, The Gravity Bar, Dublin.

ABC, 'Prince Philip eyes Guinness during bar visit', 15 December 2011. Available at: <http://www.abc.net.au/news/2011-05-19/prince-philip-eyes-guinness/2719622> (Accessed 14 May 2019).

mirror to reawaken as the cast of advertisements and films.'[15] She cites her own presidential example of Bill Clinton's visit to the Guinness Brewery in 2001 asking whether we have 'finally gone mad and joined the cast of some giant Guinness advertisement'.[16] Obama's, Queen Elisabeth's and the Trumps visit in later years suggest a certain prophetic quality to her comments. There continues to be a notable blurring of the lines between the promotion of authentic Irish culture and the marketing of that same culture abroad. We are right to be concerned about whether we are looking into, or out of, 'Neville's mirror'. McGovern has suggested that the

> Irish Theme Bar is a commodified cultural form that has mobilised a series of signs and symbols associated with an alcohol-centred stage Irish identity .... The cultural reproduction of such ethnic signs represents a reification of their meaning. As a

15   Grace Neville, 'The commodification of Irish culture in France and beyond', in Eamon Maher and Eugene O Brien (eds), *France and the Struggle against Globalization: Bilingual Essays on the Role of France in the World* (Lewiston: Edwin Mellen Press, 2007), pp. 151–152.

16   Ibid.

consequence, an essentialised conception of ethnicity is constructed, commodified and consumed.[17]

It is the consumer's perception that has the potential to shape their attitudes to that culture and one can argue that this offers us the opportunity to influence attitudes in both a positive and a negative way. Positive, if the consumer perceives the experience of the Irish Pub abroad as being both enjoyable and a fair reflection of Irish culture. Negative, if the Irish Pub is deemed too exploitative and perhaps overly stage 'oirish'. According to Cole, cultural commodification is often viewed as very unattractive in Western society.[18] Even though Cole is referring to quite extreme examples the concept can be seen as something of a betrayal of cultural integrity for profit. Cole, however, is keen to stress that from the commodity providers' perspective there are benefits. Macdonald, cited in Cole,[19] argues that 'many people can use cultural commodification as a way of affirming their identity, of telling their own story, and of establishing the significance of local experiences'. Therefore, it can lead to an enhancement of identity, perhaps to a level that sometimes seems extreme to people originally from that culture. This might go some way towards explaining that overt 'oirishness' that is sometimes evident in Irish pubs abroad.

McGovern has also emphasised the importance of the domestic Irish pub as a key marketing 'motif'.[20] He confirms the *Lonely Planet* view and suggests that the average tourist regards the Irish Pub as a very attractive element in Irish society. It is used as a condensed version of Irish identity, one that can be explored and sampled by the tourist and which offers a somewhat stylised version of our culture. While some might suggest that the power of the Irish Pub as a signifier of Irish identity has been diminished

17   Mark McGovern, 'The Craic market: Irish theme bars and the commodification of Irishness in contemporary Britain', *Irish Journal of Sociology*, 1 (2), 2002, pp. 77–78.
18   Stroma Cole, 'Beyond authenticity and commodification', *Annals of Tourism Research*, 34 (4), 2007, p. 946.
19   Ibid., p. 956.
20   Mark McGovern, 'The cracked pint glass of the servant: The Irish pub, Irish identity and the tourist eye', in Michael Cronin and Barbera O' Connor (eds), *Irish Tourism: Image, Culture and Identity* (Clevedon: Channel View Publications, 2003), p. 83.

over the years, the more recent examples in the *Lonely Planet* guide dispute this. O'Connor [21] discusses how inbound tourists view the tourist product as a reflection of Irish culture and society, but it is McGovern who takes the argument outside Ireland's borders and relates Irish identity to the explosion of the Irish theme bar on a global scale that has happened in recent decades.

It can be argued that the role of the Irish Pub abroad in shaping people's perception of Irish culture and society has ultimately benefited Ireland through tourism, improved relations and a general affection towards things Irish. This has been helped by consumers interacting with the culture of the Irish Pub through McGovern's idea of 'tourism without travel'. It involves exposing people abroad to elements of Irish identity while they remain in their own country. There are notable international examples of hosted events that take place regularly to promote elements of one culture to another. The celebration of the Chinese New Year in many countries outside of China is a case in point as is the international exposure that Beaujolais Day receives on the third Thursday of November each year. St Patrick's Day celebrations outside of Ireland provide another vehicle for the promotion of Irish culture abroad. Inglis describes St Patrick's Day as 'a display of Irish cultural capital and something that is unique in the world in terms of scale. There are celebrations and parades held not only in every town in Ireland but in almost every part of the United States as well as numerous other countries.'[22] Inglis makes the interesting point that St Patrick's Day celebrations are actually an import into Ireland with the first recorded celebrations taking place in Boston in 1737.[23] Even our home celebrations reflect this importation, according to Donald Clarke:

> Then there's the depressing embrace of garish cod-Irish iconography. In a weird postmodern swivel, perfectly decent Irish bars take on the character of those Massachusetts taverns that – all leprechauns and shillelaghs – perennially strive and fail to look like

21 Barbara O' Connor, 'Myths and mirrors: Tourist images and national identity', in O' Barbara O Connor, and Michael Cronin (eds), *Tourism In Ireland: A Critical Analysis* (Cork: Cork University Press, 1993), pp. 68–85.
22 Tom Inglis, *Global Ireland* (New York: Routledge, 2008), p. 95.
23 Ibid..

perfectly decent Irish bars. It won't be long before we start eating corned beef and cabbage and wishing each other 'top of the morning'.[24]

An important difference between the Irish Pub abroad and the aforementioned cultural events is the fact that the Irish Pub abroad has a permanent presence in a host countries' environment. Munoz and Wood explore the role of food and beverage sites as cultural ambassadors in host countries. They cite Bailey and Tian who suggest that these themed ethnic restaurants 'function as a cultural ambassador, providing, for some, an initial exposure to and means of evaluating a country's food and people'.[25] They also cite Spang, suggesting that such themed restaurants may become a 'stand in for travel or an enticement to it'[26], which echoes McGovern's view that the Irish Pub abroad provides that important function of 'tourism without travel', as previously discussed.

The Demon Drink: An Age-Old Political Dilemma

The Irish political class have taken a confusing and dichotomous approach to drink over the years. As noted above, politicians revel in extolling the Irish Pub and the Irish pint to visiting dignitaries; they also laud the recent renaissance in Irish whiskey and gin distilleries and privately cheer-lead a drinks industry that supports 92,000 jobs, and contributes over 2 billion euro to the economy.[27] At the same time both ministers and

24   Donald Clarke, 'St Patrick's Day stimulates the nation's need to be twinkly, drunk and sentimental', *Irish Times*, 16 March 2013 [online]. Available at: <http://www. irishtimes.com/culture/heritage/st-patrick-s-day-stimulates-the-nation-s-need-to-be-twinkly-drunk-and-sentimental-1.1327639?page=1> (Accessed 24 June 2021).
25   Caroline Munoz and Natalie Wood, 'No rules, just right, or is it? The role of themed restaurants as cultural ambassadors', *Tourism and Hospitality Research*, 7 (3–4), June–September 2007, p. 243.
26   Ibid.
27   Drinks Ireland. Available at: <https://www.drinksireland.ie/> (Accessed 19 May 2019).

media frequently condemn the drinks industry and suggest that Ireland's drinking culture, of which the Irish Pub is a key part, is responsible for spiralling health bills and many of society's ills. In addition, political discourse doesn't appear to recognise or consider the important difference between urban and rural pubs. They don't take account of the fact that there are very different demands and expectations, especially when one considers the hinterland our pubs find themselves operating in. The Irish Pub, as a part of rural life, is in danger of being disneyified among an increasingly urban-centric population who tend to view rural Ireland purely in terms of leisure or to visit ageing friends and family. This dichotomous political approach is not unique to either Ireland or the times we live in. In 1952 Judge Noah Sweat gave a famous speech to the Mississippi State Legislature concerning US prohibition and whiskey that typifies Irish political attitudes to drinking culture, its potential impact and the Irish Pub. Judge Sweat said:

> My friends, I had not intended to discuss this controversial subject at this particular time. However, I want you to know that I do not shun controversy. On the contrary, I will take a stand on any issue at any time, regardless of how fraught with controversy it might be. You have asked me how I feel about whiskey.

> All right, this is how I feel about whiskey: If when you say whiskey you mean the devil's brew, the poison scourge, the bloody monster, that defiles innocence, dethrones reason, destroys the home, creates misery and poverty, yea, literally takes the bread from the mouths of little children; if you mean the evil drink that topples the Christian man and woman from the pinnacle of righteous, gracious living into the bottomless pit of degradation, and despair, and shame and helplessness, and hopelessness, then certainly I am against it.

> But, if when you say whiskey you mean the oil of conversation, the philosophic wine, the ale that is consumed when good fellows get together, that puts a song in their hearts and laughter on their lips, and the warm glow of contentment in their eyes; if you mean Christmas cheer; if you mean the stimulating drink that puts the spring in the old gentleman's step on a frosty, crispy morning; if you mean the drink which enables a man to magnify his joy, and his happiness, and to forget, if only for a little while, life's great tragedies, and heartaches, and sorrows; if you mean that drink, the sale of which pours into our treasuries untold millions of dollars, which are used to provide tender care for our little crippled children, our blind, our deaf, our dumb, our pitiful aged and infirm; to build highways and hospitals and schools, then certainly I am for it.

This is my stand. I will not retreat from it. I will not compromise.[28]

Sweat's famous speech, though delivered in a different country and context almost seventy years ago, satirically typifies the relationship between Ireland's political class and the drinks industry. That relationship is often mirrored among the general Irish population in how they view alcohol as both a positive social lubricant and as something to be wary of and potentially harmful. A culture of excess at times and absence at others adds to the confused nature of our relationship with drink. But it is not just a lack of political will that has left the rural Irish pub in its current predicament. A range of contributing factors can be identified as contributing to its marginalisation. Some of these factors have also delivered positive societal change and therefore cannot be viewed in isolation. They might best be viewed as challenges or even opportunities that the rural Irish publican might take advantage of. They can be described as both external and internal in nature. External, in that they have been imposed on the Irish rural publican and he or she had very little influence over that imposition. Internal, in the sense that the publicans themselves played a part in allowing these factors to contribute to their own decline.

Unavoidable External Factors

(1) The rise of technology
Changes in how society communicates have led to a denigration of the importance of the physical places we exist and interact in. Working from home, socialising online rather than in person and using communication apps such as Skype and WhatsApp have all led to a perceived lesser need for place and less opportunity for physical contact and interaction. The Covid 19 pandemic has accelerated this move to technological engagement. Technologies like Zoom or MS Teams are linked by the common

---

28   William Safire, *Lend Me Your Ears: Great Speeches in History* (New York: WW Norton & Co, 1997), p. 954.

freedom of not being tied to any physical place and without doubt, they have had a dramatic impact on traditional places of congregation and communication.

(2) The hollowing out of rural towns

Out-of-town retail developments have greatly contributed to a hollowed out rural place experience in many areas. They have resulted in people removing themselves from village and town centres, where they historically interacted in place settings such as local pubs or shops, to the periphery of place where opportunities for personal and continuous engagement are rare. Rural people traditionally valued daily engagement with their local publican or shopkeeper and a familiar group of customers and neighbours through continuous and connected conversations. Such daily communication is now often replaced by a single interaction once a week when people do their weekly shop in an out-of-town superstore. Frequently the zero-hour contracted person serving us changes from week to week so the opportunity for continuity in terms of relationship is lost. Even innovations in retail design seem to mitigate against community as these large out of town shops negate our sense of place, by imposing impersonal self-service checkouts and push button customer feedback stations. Policy in many supermarkets is to move through quickly and pack on your own with minimum personal interaction.

(3) Developments in transport

As people have become relatively more affluent over the years, cars have become more prevalent as the primary means of travel, particularly in rural areas. In many cases car sharing has become less popular due to security concerns. There has been less reliance on village or town services as motorway improvements have opened up more interesting experiences. As rural inhabitants drive further away from village places, modern cars have had the effect of making us more insular, cocooned and less inclined to engage. Increased security fears have led to a reluctance among drivers to stop for any reason and even that most traditional rural mode of transport, hitchhiking, seems no longer acceptable.

(4) Increased education and employment opportunities

Though welcome, the increased prevalence of third-level education has contributed to the subsequent de-population of rural villages. Younger populations from rural places are moving to more densely populated areas to live, learn and work in what they perceive as more attractive urban environments. Rural pubs are increasingly populated by older customers. Younger generations, returning home from college at weekends, have moved away from using the pub as a gathering space, preferring instead to socialise at home, often with prinks (pre-drinks), before going out to congregate in more urban social settings. In addition, the arrival of foreign direct investment, predominantly centred on urban areas, has led to a commensurate draw away from rural towns and villages. Good employment paths in multinational companies have also become a significant de-population factor that rural society has found very difficult to counteract.

All the above factors have played a significant role in disrupting the sense of place that Ireland, as a predominantly rural society, once held so dear. They can be described as imposed factors that the rural publican had little control over. However, the rural Irish pub has not simply been a passive participant in its own decline. Either through their own action or inaction, they have also played a role in their marginalisation.

Internal Contributors to Decline

(1) A failure to react to Ireland's emerging food culture
Increased exposure to extensive media influences have led to demands for the less familiar and the more exotic. There has been a dramatic shift in how Irish people engage with food and drink culture in the last twenty years. The public now travel much more and are subsequently exposed to alternative food and drink cultures outside of Ireland. A great many rural Irish pubs have failed to take account of this changed gastronomic landscape. Younger markets now demand more food driven product offerings, a greater range of local products, a much broader range of drinks, excellent (and free) Wi-Fi and an array of entertainment options including,

live music, sky sports etc. Up until now many rural pubs simply could not or were not willing to meet such changing demands.

(2) A failure to capitalise on the smoking ban
In 2004 under the stewardship of then health minister, Micheál Martin, the Fianna Fáil government introduced the pub-smoking ban to Ireland.[29] Though positive in so many ways, the ban also left gaping holes in pub demand, particularly in rural settings. The new legislation was introduced despite substantial lobbying by both the Vintners Federation of Ireland and the Licensed Vintners Association. Rural publicans viewed the smoking ban as a negative imposition on their business model and many failed to consider or capitalise on any potential benefits a no smoking ban might bring. The ban provided opportunities to expose new audiences, including more families and female customers, to a new cleaner more pleasant social environment. This new cleaner atmosphere presented opportunities to provide new food and drink experiences to help target new audiences. Suddenly the rural pub had the potential to be an attractive environment for a more health-conscious customer who may have previously viewed the smoky atmosphere as somewhat toxic. Many rural pubs failed to embrace these opportunities and their sales and customers dwindled. They were slow to engage with professional food and wine offerings that targeted previously untapped markets. This was not true of all and several rural pubs did progress following the smoking ban. In some cases, we witnessed the emergence of a new gastropub culture that helped cushion forward thinking businesses throughout the severe recession of a post-Celtic Tiger economy. In fact, the well-known Michelin guide referenced two Irish pubs in its 2020 edition, The Wild Honey Inn, Co. Clare which holds a Michelin star and Baloo House, Co Down which received a Michelin Bib Gourmand Award.[30] Both pubs are best practice examples

29 Anita Guidera, 'No smoking Ireland makes history with cigarette ban', *Independent. ie*, 17 January 2014. Available at: <https://www.independent.ie/lifestyle/no-smoking-ireland-makes-history-with-cigarette-ban-29926186.html> (Accessed 12 March 2019).

30 'Michelin guide 2020: Full list of Irish restaurants and what the judges said', *Irish Times* [online], 8 October 2019. Available at: <https://www.irishtimes.com/

of many other successful rural gastropubs that now contribute to Ireland's burgeoning casual dining market.

(3) A lack of alternatives

A decreasing societal tolerance for drink driving along with increased penalties for offenders has brought about a considerable change in Irish drinking habits. This very positive societal development has led to a proliferation of high quality low and no alcohol products. The supermarket sector has been quick to recognise the demand for such products with large sections of retail space now devoted to products such as low and no alcohol beer, Nosseco and de-alcoholised flavoured wines and gins. The rural publican has, in some cases, been slow to adapt their product range to include substantial choice in this regard along with an appropriate pricing model that reflects the opportunity that such products can offer. An additional consequence of Ireland's increased focus on drink driving has been the requirement for more isolated rural pubs to combat the lack of rural transport provision in their areas. Though frequently seen as solely a government problem many now provide an informal 'run home service' but it is often inconsistent. The recent rural link network night-time trial [31] offers an example of government policy trying to address these needs and other possible solutions such as Uber are now being explored. It is important that publicans and their representative associations continue to lobby in this regard and to assist and contribute to finding innovative solutions where feasible.

(4) A lack of competition awareness

The opportunity to enjoy food, wine and even coffee in the home has become a significant challenge to rural pubs over the last ten years. Despite well-documented construction failures during Ireland's Celtic Tiger period the standard of new rural housing has generally increased.

---

life-and-style/food-and-drink/michelin-guide-2020-full-list-of-irish-restaurants-and-what-the-judges-said-1.4043663> (Accessed 31 January 2020).

31   Kevin Doyle and Margaret Donnelly, 'Revealed: The 50 bus routes under new "drink link" plan for rural Ireland', *Independent.ie*, 8 May 2018. Available at: <https://www.independent.ie/business/farming/rural-life/article36885011.ece> (Accessed 2 February 2020).

People demanded and built bigger, warmer homes; often with extensive modern kitchens, with bar-like kitchen islands, all providing attractive dining and entertaining spaces and opportunities. In addition, the availability of well-priced dine-in offers from major retailers coupled with easy-to-use delivery services from local takeaways have encouraged people to entertain more at home. Improved technology offering cinema like experiences and high quality on demand TV services such as Netflix, Amazon Prime and Apple TV have provided additional competition for rural pubs. They have sometimes been slow to adapt and in some cases actively seek to prohibit rather than engage proactively with changing demands. Pub licenses in Ireland have always been notoriously difficult to get due to the complex protectionist nature of the sector. A separate simpler European style café bar license was first suggested by, then minister, Michael McDowall as far back as 2005. The concept failed due to significant lobbying by publican's associations and pub owners.[32] Fifteen years later many rural pubs are still quite slow to provide a café style offering. With the advent of the pandemic, younger markets actively seek out places close to home where they can access barista-style products and experiences along with fast and free Wi-Fi. This has contributed to an upsurge in the independent café scene, even in rural areas. In some cases rural publicans have failed to capitalise on these demands by adapting their product offering while continuing to provide the same products and services as they always did to an ever-decreasing older population.

32   Fionnán Sheehan, 'Under their influence: FF "gang" killed McDowell's cafe bar idea', *Independent.ie*, 28 November 2005. Available at: <https://www.independent.ie/irish-news/under-their-influence-ff-gang-killed-mcdowells-cafe-bar-idea-25958987.html> (Accessed 31 January 2020).

Coming in from the Margins: Re-imagining the Rural Irish Pub

Having explored both the external and internal drivers that have contributed to its marginalisation it is important that we consider potential paths
that might encourage the survival and even revival of the rural Irish pub.
(1) Re-imagined as a domestic cultural ambassador
During the 1990s, under the guidance of designers Mel McNally and
Darren Fagan, the Irish Pub Company designed and built more than
1,000 Irish Pub Concepts all over the world.[33] Many dislike the lack of
authenticity evident in such places but their success is undeniable. Based
on substantial research into what constituted an Irish pub, the Irish Pub
Company has been very successful in exporting their version of Irish culture around the world. This has undoubtedly had a role to play in terms
of the preservation and promotion of Irish identity abroad. These have
acted as what Munoz and Wood refer to as cultural ambassadors [34] outside their home country. A reimagination of the rural Irish pub might
draw inspiration from their success but focus on rural Ireland rather than
abroad. As such there may be a role for Ireland's existing network of rural
Irish pubs to act as domestic cultural ambassadors. This role would need
to be supported and formally recognised by government. These pubs are
ideally placed to act as important bastions of story, heritage and tradition;
living museums that provide cultural expression in a variety of forms.
There are already many examples of this with rural pubs providing spaces
for local theatre, music performances, traditional card games and local
storytelling. Alex Fegan's movie *The Irish Pub*[35] captures this potential by

---

33   'The Irish Pub Company – In 2015 is it an Irish pub or a pub from Ireland?' The Irish
     Pub Global Federation, 2015. Available at: <https://www.irishpubsglobal.com/
     irish-pub-company-2015-irish-pub-pub-ireland/> (Accessed 31 January 2020).
34   Natalie T. Wood and Caroline Lego Muñoz, '"No rules, just right" or is it? The role
     of themed restaurants as cultural ambassadors', *Tourism and Hospitality Research*, 7
     (3/4), March 2007, pp. 242–255.
35   A film by directed by Alex Fegan and shown in Irish cinemas in 2013 and also avail-
     able on DVD. Available at: <https://www.imdb.com/title/tt3229518/> (Accessed
     3 February 2020).

observing that many different rural pubs play an important role in cultural preservation.

(2) Re-imagined in touristic terms

According to Fáilte Ireland's *Food and Drink Strategy 2018–2023*, tourists now expect to have an authentic experience and it is no longer reasonable to expect tourists to be happy with simply viewing attractions.[36] The strategy document identifies four key components that almost every tourism experience can be broken down into:

The product must be authentic.

The service must be of high quality.

The story must be distinctive.

The narration must have a unique character[37]

The rural Irish pub as evidenced in numerous reviews by organisations such as The Lonely Planet can satisfy each of these components and its potential role in experiential tourism is widely acknowledged.

Conducted among 1,131 respondents between the months of September and October 2017, the EuropCar survey indicates that for four-fifths of tourists, visiting an Irish pub is an important part of their visit, with 43% saying the warm and welcome atmosphere was the best part of the Irish pub experience[38]

As noted by ITIC 2014: The Irish pub offers a unique hospitality experience that is renowned the world over. When tourists come to Ireland they want to go to an Irish pub, they want to enjoy a pint in the welcome surrounds of locals. The pub is the

36 Fáilte Ireland, *Food and Drink Strategy 2018–2023*. Available at: <https://www.failteireland.ie/FailteIreland/media/WebsiteStructure/Documents/Publications/FI-Food-Strategy-Document.pdf> (Accessed 23 April 2019).

37 Fáilte Ireland, *Food and Drink Strategy 2018–2023*, p. 19.

38 'Visiting Irish pub "essential" to 80% of tourists', *Drink Industry Ireland* [online]. Available at: <https://www.drinksindustryireland.ie/visiting-irish-pub-essential-to-80-of-tourists/> (Accessed 31 January 2020).

hub of the local town, it is the heart of the local community and uniquely provides a convivial environment for meeting local people[39]

And yet, it appears that, as a nation, we are unwilling to recognise and preserve this important piece of touristic *patrimoine*. Our conflicting attitudes to the Irish pub, as previously mentioned, have contributed to a failure by government to invest and maintain such a crucial piece of Irish heritage. It's reasonable to suggest that the pub's central role in Ireland's cultural difficulties with alcohol has contributed to an unwillingness to focus on its more positive attributes. The Food and Drink Strategy report thankfully now recognises this and says that 'the consultation and engagement with stakeholders revealed a story of underleveraged food and beverage assets, including iconic experiences – such as the Irish Pub, Guinness and Whiskey'.[40] In addition, the rural Irish pub might be viewed as an antidote to the emerging problem of overtourism given the fact that the rural pub network is spread throughout the island. Their previously mentioned role as domestic cultural ambassadors could be enhanced to take on some rural tourism office functions. They could provide places where a warm welcome is guaranteed, local information and history is dispensed and a stop off or toilet break area for tourists is enthusiastically offered rather than having to be furtively sought by the tourist as they explore the rural Irish countryside.

(3) Re-imagined as an outpost for local food and drink

Access to food and drink options for consumption at home have never been greater and increasingly people seem to be choosing to stay in rather than have the traditional night out in the rural pub. However, just as eating and drinking in the home disrupted the traditional role of the rural Irish pub, that same pub can now provide something that might encourage people back out from their comfortable kitchens. It can be re-imagined as an outpost of local quality food and drink in an era where

---

39   Anthony Foley, 'The contribution of the drinks industry to Irish Tourism,' 2017, p. 14. Available at: <https://vfipubs.ie/wp-content/uploads/2017/09/DIGI-Tourism-Report-2017-1.pdf> (Accessed 4 May 2019).

40   Fáilte Ireland, *Food and Drink Strategy 2018–2023,* p. 30.

people, for various reasons, are reluctant to travel too far on a Friday or Saturday night. The global pandemic has encouraged this phenomenon as people have become more familiar with their local area due to imposed restrictions. There are many best practice examples of this and some rural pubs are experimenting with interesting food and drink offerings at certain times of the week. These include things like curry nights, pizza nights and tapas evenings. A case in point is Casa Tapas located at Moore's Pub in Grangecon, County Kildare. This 4th generation pub, in a remote rural area of South Kildare, has changed its focus by providing authentic tapas on Friday and Saturday evenings. This, along with other initiatives, has helped develop a thriving food business and a reinvigorated drinks trade.

> Set in the cosy, rustic surroundings of Moore's Pub, Casa Tapas offers a diverse selection of international tapas ... Serving locally sourced produce, a range of craft beers, wine and cocktails, you'll enjoy a unique atmospheric restaurant ... We also proudly support our friends in our local microbrewery in Grangecon; Beaky Dargus Brewery.[41]

Innovations like this, if set up and managed correctly, can draw people back to the local pub, by satisfying current market demands for using locally produced food ingredients and beverages.

(4) Re-imagined as a Community Café

Increasingly, we are seeing the development of community space projects in rural Ireland. Supported by government funding, such spaces provide a local community meeting place, frequently in the form of a community café, and a place for local food and craft businesses to use and display their wares. One of the most prominent examples of this is Billy's Tea Rooms in Ballyhale, Co Kilkenny which has received a lot of media attention of late. In a recent article Anne Fitzgerald of *Farming Independent.ie* wrote:

> I have seen Rock and Roll's future and its name is Bruce Springsteen. With these rousing words, the world was introduced to 'The Boss' in 1974. Recently, I was struck

41   Moore's of Grangecon website. Available at: <https://www.mooresofgrangecon. com/> (Accessed 28 May 2019).

by a similar feeling, regarding the future of rural Ireland, when I visited Billy's Tea Rooms and Shop in Ballyhale, Co Kilkenny.[42]

Local initiatives like Billy's Tearooms are being developed throughout rural Ireland with a particular community focus and social remit in mind. Their value lies not in monetary gain but in the provision of a social hub where a rural community can value their own sense of place. Rural pubs have the potential to engage with community projects like this. The traditional rural pub as described in this chapter has historically fulfilled many of the roles that these new community spaces now strive to provide. Although a relatively recent phenomenon, rural community cafés are often in competition with the local pub and in some cases might have the potential to contribute to their demise. Ironically, as the local community strive to fundraise so that their community cafés can be furnished with the fixtures and fittings such an enterprise requires, the local pub, often located nearby, has so much of their practical requirements already in place. Yet in many cases, the pub is considered as 'other' and is becoming slowly marginalised while the community focus shifts to the newly developed community café. This irony is marked even further when one considers that these community cafés usually operate on a 10 a.m.-5 p.m. schedule, the very hours the rural pubs are now closed due to lack of business. The logical solution would be to combine the local community café ethos with the local rural pub thus encouraging the development and survival of both.

42   Ann Fitzgerald, 'After losing five shops, three pubs and the post office, how this rural community is revitalising itself', *Farming Independent* [online], 24 March 2019. Available at: <https://www.independent.ie/business/farming/rural-life/after-losing-five-shops-three-pubs-and-the-post-office-how-this-rural-community-is-revitalising-itself-37926624.html> (Accessed 28 May 2019).

Conclusion

It is evident therefore that the rural Irish pub is facing an existential crisis in many places throughout Ireland. Unlike the Na Fianna example mentioned at the beginning, key decision-makers in government appear reluctant to fully appreciate the many social advantages that the rural pub can bring. *The Social Value of CLG Na Fianna Report* [43] used several original metrics to calculate, in a systematic and quantifiable way, the estimated social value output that the club introduced to its surrounding community. It is reasonable to draw comparisons with the rural Irish pub in terms of the monetary value that the report placed on the development of things such as friendship, mental well-being and a sense of belonging. Such outcomes are frequently mentioned during discussions on the role of the traditional Irish pub in rural communities. The dichotomy of approach to the pub by Ireland's political class has led to inertia in terms of protecting and promoting this valuable aspect of our country's cultural heritage. Even though many have come to informally recognise its economic value, its underlying social significance remains largely unrecognised. Even the pub's popularity among visitors and locals alike is often more quietly celebrated by politicians rather than lauded openly. Such an approach has undoubtedly played a role in the stark decline of rural pubs and, when coupled with the internal and external contributory factors discussed above, seems to point to a bleak future for one of Ireland's most traditional social spaces. Between 2005 and 2017 the number of pubs declined by 17.1%.[44] This has been further exacerbated by the pandemic which has brought about the closure of another 349 pubs.[45] However, it

---

43   Velthius, *The Social Value of CLG Na Fianna.*

44   'Report finds every county in Ireland has fewer pubs than in 2005', *Irish Examiner* [online], 5 September 2018. Available at: <https://www.irishexaminer.com/news/arid-30866864.html> (Accessed 27 November 2021).

45   Melanie Finn, 'Almost 350 pubs have closed down since pandemic began', *Irish Independent* [online], 17 October 2021. Available at: <https://www.independent.ie/irish-news/almost-350-pubs-have-closed-down-since-pandemic-began-40957271.html> (Accessed 21 November 2021).

is also noticeable that some rural pubs are attempting to bring new life to twenty-first-century rural life. The reimagined examples discussed here offer considerable hope that pubs are adapting their offering to a changing Ireland while still maintaining an authentic grip on past traditions. These examples demonstrate that Ireland can maintain its pub tradition into the future and with appropriate government focus and support the Irish pub might once again become the 'beating heart' of rural Irish life.

CHAPTER 6

The Traditional Irish Butcher Shop: Harnessing the Power of *Patrimoine*

This chapter deals with a place that was such a large part of my life growing up. As already mentioned, my earliest memories are bound up in the sounds and smells of the family butcher shop. We all lived over the shop until I was seven and I continued to work there alongside my siblings during weekends and summer holidays through both school and college years. Even after I left for London, I returned at times to help out in the shop when my mother and father took time away for a well-deserved break. At first, I was reluctant to include personal stories like this in my work and yet it was this chapter that made me realise that a book exploring how Irish society engages with food and drink must include parts of my own food memory. It would be dishonest to treat many of the topics discussed throughout the book in a dispassionate and impersonal way. This picture was taken by my sister, Deirdre, and is the only one I have of me working in the shop. Along with my father's old meat saw, cleaver and knife, which now hang proudly in my kitchen, these are the only material items I have left from the family butcher shop at 50 Bulfin Road, Inchicore.

The Irish pub, as explored in the last chapter, is perhaps one of the most obvious places that springs to mind when one is exploring food and drink culture in Ireland, but there are others. This chapter examines a sometimes overlooked site of food engagement, namely the traditional family butcher shop. For many years, in a similar way to the pub, the small family butcher shop has been disappearing from our village centres and our urban main streets. It has been subsumed into the meat counters of large international retailers where the traditional aspects of the Irish butcher shop have all but disappeared and been replaced by an often *faux*-authentic approach to butchery. The impression of the traditional shop is created but there is little in terms of traditional Irish butchering heritage evident. This chapter explores how the authentic Irish family butcher shop can

Image 6. M. J. Murphy's Butchers, 50 Bulfin Road, Inchicore, Dublin.

This photo was taken by Deirdre Doyle on the day before M. J. Murphy's Butchers was handed over to its new owners after thirty-five years and includes from left to right, Brian J. Murphy, Lucy Murphy and Michael J. Murphy.

exploit its sense of *patrimoine*. It explores where this sense of *patrimoine* comes from and how these origins can be utilised to best effect. The chapter argues that for a traditional food business to survive in contemporary Ireland's open and competitive marketplace it needs to exploit and promote its cultural heritage qualities.

The theoretical framework that is used for discussion and analysis throughout the chapter is based on the Fourth Space model.[1] This model was explained in the introduction of the book and provides an engagement

---

1   Brian Murphy, 'Communicating new definitions of terroir to a millennial audience through the medium of fourth space', in *Kulinarischer Tourismus und Weintourismus* (Wiesbaden: Springer Gabler, 2017), pp. 85–92.

template for how any modern food and beverage site might interact with its audience and successfully communicate a true sense of that illusive quality, *terroir*. The traditionally defined French concept of *terroir*, which has become a touchstone for many disciplines such as sociology and cultural theory,[2] has recently become an overused phrase. We now have *terroir*-driven restaurants, *terroir*-focused chefs and *terroir*-based cuisines. In November 2016, Dublin hosted the inaugural *Tourroirs: Food Tourism and Culture* conference in Croke Park.[3] *Terroir* means so much more than simply a reflection of land or soil and according to Trubek 'culture, in the form of a group's identity, traditions and heritage in relation to place, must also be part of the equation'.[4] Such concepts are perhaps less tangible than our traditional understanding but they are nonetheless valid and align the concept of *terroir* closer to a sense of *patrimoine* as understood in French culture. The difficulty arises when one attempts to communicate such *patrimoine* to increasingly gastronomically aware audiences. This is where the Fourth Space model can be of particular use. It provides a simple to understand framework for developing a strategy that will help any small food or drink business identify key aspects of their cultural heritage and subsequently convey these to an audience. The overview diagram below reminds us that the model has five key strands.

Each of these strands has several subheadings as previously detailed in the Introduction. This chapter overlays Strand 1 and 2 of the model onto two business examples. Both places are similar in origin but as we shall see, become separated by time, location, scale and success.

The first business examined is the small M. J. Murphy's family butcher shop located at 50 Bulfin Road, Inchicore Dublin, which my own family operated for thirty-five years. My first-hand experience of this business provided me with the impetus to explore the second case examined in

2   Marion Demossier, 'Beyond Terroir: Territorial construction, hegemonic discourses, and French wine culture', *Journal of Royal Anthropological Institute*, 17, 2011, p. 685.

3   The title of this annual conference itself being a play on words and emphasising the inextricable links between *terroir*, culture and food.

4   Amy Trubek, *The Taste of Place: A Cultural Journey into Terroir* (London: University of California Press, 2009), p. 91.

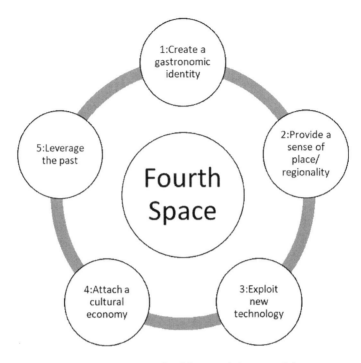

Image 7. Five Strands of the Fourth Space model.

this chapter, James Whelan's Butchers from Clonmel in Tipperary, a very successful butchery business that now employs more than 100 people and whose heritage products are recognised internationally. Like M. J. Murphy's, the business began life as a small family butcher shop in Clonmel. When James Whelan's son Pat took over from his father in the late 1990s, this small shop employed just four people. Both butcher shops have something to offer in terms of how we understand the application of a Fourth Space model but our analysis is particularly focused on how, over a relatively short period, James Whelan's Butchers managed to successfully harness and monetise key heritage attributes while M. J. Murphy's did not.

Case 1-M. J. Murphy's Butchers, 50 Bulfin Road, Inchicore, Dublin

In 1963 my parents returned home from Canada after several years abroad. Soon after, they purchased and opened M. J. Murphy's Butchers at 50 Bulfin Road, Inchicore, Dublin 8. The small flat above the shop was to become our family home for the next ten years and the shop would remain in our family for the next thirty-five years. My father Michael J. Murphy started working as a butcher's apprentice after primary school, served his time in Ireland and travelled over subsequent years with his craft through the UK and Canada. Throughout a career that spanned more than fifty years he became a highly skilled practitioner. During my early teens, I recall how every couple of days he would visit the nearby Red Meats Abattoir in Clanbrassil Street to select cattle, pigs and lambs for delivery the following day. These animals would be hung on heavy racks in the shop. They would be skilfully broken down in the shop in full view of the customers, before being carried into the walk-in fridge where appropriate ageing techniques and monitoring would ensure meats of the very highest quality. Twice a week he would render down beef suet in a large boiler out the back of the shop and prepare individually wax-packed beef dripping. I can vividly remember him hand rubbing what seemed like secret mixtures and compounds to brine his own corned beef. He would also pickle and hand-pump hams in a freezing and bloody pickle barrel that also doubled as a fast chiller for large bottles of TK lemonade on hot summer days.

At Christmas, he would regularly go to my aunty and uncle's small farm in Co. Kildare, where we would select freshly killed turkeys with individual client needs in mind. They were killed and plucked in the adjacent sheds by my uncle and his team. He would load the turkeys into his car and drive back home to the shop in Inchicore. The whole family pitched in during Christmas week. The turkeys had to be cleaned and dressed, ready for customers a day or two before Christmas day. When I look back now, I can see that the shop in Bulfin Road was built on a strong 'place and story' foundation. Although we used local produce that strongly reflected the local region, we would certainly never have used words like *terroir*. My father probably wouldn't have considered himself an 'an artisan'. He was, in his words, a butcher, a tradesman, a shopkeeper. My siblings and I all lived and worked in the shop throughout our teens and into our early 20s. The family remained anchored to that shop for thirty-five years until it was sold in 1998 due to my father's ill health. Words like authenticity, sense of place, story and indeed *terroir* are now frequently deployed when discussing many aspects of food and drink. Businesses increasingly want to differentiate themselves from others by conveying a true sense of *patrimoine* as one of their key signifiers. The analysis below examines whether M. J. Murphy's could, in some ways, be described as a Fourth Space.

Case 2-James Whelan's Butchers, Clonmel, Co. Tipperary

The Whelan family followed a similar track to M. J. Murphy's up until the late 1990s, when their small independent butcher shop in Clonmel found itself employing just four people and fulfilling predominantly local needs. The Whelans also lived over the original family business in Clonmel and the family were raised as part of that same small shop tradition.

> We lived over the town shop. If there was a leg of lamb needed in Oakville, I went on my bike to drop it over. This was a continuum of family life. We ran a quality butchers and it was understood that this was part of who we were.[5]

The similar background stories of M. J. Murphy's of Inchicore and James Whelan's of Clonmel diverge in 1999. That year M. J. Murphy's was sold due to my father's ill health. Around the same time Pat Whelan returned home to Clonmel from Dublin, where he had enjoyed a successful

---

5   Mark Paul citing Pat Whelan, 'Hooking up with Dunnes Stores helps butcher Pat Whelan raise the steaks', *The Irish Times* [online], 13 October 2017. Available at: <https://www.irishtimes.com/business/retail-and-services/hooking-up-with-dunnes-stores-helps-butcher-pat-whelan-raise-the-steaks-1.3252491> (Accessed 3 January 2018).

business career, to take over the small family business. In the space of twenty years, Pat brought this once traditional Irish butcher shop on a journey that would see it develop and fully integrate its adjoining farm and abattoir. It would go on to forge links with iconic Irish retailers such as Avoca opening James Whelan's butcher's shops in Monkstown and Rathcoole. It would become an early adopter of online technology and would promote its local produce throughout Ireland and the UK. It would develop heritage products that would go on to be recognised as expressions of Irish identity. The business has recently joined forces with another iconic Irish retailer, Dunnes Stores and has collaborated on opening several high-end butcher stores in their outlets. James Whelan's Butchers now employs approximately 110 people across all its businesses. Pat Whelan himself has always focused on developing what he frequently refers to as 'a legacy brand'.

> My mother would always have preached about the lifetime value of a customer re-
> lationship .... I am still running the business that I took over from my parents all
> those years ago .... My objective is to make sure that it's a legacy brand that people
> will recognise around great meat long into the future.[6]

In a sense the drive to create what Whelan refers to as a legacy brand does, by necessity incorporate the successful communication to the client of an authentic sense of *patrimoine*. The Fourth Space model provides a framework to help understand this.

Viewing the Traditional Irish Family Butcher Shop through a Fourth Space lens

Strand 1 - Creating a gastronomic identity
(1.1) Incorporating a Third Place function

6   Brendan Byrne citing Pat Whelan, 'Pat Whelan-building a legacy brand in but-
     chering', www.Think Business.ie, n.d. Available at: <https://www.thinkbusiness.ie/
     articles/pat-whelan-butcher/> (Accessed 5 January 2018).

The small family butcher shop is at the very heart of traditional Irish society. Though disappearing in more recent times from its rural or semi-rural settings, it is still viewed as an important focal point of the local community, a meeting place, a place in which to gossip, a place where staff and clients frequently engage in banter. From experience, it was a place where regular customers had set family orders that were fulfilled by the family butcher and where weekly supplies were sometimes provided 'on tick' and recorded in a small blood-stained notebook until they could be scratched off in pencil when payment was eventually made. Ray Oldenburg has written extensively on what he refers to as the Third Place, and this attribute is an important element in our Strand 1 analysis.

A Third Place is a place that exists outside of both the home (the First Place) and the work environment (the Second Place). Oldenburg is keen to stress that Third Places 'exist on neutral ground and serve to level their guests to a condition of social equality'.[7] His examples of good Third Places include the English pub, The French Café and the German/American beer gardens, but one could argue that there are many aspects of Oldenburg's Third Place that might also apply to the local family butcher shop. Oldenburg suggests some key phenomena that qualify a location to be classed as a Third Place. They include:

1. The Third Place has to be on neutral ground.
2. The Third Place is a leveller.
3. Conversation is the main activity.
4. Regular customers are key.
5. As a physical structure it often has a low profile.
6. The mood is playful.
7. It acts as a home away from home.[8]

Many of these criteria fit with the role of the traditional family butcher shop and it would seem eminently qualified to be considered one of Oldenburg's Third Places. My own experiences, though anecdotal,

---

7   Ray Oldenburg, *The Great Good Place,* p. 42.
8   Oldenburg, *The Great Good Place*, pp. 20–42.

confirm this view. M. J. Murphy's was located in an unassuming block of shops on Bulfin Road, Inchicore. Like many local shops, its shop front, was traditional and small. In fact, the shop itself could only accommodate 2-3 workers comfortably and had very limited customer space. It dealt predominantly with local and regular customers, many of them from large families. There was no sense that some clients were more important than others and all were treated with similar respect regardless of circumstance. One of my overriding memories was of the 'banter' in terms of how many of the customers were dealt with. This type of engagement was not contrived but was important in making people feel welcome. I can still remember how my father would lean with one arm up on the end of the display counter as he engaged in long conversations with people, often to the annoyance of my mother, who was frequently left to busily run around after other customers while he chatted.

(1.2) Conveying the story of place

The traditional family butcher shop usually provides locally sourced produce that reflects the place it's situated in. This was always true of family shops who produced their own sausages, pudding, beef dripping, etc. on site. It was certainly true of M. J. Murphy's in Inchicore. The fact that such products and processes were produced under the gaze of clients, young and old, also added to the rich story of place that these traditional shops revelled in. Modern supermarket butcher's counters have to a large extent forgone this tradition, and now little skilled work is carried out on-site and produce tends to arrive pre-cut and pre-packaged thus detracting from the sense of place associated with meats produced on site. Traditional butcher businesses like James Whelan's are keen to enhance their story of place even further by using only their own livestock from their own farm, processed through their own abattoir. They frequently stock other locally made produce from chutneys, jams, eggs and potatoes to home baked breads and goods which again reflect the authentic story of their place. Walls and counters are often adorned with pictures and objects associated with local sports teams and local events etc. The shop window, in many ways, acts as a community notice board for local interactions. The business is often a key supporter of such events and as such acts as an important part of local communities. All these elements contribute towards the story of the place the butcher shop is located in. They anchor the shop to its place which in turn accentuates the associated sense of *patrimoine* that the site conveys.

(1.4) Acting as a cultural ambassador

Whelan's Butchers has become renowned, both in Ireland and abroad, for its uniquely Irish award-winning product 'Beef Dripping'. They have taken what was once a very traditional butcher's product, followed an old family recipe and re-energised the product for both the domestic and international market. Like Irish Whiskey and Guinness such products can be especially powerful in conveying a sense of Irishness when associated with such family heritage. According to *Irish Times* food writer Marie Claire Digby:

> Whelan's winning product, beef dripping made in Clonmel from suet from his grass-fed Irish Angus and Hereford beef, rose to the top from 10,000 entries in the annual awards, and Whelan says he created it with 'more than a little guidance' from his mother.[9]

The links between local family food businesses and Irish identity are strong and in recent years the expansion of locally produced products that reflect the place from which they came has also influenced how people abroad view our gastronomic identity. These products have managed to successfully expose Ireland's sense of place to people both living in and outside of the country. Though not always positive, this sense of place has impacted on the image of Ireland. It is the consumer's perception of award-winning products like Whelan's Beef Dripping that has the potential to shape attitudes to a place and influence them in positive ways. The beef dripping itself is an interesting heritage product in that it was traditionally very common for small family shops to produce their own beef dripping. This practice became less common in recent years, but James Whelan's revived and reinvigorated it. Whelan's Beef Dripping is now brought to new markets across the UK and Ireland. By locating satellite

---

9   Marie Claire Digby, 'Irish butchers beef dripping wins best food product in UK and Ireland', *The Irish Times* [online], 8 September 2015. Available at: <https://www.iri shtimes.com/life-and-style/food-and-drink/irish-butcher-s-beef-dripping-wins-best-food-product-in-uk-and-ireland-1.2344248> (Accessed 12 December 2017).

shops in places like Avoca Hand Weaver's in Rathcoole and Monkstown he again aligned his produce with a heritage brand that is synonymous in retail terms with reflecting Irish culture to tourists and domestic customers alike thus fulfilling an important cultural ambassador role.

(1.4) Providing Authentic People

The small traditional butcher shop was always staffed by local people. Often the butcher and their family lived over the premises and were key members of the local community. Frequently local teenagers were employed during school holidays and unlike larger retailers rarely were staff brought in from outside the area. Often immediate family members and spouses were trained up to work in the family business. There was frequent local banter between staff and customers with the result that the shop developed a reputation for having the 'craic' with the customers. Grantham[10] suggests that 'having the craic' has become the quintessential term among the Irish for having a good time. Some would contend that the craic in an Irish context can only be achieved by having local staff with an innate sense of hospitality and warmth. From memory, this is very true of staff/customer relations in the shop growing up. It is an intangible aspect of Irish culture that is very difficult to plan for or structure. Visitors from abroad have always associated Ireland as a place where the Irish welcome could be guaranteed. It is difficult to describe the intangible hospitality and warmth that one associates with a true Irish welcome and yet without these qualities it is difficult to see how any local butcher shop can become a true Fourth Space. James Whelan's shop also provides high quality service which is fundamental to its success however it must be noted that success and expansion has the potential to dilute an otherwise authentic family welcome and experience. One of the consequences of an expanding business is that one can no longer expect to be served by a family member when visiting the family butchers. A family business such as Whelans that has managed to move beyond its original single shop structure must by necessity work much harder to maintain a traditional family approach through the qualities and attributes of the

10   Bill Grantham, 'Craic in a box: Commodifying and exporting the Irish Pub', *Journal of Media and Cultural Studies*, 23 (2), 2009, p. 257.

staff it employs. James Whelan's does quite well in this regard but inevitably some personal identity is lost as the business grows bigger and develops new sites.

Strand 2 - Providing a sense of place/regionality
(2.1) Emphasising place of origin/regionality
Place and a sense of belonging to that place are essential ingredients when striving for *patrimoine*. The promotion of cultural heritage requires such heritage to be connected to a particular region or place. Most traditional family butchers reflect this reality to varying degrees. However, what makes some butchers different is a consistent message that their produce is regional and overtly reflects where it comes from, thus offering an authentic sense of *terroir*. This was reflected in M. J. Murphy's, as described earlier, but was never really capitalised upon perhaps because the business existed in another era where many commercial products sold expressed a natural sense of place. It was a period of fewer imports and more home-produced goods. In a sense, place-integrity was expected through circumstance. James Whelan's business, on the other hand, thrives in a much more open economy, one where homogenous and generic goods flood the market. To compete, James Whelan's clearly reference place and regionality with almost all their products. In cases where they don't supply from their own local farm, they are still keen to emphasise the place and region in the pursuit of gastronomic credibility.

French attitudes to place and regionality have long been at the forefront of gastronomic culture. The strength of the *Appellation Contrôlée* laws that were first introduced in 1935 formed an essential bedrock for lots of place-based foods. Ireland is only now beginning to learn from French attitudes to place and regionality in terms of our food and drink products. The European system of place classification, where products are certified and labelled as having a protected designation of origin (PDO) or a protected geographical indication (PGI) has recently started to gain traction in Ireland. Like the *Appellation Contrôlée* system, PDO and PGI classifications allow for food and drinks to be aligned with places and regions once certain strict criteria are achieved and a quite complex application procedure is successful. Currently France has 113 separate food products registered which have achieved PDO designation while Ireland only has

5.[11] However, increasingly Irish food producers are beginning to understand the importance of having recognised certification that formally ties foods to places. A collection of Waterford bakers garnered considerable publicity in 2013 when they were awarded PGI designation from Europe for producing their unique and traditional Waterford Blaa breads and there we will undoubtedly be more Irish food products seeking similar place and process certification from Europe in the coming years.[12]

(2.2) Avoiding fauxthenticity

Authenticity is key when any food business is attempting to portray a sense of place. Though difficult to define there are many examples of food and drink businesses using exaggerated back stories. Attempts to use these should be treated with care and often producers would be better served by emphasising more authentic elements of story even if it is more contemporary in nature such as the story of the ingredients used, the story of the people who supply the product or the story of the processes used to make the product. James Whelan's does this to great effect while maintaining a sense of authenticity due to the verifiable links that the business has with five decades of history. Firstly, the direct and consistent link with the original family butcher shop in Clonmel provides the brand with authenticity. Secondly, the link with their own farm and abattoir substantiates this claim. There are other less obvious authentic story elements that are particularly interesting. As part of their design in their butcher outlets in both Avoca locations, and more recently in Dunnes of Cornelscourt, they have presented their staff butchery skills in a very interesting manner. Unlike more traditional butcher shops, the skilled aspect of production is clearly visible to the consumer, thus providing authenticity in terms of the meat produced and skills used on site. The butcher faces the consumer through a floor to ceiling glass window

11 All European products that have achieved PDO and PGI status are detailed on the European Commission's Agriculture and Development site which is available at: <https://ec.europa.eu/info/food-farming-fisheries/food-safety-and-qual ity/certification/quality-labels/geographical-indications-register/> (Accessed 12 December 2021).

12 Marie Claire Digby, 'Waterford Blaa awarded special status by EU', *The Irish Times* [online], 19 November 2013 (Accessed 2 January 2018).

which resembles a viewing stage. Behind the viewing window three butchers work on three separate cylindrical blocks ensuring that customers
can see both the skill and the care that goes into the presentation of their
products. Modern versions of less authentic butcher shops provide no
visibility at all regarding the preparation of meat products which are frequently brought into the shop pre-prepared and pre-packaged at a factory
location. An authentic approach was always evident in traditional Irish
butcher shops such as M. J. Murphy's, when all skilled handling and preparation of meat products was carried out in full view of the clients. James
Whelan's have taken this concept to a new level thus enhancing their own
sense of authenticity.

(2.3) Providing an educational medium/enables decodification

One of the challenges faced by a food or drink producer rests in the codified nature of the product and the difficulty that can occur in helping
understand key product attributes. The Fourth Space approach attempts
to address such challenges by focusing on opportunities for educational
engagement with the product in question. French *appellation contrôlée*
wines provide perhaps our best example of the need for such educational
engagement. Aside from the obvious language differences, quite complex
legislation and labelling systems can often pose problems for consumers
when it comes to interpreting a French wine fully. Grape varieties are
traditionally not mentioned on the label and the complexities of their *appellation contrôlée* systems are often not apparent. Terms such as *Premier
Cru* and *Grand Cru* mean different things in different regions and represent other aspects of the wine's story that need decodification. For the individual to fully appreciate such a culturally charged product, they need
some wine knowledge. Though not quite as complex as French wine, the
whole area of the meats we eat also has layers of understanding that consumers find difficult. In the introduction to the book *Distinction*, Pierre
Bourdieu suggests, when referring to a work of art, that 'a beholder who
lacks the specific code feels lost in a chaos of sounds and rhythms, colours
and lines, without rhyme or reason'.[13] He is suggesting that a piece of art

13   Pierre Bourdieu, *Distinction: A Social Critique of the Judgements of Taste*, translated
      by Richard Niece (Abingdon, Oxon: Routledge Classics, 2010), p. xxv.

or music can be consumed on different levels. Without the appropriate code, Bourdieu maintains that

> he cannot move from the 'primary stratum of the meaning we can grasp on the basis of our ordinary experience' to the 'stratum of secondary meanings', i.e., 'the level of meaning of what is signified', unless he possesses the concepts which go beyond the sensible properties and which identify the specifically stylistic properties of the work.[14]

A similar approach might be suggested regarding understanding meats and butchery processes that have become hidden as the traditional Irish butcher shop has faded from prominence. Increasingly consumers are separated from the meat production process and have become familiar only with the finished product which is sometimes deliberately disguised to hide its true origins. James Whelan's butchers have been innovative in how they have introduced elements of formal and informal education into their engagement strategies. Firstly, they started running butchery courses targeted at the lay market that encourage consumers to become proficient in the art of butchery. These three-hour programmes are de-livered in relaxed but educational manner on site in their butcher shops to small groups of 10/12 people. The course itinerary includes the following topics: Meet and Greet, Overview of James Whelan Family History, Knife Play, Celebration of Pork, The Sweet Secrets of Beef, Chicken at its best, Nibbles and Natter.[15] Other examples of informal education can be found in the transparent way that the James Whelan's butchers carry out complex butchery task on customer-centric display blocks as previ-ously described. They have also been innovative in their development of the Butcher Academy concept which has recently provided more formal butcher training to young career butchers that they have taken on. As outlined in the quote below such educational strategies are deliberately used to perpetuate the legacy of the butchery business:

---

14   Ibid., xxvi.
15   This is the events course outline for their next upcoming butchery demonstra-tion on 26 February 2018 to be held in the butcher shop. Available at: <http://www.jameswhelanbutchers.com/info/butchery-demonstrations/> (Accessed 8 February 2018).

But he has other strategies in play to help him reach his goal of turning James Whelan Butchers into a 'legacy brand' in Ireland. One has been to establish a 'butchery academy' under the brand, a move which he feels will also help protect the business against skills shortages in the future.[16]

By passing on the traditional skills of the butcher in the James Whelan's Butchery Academy Pat Whelan is ensuring that the traditional craft of butchery stays relevant. By developing their own educational framework, they are also enhancing a sense of *patrimoine* because this framework is being used to ensure that the unique James Whelan's butchery ethos is perpetuated.

(2.4) Allowing for a food and drink place link

Given the gastronomic developments that have occurred in Ireland in recent decades, it is difficult to see any individual food product in isolation and other foods and drinks must form part of any Fourth Space strategy. It is interesting to note that modern butchers like James Whelan's have started to align themselves with other food and drink categories not traditionally associated with the butcher's domain. Many have broadened their ranges to include high-end deli goods such as jams, chutneys, gourmet cheeses, sauces and oils. Examples from James Whelan's shop include innovative ancillary food products such as their slim line meats range and their extensive Party-to-Go menu for outside catering. Some beverage product categories are also natural bedfellows for different meats and there are other examples within the traditional butcher shop arena such as Nolan's Butchers in Kilcullen Co Kildare who offer extensive high-end wine selections within the confines of their traditional butcher shop as well as the expertise to describe and match those wines to various meats.

---

16   Killian Woods, 'Why this Tipperary butcher sold his five-decade-old family business to Dunnes', *The Journal.ie*. Available at: <http://www.thejournal.ie/james-whelan-butchers-dunnes-stores-2-3713094-Nov2017/> (Accessed 20 December 2017).

Conclusion

Meat is a complex and culturally laden product. It offers more than simple nourishment. At its worst meat can be heavily processed, uniform and cynically lacking in authenticity. At its best such foods are a combination of people, place and story. The examples used in this chapter have demonstrated that traditional Irish butcher shops can be successful Fourth Spaces by emphasising aspects of cultural heritage. M. J. Murphy's held within the confines of its walls many elements of what we now describe as *terroir*. It had the benefits of a family heritage that spanned fifty years. The skills, the processes, the products, the authentic people were indeed all present at 50 Bulfin Road Inchicore but its sense of *patrimoine* was never truly exploited. The James Whelan's example tells a different story. Although it started out in the same way as M. J. Murphy's, it ultimately exploited the essence of Fourth Space engagement. Due to time constraints, the chapter limited its analysis to the first two strands of our Fourth Space model but other strands reveal additional approaches that involve similar cultural engagement strategies. These include the early adoption of online technology to enhance the business story and an appreciation of cultural economy through the release of two beautifully produced and illustrated butchery books by Pat Whelan himself, *An Irish Butcher Shop* [17] and *The Irish Beef Book*.[18] To make use of a truly successful Fourth Space strategy, one must not be driven solely by the desire for monetary success. The true passion of the individual artisan operator must shine through. The combination of the product's authentic place and story elements can create a bond between product and customer and James Whelan's Butchers, through the unique vision of Pat Whelan, has managed to do this.

In a world where profit has become the only real key driver of success, it is perhaps unlikely that every aspect of an authentic Fourth Space can be realised. As soon as the strands of that Fourth Space are seen as a

17   Pat Whelan, *An Irish Butcher Shop* (Cork: The Collins Press, 2010).
18   Katy McGuinness and Pat Whelan, *The Irish Beef Book* (Dublin: Gill and McMillan, 2013).

route to monetary gain, the game is lost. The spell that binds the person to the product's authentic place and story can start to loosen. We live in a post-truth world filled with fake news and alternative facts. For any food or drink product to maintain its standing, place and story have got to be authentic and true to their origins. Marketing specialists continue to dilute authenticity in the understandable pursuit of profit. There is sometimes little reference to real people and their stories unless it fits in with an agreed marketing back story. It seems to matter less and less whether our food stories are real or the place exists at all. On reflection, when I overlay the Fourth Space approach on to M. J. Murphy's, I can see that the shop stayed true to its original ethos of providing quality local products to a local community. It was a traditional butcher shop that fulfilled but never capitalised on many of the Fourth Space strands discussed here. True Fourth Spaces are becoming relatively rare given our recent economic history but there are now real signs of a revival. There is evidence of a gastronomic world willing to at least consider holding more dearly the role that people, place and story play in our food and drink culture. We have had the rise of the Slow Food movement spreading to all parts of the globe, including Ireland. There has been an increase in organic food and drink production as people seek out surety about their ingredients and information on their food's origins. The popularity of independent craft breweries, gin and whiskey distilleries is on the increase. A new locavore has emerged who expresses a desire to know exactly where their food and drink has come from with an almost evangelical insistence that it be steeped in the local. As these trends emerge, large producers are already seeking to appropriate the smaller producer's people, place and story status. Small operators like the traditional family butcher shop are being subsumed so that larger multinationals can create impressions of individuality. These large global entities desperately need to be associated with true stories. They sometimes maintain façades of authenticity, but as soon as they subsume an individual operator into their collective *terroir* brand, any sense of *patrimoine* is lost. It is perhaps through businesses like James Whelan's Butchers that real associations between products, people and place can be sustained and nurtured in an increasingly competitive environment. The idea that the traditional family butcher can provide *patrimoine* in such a world may yet prove to be one of the few ingredients that allows for true distinction in an ever-shrinking world of sameness.

CHAPTER 7

The Whiskey Distillery: A Fourth Space Case Analysis

In 2017, I travelled to Bordeaux to visit one of the world's great beverage tourism attractions, *Cité du Vin*. This impressive 81 million euro development demonstrates the importance the French nation places on its most renowned beverage. Ireland also has an iconic beverage of its own in whiskey but it is only recently that the country has started to re-discover the importance of this drink and its places of production. Up until the dawn of the second millennium, Ireland was dominated by a limited range of large players, both in terms of whiskey and indeed beer. This chapter speaks to the many smaller whiskey producers and craft brewers that have emerged since then. They may not have the tourism development budget of the large corporate players but they do have advantages in terms leveraging their sense of place. What follows seeks to highlight this, by examining two different distilleries using a Fourth Space paradigm.

The final place that is explored in this section of the book relates to a relatively recent addition to Ireland's food and drink cultural landscape. Up until the early 2000s there was a limited number of whiskey tourism sites in Ireland, with only Midleton, Jameson, Bushmills and Kilbeggan (formerly Locke's) distilleries in active production. This chapter examines the impact of the whiskey renaissance in Ireland and how dramatic growth in the sector has led to a new focus on the distillery tourism experience and on the new players who have entered the fray.

In 2019, then Minister for Agriculture, Food and the Marine, Michael Creed, launched a new brand home and strategy for Irish Whiskey called *IrishWhiskey360°*.[1] It proposed that 'visitors to Irish whiskey distilleries

1   *Irish Whiskey Magazine* [online], 10 September 2019. 'IrishWhiskey360° the Irish Whiskey initiative unveiled' Available at: <https://www.irishwhiskeymagazine.

and visitor centres would break one million as industry targets 1.7 million visitors by 2025 and *IrishWhiskey360°* aims to make Ireland the No. 1 destination in the world for whiskey tourism'. This ambitious goal stemmed from the fact that Irish whiskey has recently been cited as the fastest growing subsection of the entire whiskey category globally over the past decade.[2] Concepts like authenticity, place, story and indeed *terroir* are often deployed when considering many aspects of contemporary whiskey tourism sites but interpretation and analysis of these sometimes nebulous concepts can vary considerably and they can prove very difficult to define. As we have seen previously, concepts like *terroir* can prove particularly challenging, not only in terms of definition, but also in terms of how to communicate a sense of *terroir* to an audience. And yet a clear understanding is necessary when developing appropriate strategies. This chapter explores the concept further with a view to providing insights into how contemporary drink tourism sites might successfully engage with visitors through a variety of mediums to convey that true sense of *terroir*. As with the previous chapter's butcher shop example it uses the Fourth Space model, described in the introduction, which draws on the long-lived success of the French wine sector's portrayal of *terroir* to consumers. It provides a framework to help explore how beverage tourism sites can both analyse and communicate *terroir* elements to visitors. Using a comparative analysis of two distillery tourism sites in Ireland, the study maps their level of *terroir* engagement across several different strands as determined by the Fourth Space model. The analysis helps further demonstrate the potential benefits of such a model in developing strategies that can be of benefit to a broader range of food and drink sites. It shows how they can enhance their ability to convey a strong and authentic sense of *terroir*, thus allowing them to compete in an increasingly competitive market.

　　com/news/latest-news/irishwhiskey360-the-irish-whiskey-initiative-unveiled/> (Accessed 3 September 2021).

2　'Irish whiskey sector back on track with further success in sight' Cantillon, *The Irish Times* [online], 9 September 2021. Available at: <https://www.irishtimes.com/business/agribusiness-and-food/irish-whiskey-sector-back-on-track-with-further-success-in-sight-1.4668585> (Accessed 27 November 2021).

Some years before *IrishWhiskey360°*, an early *Scottish Whisky Association Report* heavily emphasised the crucial link that exists between the promotion of Scottish whisky and the promotion of tourism in Scotland. It coined the term 'the distillery effect' where 'clusters of tourism and culture related activities have developed around whisky distilleries across Scotland'.[3] It could be argued that the distillery effect as identified in Scotland also has a considerable role to play in Ireland, a country where tourism has always featured as a key economic driver and an increasingly important growth sector for the economy. 'In 2018 there were 923,000 visitors to Irish whiskey distilleries, up 13% compared to 2017 and up 41% compared to 2015. 45% of visitors in 2018 came from North America, 14% from Great Britain, 12% from Ireland, 8% from Germany and 7% from France.'[4] Obviously the Covid 19 crisis has caused unprecedented disruption to all tourism sectors but as key markets slowly emerge from the global pandemic, travel consumers are becoming ever more sophisticated. Ireland is increasingly turning its focus on visitors who want to immerse themselves in local culture and heritage. The experiential nature of any tourism site has become very important and consideration of how best to communicate that experience is key.

It has often proved difficult to define the idea of *terroir* and yet it appeals strongly to any tourism market interested in place, and reflection of that place through a food or drink product. One of the most authoritative reference texts in oenological studies is the *Oxford Companion to Wine* by Jancis Robinson. In its analysis of the term *terroir*, it suggests that although there is no specific English translation for the word, it refers to the total natural environment of any viticultural site.[5] As such, the idea of *terroir* offers little in terms of application for the whiskey tourism business. Increasingly

3   VisitScotland (2011), *Scotch Whisky and tourism*, Available at: <www.scotch-whisky.org.uk/.../scotchwhiskyandtourismreport.pdf> (Accessed 3 September 2018).

4   *Irish Whiskey Magazine* [online], 10 September 2019, 'IrishWhiskey360° the Irish Whiskey initiative unveiled'. Available at: <https://www.irishwhiskeymagazine.com/news/latest-news/irishwhiskey360-the-irish-whiskey-initiative-unveiled/> (Accessed 3 September 2021).

5   Jancis Robinson, *The Oxford Companion to Wine* (Oxford: Oxford University press, 2015), p. 737.

however the definition is being broadened by authors to include other cultural markers that allow products to be somewhat more distinctive. Overton and Heitger, citing Vaudour in their analysis, emphasise cultural resources in their definition of *terroir*.[6] Tomás Clancy, one of Ireland's foremost drinks writers, suggested that the French would think you crazy if you suggested that *terroir* relates to soil alone.[7] According to Clancy, it is ironic that although it is generally perceived that the marketing of varietal wines and the dismissal of the French understanding of *terroir* is usually embraced by the New World, it is to Old World history that one must look for the first example of the mass marketing of varietal wines. Bohmrich stresses the important link between the concept of *terroir* and its relationship to wine quality[8] and it is the link between *terroir* and perceptions of quality that is of most use when applying *terroir* concepts to the whiskey business.

In terms of whiskey tourism, we can refine our definition even further. In addition to the necessary ingredients that make up a good Irish whiskey namely barley, water and yeast there are several additional elements that one must consider, to ensure the finished product reflects the place from which it came. These include clearly identifiable factors such as the master distiller's skill, maturation and blending methods, storage etc. But they also include less tangible concepts such as heritage, the story of the makers and the ingredients, cultural economy, authenticity and distinction. These too must be incorporated into definitions of whiskey *terroir*. Each element of this definition has potential benefits in terms of how it engages a tourism audience and it is the analysis of how this is communicated to the whiskey tourist that takes up much of this chapter. As we have seen earlier, concepts of *terroir* have been framed in terms of either a geographical approach or a more socio-cultural interpretation. Despite extensive discussion about its historical origins the current literature lacks analysis on ways attractive

6   John Overton and Jo Heitger, 'Maps, markets and merlot: The making of an antipodean wine appellation', *Journal of Rural Studies*, 24 (4), 2008, p. 441.
7   Tomás Clancy, 'Around the world with pinot noir', *The Sunday Business Post*, 8 March 2009, Available at: <http://archives.tcm.ie/businesspost/2009/03/08/story 40007.asp> (Accessed 15 July 2018).
8   Roger Bohmrich, 'Terroir: Competing perspectives on the roles of soil, climate and people', *Journal of Wine Research*, 7(1), 1996, pp. 33–34.

but hard to define concepts like *terroir* might be communicated to an audience. The case study below proposes that whiskey tourism sites can act as locations for such engagement and the Fourth Space model as defined in earlier chapters can provide a vehicle to help explain and describe ways in which *terroir* benefits can be realised.

A Tale of Two Distilleries

Two distilleries have been chosen for investigation. To protect the rights of these businesses and to allow for comprehensive discussion and analysis, the identity of the distilleries in question have been anonymised. For the purposes of this research, they are referred to as: Distillery A and Distillery B.

There are several established and more recently opened distilleries in Ireland but in terms of selection criteria these two were chosen for the following reasons:

1. They are both contemporary interpretations of the Irish whiskey tourism experience and are reflective of the recent renaissance in Irish Whiskey.
2. Both have had substantial investment within the last two years.
3. Both distilleries have a substantial focus on using whiskey tourism as a method of audience engagement. Distillery A is a newly opened distillery with some production on site but with much emphasis being placed on the touristic experience. Distillery B historically produced on-site but has recently been reimagined as a new tourism experience.
4. They are both positioned in a Dublin, in what has recently been referred to as Whiskey's 'Golden Triangle' and are therefore reflective of many additional distillery investments taking place in the immediate vicinity.

5. Even though they have considerable scale differences in terms whiskey production both distilleries are attempting to convey to markets their true sense of *terroir*.

Distillery A and Distillery B were visited and analysed using the Fourth Space model[9] as described in the introduction to this book. Each visit took approximately one hour and thirty minutes. After each visit a separate analysis was drawn up using the Fourth space template. Using notes, observations and photographs from each visit the analysis was written as detailed below. In this instance only 4 of the 5 strands of the Fourth Space model were used. Strand 5 deals with 'Leveraging the Past' and because of the deep tradition and history inherent in the whiskey sector this final strand is already well integrated into the main analysis.

Strand 1 - Creating a gastronomic identity
(1.1) Incorporating a Third Place function
The Fourth Space model suggests that four key elements are necessary, as listed under this first strand to successfully convey of a unique gastronomic identity. As mentioned earlier Third Place elements stem from the work of Oldenburg who defined Third Places as having a number of important characteristics typified by a sense of local hospitality where the Third Place is a leveller, all people are treated equally, conversation is a key activity, the mood is playful and it acts as a home away from home.[10] Obviously creating a home away from home is not the purpose of a beverage tourism site however the Fourth Space model attempts to encapsulate some Third Place elements in terms of a sense of true hospitality delivered. Both distilleries offered a warm welcoming atmosphere. There was a pleasant mixture of personal welcome on the part of reception and tour guides alike and pleasant relaxed surroundings that demonstrated some

---

9   Brian Murphy, 'Communicating new definitions of terroir to a millennial audience through the medium of fourth space', in Daniella Wagner, Michael Mair, Albert Franz Stockl and Axel Dreyer (eds), *Kulinarischer tourismus and weintourismus 2015* (Wiesbaden: Springer Gabler, 2017), pp. 237–235.

10   Ray Oldenburg, *The Great Good Place* (Philadelphia, PA: Da Capo Press, 1998), pp. 20–42.

of the Third Place qualities mentioned above. However, the Distillery A experience lacked warmth in terms of the physical surroundings of the reception and waiting area. Seating was limited, the area was cold and quite clinical in terms of its décor and it lacked any ancillary services. Given the substantial waiting times that are likely to be a feature of any scheduled tour business this could present a problem. The Distillery B experience offered considerably more interaction in terms of Third Place qualities with visitors being greeted by several busy service operations offering personal interaction, ample casual seating, serving a range of whiskey associated drinks, tea/coffee etc. in a 'local pub' like atmosphere to both visitors and importantly locals. The tour ticket price in Distillery B also included a drink at what they referred to as their Daily Grog Bar. This provided an opportunity for clients to engage with each other and the site itself while waiting for the scheduled tour to start thus enhancing their Third Place atmosphere.

(1.2) Conveying the story of place

The story of place is another one of the criteria emphasised in the Fourth Space model and refers to the way in which any beverage site communicates a sense of physical place to the audience. This can be done in many ways. By necessity the story of place requires the beverage site to be rooted to on individual location. This rootedness is then conveyed to the audience. Distillery B was lacking in terms of this strand in that it was essentially telling the story of a place that is no longer a site of whiskey production. The tour guide was up front and honest in their insistence that all its whiskey was now made at an alternative site. Such honesty emphasises authenticity. The guide than mitigates this by stressing that their more contemporary production facility is located just a few short hours from Dublin because of the quality of the barely grown in that region which all comes from within a 100-mile radius and the quality of the water that comes from the local river that runs through the site. The place story is further emphasised on the Distillery B website where it elaborates on the local river, the local barley, the proximity of suppliers and the unique traditional and local production processes that go into making their whiskey. Distillery A's tour guide also clearly conveyed the story of place by stressing that their whiskey is produced on site in the distillery. This was heavily emphasised with two of their branded whiskies on display. Because they are newly opened many modern distilleries in Ireland have had to buy in whiskey produced at other locations due to the necessity for Irish whiskey to be aged for a minimum 3 years. Many therefore struggle to convey a sense of place. In fact, when one looks closely at the product descriptors on Distillery A's website, we can see that they mention that each whiskey contains some single malt whiskey that has been produced on the stills at the actual site. They don't stipulate how much of their blend was produced on-site but it still allows them to claim and convey that sense of place and thus claim a unique gastronomic identity.

(1.3) Acting as a cultural ambassador

One of the potential benefits of any gastronomic tourism site is that it has the potential to act as an ambassador for cultural expression to visiting tourists. As such the attraction steps beyond its remit of selling the product and offers a more symbolic interpretation of Irishness. Both distilleries performed well in this regard but for different reasons. Distillery A offered quite an intimate tour-guiding experience that focused as much on the area's social history as it did in terms of the whiskey product. It emphasised the personal connections between the distillery's founder and the social history of the surrounding area. Through the medium of the local tour guide, visitors are presented with an authentic interpretation of Dublin. The fact that the distillery is located in a church links religion and whiskey together in a way that mirrors the origins of distilling in an Irish context and demonstrates that the religious have always been associated with distilling down through the centuries. Such links are emphasised more overtly by other Irish distilleries such as the Glendalough Distillery which relies heavily on religious iconography in terms of portraying its sense of Irishness to consumers. The Distillery B experience also moved beyond the actual product and portrayed a sense of Ireland that could be clearly understood by visiting tourists. It was apparent at an early stage that it was targeting an international audience and one of the first things the tour guide established as part of a scripted performance was the range of nationalities that were present in his audience. He also established his Irish credentials clearly stating where he was 'born and bred' before going on to make frequent references to reasons why Ireland was different in terms of our approach to whiskey and indeed alcohol more generally. The tour guide script was peppered with references to Ireland's cultural reputation for drinking and the craic with quite stereotypical statements such as 'as you know we Irish love a drink!' A sense of Irishness was also demonstrated in Distillery A through the process description when Ireland's unique methods of making whiskey were highlighted. Secondly the comparative tasting at the end made it clear that Ireland, Scotland and America were very different in terms of their approach to making whiskey and the subsequent flavour differences that emerged. A Wall of History at the very start of the tour where groups were waiting also portrayed Irish history more generally and posters and advertising campaigns helped reflect Irish identity down through the years. The lobby bar area was open to the public and this offered the space for a more authentic Irish atmosphere which was enhanced by the fact that this area was open for locals and non-tourists as well as tourists.

(1.4) Providing authentic people

Both distilleries offered interactions with people who seemed passionate and tied to the visitor experience but they were very different in how they engaged. The tour guide in Distillery A was much less scripted than the one in Distillery B. He also conveyed a genuine affiliation to, and knowledge of, the place in which the distillery was located. This offered an authentic sense of identity during the tour. The stories he recounted were all associated with the place, and the attached historic church graveyard which has been reclaimed as part of the distillery development project. The Distillery B guide was much more scripted and professional in their delivery of knowledge and story. An overtly scripted presentation led to diminished authenticity when it came to conveying a true sense of gastronomic identity. This may be due to the bigger scale of tourist operation on the Distillery B site compared to Distillery A and the necessity for the efficient operation of tours and guest interactions.

Strand 2 - Provide a sense of place/regionality

(2.1) Emphasising place of origin/regionality

Certain drink products successfully emphasise their place of origin and sense of regionality. If we take the example of single malt whisky in Scotland, we can see that it trades very heavily in terms of its *terroir* distinction. Like the *Appellation contrôlée* wines of France, they have a strong association with place and possess a very specific sense of regional gastronomic identity. Scotland has five key whisky regions. They include Highland, Speyside, Islay, Lowland and Campeltown. Each region produces whiskies of a defined style with certain common characteristics. Speyside offers the consumer a unique insight into its place-based identity with over half of all single malt distilleries in Scotland situated there.[11] Tourism plays a large part in the expression of Scottish single malt's regionality. Irish whiskey on the other hand has historically lacked a similar sense of regional identity. It all trades under the one place designation 'Irish Whiskey' with no official regional recognition so both whiskey products from Distillery A and Distillery B have a national classification of Irish Whiskey once they fulfil certain legal requirements regarding minimum aging and minimum alcohol by volume. At first glance, the whiskey for Distillery A and Distillery B are lacking in terms of regional identity even though Distillery A was particularly keen to emphasise its association with the 'Golden Triangle' of distillers that has existed in that region of Dublin for over 200 years. One of the first images the visitor is presented with on arrival at Distillery A is an infographic entitled *Brew, Boots and Biscuits* that clearly emphasises Distillery A's association with the Golden Triangle. Such emphasis allows the distillery to claim association with a distinct regional area thus enhancing their sense of place. This is mirrored in their brochure where they convey a similar sense of regional identity: 'In a remarkable 21st century revival of The Golden Triangle, several new distilleries have been opened in the liberties'.[12] Distillery B, although it also refers to the Golden Triangle as part of the tour guide's script, seems more interested in maintaining Irish whiskey's national identity as opposed to any regional identity. This is not surprising given that their whiskey is a very dominant player in terms of Irish whiskey exports and further regionalisation of their identity might

11   Brian Murphy, 'Cognac, Scotch and Irish: Lessons in gastronomic identity', in Frank Healy and Brigitte Bastiat (eds), *Voyages between France and Ireland: Culture, Tourism and Sport* (Bern: Peter Lang, 2017), p. 245.

12   This appears in the extensive marketing brochure for Distillery A, 2017, pp. 32–33.

not be to their advantage. The fact that their whiskey is produced at a location removed from the distillery tourism site also limits any engagement they might have with regionalisation. One interesting expression of place identity occurs during their three-whiskey tasting at the end of the tour. Obviously, visitors taste Distillery B's own whiskey but interestingly they are encouraged to compare it against Johnny Walker Scotch and Jack Daniels Bourbon. One could argue that they are attempting to differentiate their product as tasting distinctly Irish when compared to other nationally identified products like Scotch and American whiskey, thus re-enforcing their national rather than regional identity.

(2.2) Avoiding fauxthenticity

Authenticity is key when any beverage is attempting to identify with their sense of place. Though difficult to define there are examples of beverage sites such as craft breweries or whiskey and gin distilleries aligning themselves with stories that are quite thinly veiled in reality. We can refer to this phenomenon as 'Fauxthenticity'. Attempts to use falsely created back stories should be treated with care and often producers might be better served emphasising more authentic elements of food or drink product's story even if such story is more contemporary in nature, for example, the story of the ingredients used, the story of the people who supply the product or the story of the processes used to make the product. Distillery B uses interesting tools to help avoid accusations of fauxthenticity with references to their distillery archive, the employment of a full-time archivist and the fact that they possess examples of their founder's own handwritten distiller's notes along with many other historical artefacts including ancient grains that were found between the pages of ancient distillery mash bill recipe notebooks. Distillery A appears to use the adjoining historic graveyard as a tool with which to express its own sense of authenticity. It references several well-known people who are buried there along with members of the distillery founder's family. Such accounts of well-known historic burials provide a certain authenticity to their distillery site. An association with religious pilgrimage appears less successful in terms of expression of authenticity. These associations were heavily emphasised as part of the tour but further evidence regarding this place connection would enhance Distillery A's authenticity credentials.

(2.3) Providing an educational medium/enable decodification

One of the challenges faced by many high-end beverage products in terms of communicating their place story rests in the codified nature of the product and the Fourth Space model of *terroir* engagement addresses such challenges by focusing on opportunities around educational engagement with the product in question. For the individual to fully appreciate such a culturally charged product, it is often necessary to have a certain level of knowledge. This can be viewed as a challenge or an opportunity. In recent years there has been a considerable uptake in terms of formal beverage education courses organised by companies such as the Wine and Spirit Education Trust.[13] There are also a wide range of more informal courses offered in beverage areas such as coffee, wine and whiskey. Such educational opportunities encourage audiences to become more expert in their appreciation of products. Both Distillery A and Distillery B held tastings as part of the tour but Distillery B's tasting experience was superior in terms of decodification in that it clearly emphasised tasting technique as well as distinctive elements of each comparative whiskey. It also offered considerable decodification knowledge in terms of its process description using experiential methods to educate visitors regarding malting techniques, maturation stages and guide-led comparisons between pot still whiskey aromas and column still whiskey aromas. It was successful in terms of allowing visitors to feel a real sense of knowledge development when it comes to whiskey in general. On the other hand, Distillery A's tasting lacked decodification knowledge in general, the tasting was quite brand specific and lacked depth in terms of understanding the whiskey process and classification. Distillery B also offers a ladder system of courses and experiences at their visitor site that are in addition to the standard tour and charged for separately. While the standard tour concentrates on story, process and tasting, the more advanced and expensive experiences have themes such as the whiskey producer's experience, whiskey cocktail creation and advanced tasting techniques. These increasingly complex experiences allow Distillery B to provide a very substantial educational

13   WSET Global.com (n.d.). Available at: <https://www.wsetglobal.com/> (Accessed 20 September 2021).

aspect to their visit which significantly enhances the visitor's *terroir* engagement when viewed through the lens of the Fourth Space model. Such specialist knowledge attainment emphasises the pleasure for some consumers and helps them move beyond the drink's primary meaning, to another level of understanding which is contained within the many layers of complexity associated with the drink such as regionality, nuances of taste and production aspects.

(2.4) Allowing for a food place link

Given the major gastronomic advancements that have occurred in Ireland in recent decades, it is very difficult to envisage any beverage product in isolation and food must form part of any *terroir* engagement equation. Some beverage products like wine or even Scottish single malt whiskey have natural food bedfellows. There are numerous references to matching certain foods to certain whiskies. This is particularly true when we deal with regional specificity. One of the strengths of a whisky tourism leader like Scottish whisky is that it possesses regional specificity, and this allows much more interest from a food perspective. Take, for example, the smoke-laden whiskies that hail from the regional appellation of Islay. Because of their regional identity they provide ample opportunity for specific associations with food:

> On the other side of the whiskey spectrum is Islay Scotch. This may seem at the outset to be a more difficult whiskey to pair, but it is really just as easy to match as bourbon. The signature note of an Islay whisky is peat smoke. Work with that.[14]

Other food perspectives can also be considered. Scottish single malt is a popular ingredient in Scottish regional foods such as jams or chutneys. It is also frequently used to promote associated regional food such as Scottish smoked salmon through promotional materials or tasting masterclasses. There was little evidence regarding the integration of whiskey into Ireland's food culture during both distillery visits. Distillery A, unlike many beverage tourism offerings did not include even the most basic

14   Thewhiskeywash.com, 'Whiskey and food pairing: The fine art for beginners'. Available at: Retrieved from <https://thewhiskeywash.com/american-whiskey/ whiskey-and- food-pairing-the-fine-art-for-beginners/> (Accessed 20 June 2017).

food outlet. This presented problems in terms of ancillary facilities for visitors as they waited for the scheduled tour departure times. However, this problem is likely to be addressed given that the distillery has also purchased an existing pub that adjoins the site. As this beverage site was a very new development with some elements under construction it is likely that food perspectives will be addressed in the future and more evidence of Distillery A's interactions with food will become clear. Interestingly during recent renovations Distillery B removed its principal restaurant and now focuses predominantly on their drink's experiences. However, they still engage indirectly with food through several special events and festivals. Their event space is also used for food and drink functions. In general, associations between both distilleries and food seem to be somewhat limited and there is considerable potential for developments in this area which will allow consumers to benefit from a more enhanced relationship with the product's *terroir*.

Strand 3 - Exploit new technology

(3.1) Using technology to bridge the place and story gap

Because of the strong associations between beverage and place, the story of that place has taken on a particular relevance in the drink's world. New technology is rapidly changing our storytelling capacity and a newly emerged millennial generation now imbibe their stories through platforms like TikTok, Snapchat, Facebook, Twitter, Instagram and YouTube, rather than through traditional channels. It is essential that beverage tourism sites use technology to help tell the story of their product to contemporary audiences. Distillery A was relatively weak in terms of its use. The entrance/waiting hall offers some limited technological engagement through a series of screens that tell a linear story of the distillery founder and others that offer an interactive quiz testing visitor's existing knowledge. There was also a selfie photo opportunity frame that encouraged visitors to engage with the product through mediums such as Instagram. In addition, the website was quite weak in terms of its story engagement and stories were limited to associated church and graveyard themes at the time of the visit. This limited technological engagement may be due to the distillery and the website being so new although the visitor experience itself was also lacking in technological engagement. Distillery B on the other hand uses technology to good effect both through online engagement on its website and various social media channels as part of its storytelling experience. The tour guide himself engaged and with interactive screen displays which told the distillery's historical story as well as their process story. There was also engagement with sound and smell that encouraged a more experiential tour. Light systems in each of the three tour rooms enhanced the experiences in terms of the story being told. In addition, there was considerable opportunity for technological story engagement in the communal waiting area with visitors encouraged to experience the distillery through Facebook, Twitter and Instagram. There were also computer terminals where visitors could register to receive a certificate as a memoir of their visit. This was emailed to visitors immediately. All these technological elements were subtle and well-integrated into the visitor experience which is important when one considers a heritage product like whiskey.

(3.2) Facilitating elements of tourism without travel

The technological strategies mentioned above help develop potential markets and are aimed at promoting and giving specific exposure to the story of the whiskey's place. Many food and beverage tourism sites however now also use technology to achieve, to some degree, what McGovern has previously referred to as Tourism without Travel.[15] That is to say, the consumer is given the story of the place without the necessity of being physically present in that location. Social media and similar interactions with a product that are not dependent on being physically present can be of important benefit to any whiskey brand in a competitive global market. As we shall see in a later chapter, Scottish distilleries like Laphroaig use the story of place to excellent effect with continuous technological engagement with the distillery through live websites monitoring the distillery processes in real time along with outreach initiatives such as live

---

15   Mark McGovern, 'The cracked pint glass of the servant: The Irish pub, Irish identity and the tourist eye', in Michael Cronin and Barbara O' Connor (eds), *Irish Tourism: Image, Culture and Identity* (Clevedon: Channel View Publications, 2003), p. 91.

place-based virtual events. Although Distillery B uses technology quite well and does so in a much more integrated manner than Distillery A, there is little evidence of both subjects allowing audiences to engage with their physical locations without the need to travel there. There are good opportunities for both locations to benefit from enhanced technology engagement as will be demonstrated by some of the more technologically engaged examples in the coming chapters.

(3.3) Providing personal interactions before and after the touristic experience

Technology can also be used to encourage personal relationships between the consumer and the tourism site. Examples may include engagement with key personnel such as the master distiller or the distillery founder. Laphroaig distillery in Scotland offers direction in this regard in the way it uses the persona of distillery manager John Campbell. He is consistently presented as the human face of the distillery and engages with consumers through email and scheduled live internet tastings and broadcasts. Even though consumers may not get an opportunity to travel to the distillery they still manage to form a personal bond with the site through communications with the personnel working on the site. Again, there was little evidence from both distilleries regarding such provision and there are considerable opportunities in this regard.

(3.4) Targeting millennial audiences

The emergence of the digital native generation requires tourism sites to engage even further with technological advances. A digital native can be described as 'a person born or brought up during the age of digital technology and so familiar with computers and the Internet from an early age'.[16] As younger generations come of age, tourism sites such as Distillery A and Distillery B may need to re-think and enhance their approach to technology. Countries like Germany which have long traditions of advances in wine tourism are already exploring the potential of using augmented reality technology to enhance the touristic experience. Whiskey

---

16   Oxford Dictionary.com (n.d.). Available at: <https://en.oxforddictionaries.com/ definition/digital_native> (Accessed 20 August 2019).

tourism sites have also begun to take tentative steps in terms of similar audience engagement approaches. Because whiskey is a product steeped in tradition and history there is perhaps a reluctance on the part of distilleries to portray their product through a technological lens, but we have already seen that some, like Laphraoig, have shown leadership in this regard. One interesting Irish example of using augmented reality concerns The Walsh Whiskey Distillery who provide a virtual reality whiskey experience at Dublin Airport that allows passengers to avail of a virtual tour of its picturesque distillery in Royal Oak in County Carlow while indulging in an physical tasting of one of their premium whiskeys.[17] Increasingly, the early adoption of new technologies will be a key differentiator for all beverage tourism sites as target markets change and audiences become more digitally aware.

Strand 4 - Attach a cultural economy

(4.1) Providing authentic links to a product's culture

David Aylward describes the increasing demand among consumers to experience value-added elements when consuming drinks products. Using the wine industry as an example he makes the argument that the art of winemaking in Australia has been replaced by purely economic thinking and this has reduced the practice to formulaic assembly line production. Such a commodity-based approach fails to satisfy increasingly educated customers. Aylward argues that wine producers should understand

> the way in which a wine's cultural and economic qualities can be woven into a more enriched fabric. This would not simply assign cultural elements to an economically oriented product. Rather, it would weave individual and community values, passion, care, identity and *terroir* together with the more tangible aspects of production, distribution, price points and marketing[18]

---

17 'Dublin Airport passengers offered tours of Walsh Whiskey Distillery – virtually', *Sips and Stories*. Available at: <https://www.walshwhiskey.com/1277/dublin-airp ort-virtual-walsh-whiskey-distillery-tours/> (Accessed 9 October 2021).

18 David Aylward, 'Towards a cultural economy paradigm for the Australian wine industry', *Prometheus*, 26 (4), 2009, p. 373.

The cultural economy strand of our *terroir* engagement model draws from Aylward's definition described here. It suggests that beverage tourism sites should explore the value of expressing the story of the product not only in terms of its tangible attributes but also in terms of its associated people, its history and its place. These are the elements that allow a whiskey to provide additional value-added elements. Both Distillery A and Distillery B have exploited cultural economies like these to good effect, as discussed earlier in the analysis of Strand 1 and Strand 2. The cultural economy of a drink product can also be expressed through its association with other cultural spheres which can in turn contribute additional attributes to the drink product in question.

(4.2) Conflating with other cultural activities

The Fourth Space model includes ways in which beverage tourism sites and associated products conflate their identity with more traditional cultural signifiers such as literature, music, art and architecture. This type is of cultural conflation is increasingly seen in the wine tourism world and whiskey tourism sites are also beginning to avail of the many advantages it can bring. The newly opened Cité du Vin in Bordeaux and the previously mentioned Chateau La Coste vineyard in the South of France offer good examples of such conflation. Both sites successfully blend wine tourism with the worlds of art, literature and architecture. The former provides architectural tours, wine libraries and a schedule of on-site cultural events[19] and the latter emphasises its series of Art and Architecture Walks as part of their wine tourism experience.[20] Distillery A certainly provided evidence of this through its association with, and emphasis on, religious art using elements such as its stained glass windows to combine art, religious story and distilling. They incorporated the structure of the distillery into the architecture of a church building and the installation of an iconic glass pyramid as the centrepiece on their distillery steeple. Distillery B was also quite advanced in terms of its cultural economy provision. There

---

19   Laciteduvin.com, Available at: <https://www.laciteduvin.com/en> (Accessed 4 October 2021).

20   Chateau La Coste.com, Available at: <https://chateau-la-coste.com/en/art-archi tecture/art-and-architecture-walk.html> (Accessed 4 October 2021).

were considerable artistic references in the bar waiting area in the form of hand painted whiskey casks, bespoke sculptural light fittings forged from whiskey bottles and backlit displays of rare and ancient whiskies. There were gallery displays of historic advertising campaigns in the waiting hall and several engraved oversized oak tables adorning the premises with the names of distillery workers carved around the edges. In addition, there were frequent references to distillery engagements with the world of arts, crafts and music. These communications tell the story of various groups of designers, artists and musicians that the distillery collaborated with. They included famous leather designers, contemporary furniture makers, art and fashion houses, artists and illustrators who designed limited edition labels. There is also reference to the distillery's involvement with music sessions on-site and other events such as distillery film clubs. All these elements point to an advanced appreciation of their whiskey's cultural economy. Sociologists have long emphasised the importance of cultural capital and its relationship to economic capital and many have sought to define such a link and its importance.

> By conceptualising the interactions between 'culture' and the 'economy' in this way, we might transcend the narrow focus of looking simply at the economy as a self-serving entity, or at culture as bearing no relationship to anything but itself, and replace these piecemeal models with a broader interactive framework in which all relevant economic and cultural variables could be accounted for simultaneously.[21]

(4.3) Striving for cultural capital while avoiding exploitation

The Fourth Space model stresses the necessity for beverage tourism sites to provide links to cultural aspects of their touristic experience while minimising blatant exploitation. According to Aylward the conceptualisation of theorists like Bourdieu 'rest on the premise of independent or segmented variables whereby economic capital and cultural capital are seen as two distinct and self-contained entities that can and should complement each other'.[22] Both Distillery A and Distillery B are successful in

---

21   David Aylward, citing Geursen and Rentschuler, in 'Towards a cultural economy
      paradigm for the Australian wine industry', *Prometheus*, 26 (4), 2009, p. 380.
22   Ibid.

this regard although it should be noted that Distillery A appears considerably more blatant in its exploitation of cultural economy elements particularly with regard to how religious art and architecture are incorporated into its visitor experience. Distillery B also does well in its provision of cultural capital benefits but in a less obvious way where the distillery and the whiskey itself appear secondary to the linked cultural aspect and more focus is placed on the philanthropic nature of such associations.

Conclusion

Although whiskey distilleries have experienced considerable growth in recent years they increasingly have to compete with other more advanced and established beverage tourism offerings. These include long-established wine destinations, Scottish whisky sites and more recent gin and craft beer tourism locations. With over 1.7 million visitors, the Guinness Store House is the most visited paid tourism attraction in Ireland.[23] Traditionally, tourism attractions have placed a strong focus on areas such as on-site facilities, transport infrastructure, tour guiding/information and technology. While recognising the importance of these to any beverage tourism site's success, the analysis presented here has turned its gaze on the less obvious benefits of communicating a sense of *terroir* to increasingly gastro-aware tourists. It identifies key factors that mark modern drink tourism sites out as being distinctive and *terroir* focused. It presents ways that a sense of *terroir* can be communicated successfully to a whiskey tourism audience. The academic literature has clearly demonstrated that the idea of *terroir* is difficult to explain, and authors define the term in many ways. While some tend towards a more geographic understanding of scientific factors that influence the quality of the liquid

23   Fáilte Ireland, 'Key tourism facts 2019', 21 March 2021. Available at: <https://www.failteireland.ie/FailteIreland/media/WebsiteStructure/Documents/3_Research_Insights/4_Visitor_Insights/KeyTourismFacts_2019.pdf?ext=.pdf> (Accessed 30 November 2021).

in the glass, others have tried to broaden that definition to include cultural markers such as place, story and authenticity. The Fourth Space model employed here is designed to reflect this latter definition and has allowed these cultural markers to be discussed, analysed and subsequently communicated to a tourism audience. The model proposes one way of exploring difficult to understand and yet important beverage tourism attributes. The French wine sector has been very successful at communicating its own sense of *terroir* to audiences since the inception of its *Appellation Contrôlée* laws as far back as 1935 and the model proposed here has drawn on this success. It includes in its framework many of the key *terroir* attributes that wine tourism culture has exploited over many years. Once these attributes can be identified and discussed it becomes easier for whiskey tourism sites to assess whether tourists are engaging with, and are attracted to, these elements.

The Fourth Space model is conceptual, and the limitations of the case study approach used in this chapter are recognised in that only two distilleries are used for analysis and that analysis is explored from only one standpoint. However, the research does indicate that engaging with a Fourth Space model does allow a deeper interpretation of the complex approach taken by modern beverage sites in terms of expressing their story, their place, their people and their product. Though relatively recently re-developed, Distillery B has a long association with whiskey tourism in Dublin and it can be clearly seen from the analysis presented here that it has considerable *terroir* engagement advantages over the newly opened Distillery A. The *terroir* message emanating from Distillery A is more disjointed and inconsistent in terms of the strands explored here. This is perhaps unsurprising given it is a newly developed tourism site and will undoubtedly change substantially in the coming years. Distillery B has also had considerable capital investment in its redevelopment and such a spend is reflected clearly in how the visitor attraction is successful under much of the Fourth Space analysis. We cannot measure or score exact achievement when using a model such as Fourth Space and it is therefore best employed as a critical analysis tool. There is considerable opportunity for further research to be undertaken into how concepts like *terroir* are communicated to, and received by, tourism audiences and the research presented here has merely begun to frame a narrative around this emerging concept. Investment levels have proved to be an important factor. Both Distillery A and Distillery B had substantial investment in their development; 7 million euro in the case of Distillery A and 11 million euro in the case of Distillery B, but many smaller beverage tourism sites in Ireland don't have access to that same level of investment or expertise. And yet just like the larger players they too need to consider similar *terroir* engagement approaches if they are to become distinctive in such a competitive tourism market. The Fourth Space approach presented in this and earlier chapters can help provide discussion and analysis regarding such levels of engagement. Conclusions drawn should assist all beverage tourism sites, large or small, in developing strategies to enhance and communicate their own true sense of *terroir* to an increasingly sophisticated food tourism audience.

PART III

Products

CHAPTER 8

Irish Single Pot Still Whiskey: Advertising in an Epicurean World

I first encountered Irish whiskey historian, Fionnán O' Connor, at the Dublin Gastronomy Symposium in 2016 when we invited him to lead a unique whiskey tasting as part of the events we arranged for delegates that year. Fionnán's work includes the excellent 2015 book *A Glass Apart: Irish Single Pot Still Whiskey*. This book provided the impetus for this chapter. In it Fionnán emphasises the importance of Irish Single Post Still whiskey, its unique qualities and how as a style, it has only recently come back to prominence after a long period of exile. As the chapter explains the Irish Single Pot Still designation offers a unique and authentic story in an increasingly crowded marketplace. I am a strong supporter of all Irish food and drink products but the story of Irish Pot Still Whiskey stands out as an example of a drink that is uniquely Irish and one that can't be recreated outside the island. As such it deserves a special place in our hearts.

Having dealt with important places of food a drink engagement in section 2, this section of the book narrows our focus even further by examining how products that are traded in these places demonstrate additional attributes that help connect with gastronomic audiences. Using the example of Irish Single Pot Still Whiskey this chapter draws on the success of such attributes and their strong sense of gastronomic identity to argue that these uniquely Irish qualities are exactly what the Irish whiskey sector must promote if it is to meet the provenance demands of an increasingly gastro-aware society.

In March 2016, *The Irish Times* reported that an Irish Single Pot Still Whiskey bottled 100 years earlier in 1916 would achieve in the region of €15,000 at an auction to be held by Irish auctioneers, Adams.[1] There are

---

1   Conor Pope, 'Bottle of Whiskey blessed for spirit of kindness expected to fetch

several reasons why this single bottle of whiskey might achieve such an extraordinary price. Rarity and its centenary year of production play an important part but there are other less obvious aspects at play. Firstly, the bottle is surrounded by a legend and a story that endows distiller Richard Allman, and hence the whiskey itself, with a unique and authentic pedigree:

> Richard Allman, the owner of the Bandon Distillery, was a liberal MP during the years of Charles Stewart Parnell's Home Rule movement and, legend has it, owed his whiskey fortune to the blessing of a Catholic priest. In 1820 a Fr. Collins was pursued by an Orange mob and given sanctuary for three days by the Allman family. To thank the woman of the house for her kindness he prayed 'that your children may make riches out of water'. Six years later her son James C. Allman converted a mill in Bandon and made his fortune from the water of life.[2]

Secondly, the bottle in question is a rare unopened example of an Irish Single Pot Still Whiskey which means it was made using a uniquely Irish distillation method incorporating malted and un-malted barley. It is precisely because of the whiskey's unique combination of place, production method and story that this bottle achieved such exalted status.

Irish Whiskey has had a turbulent time throughout much of the last 100 years. At its height, the country was home to eighty-eight licensed distilleries and the world leader in whiskey production.[3] Due to a combination of misfortune and misjudgement during the twentieth century, the island would ultimately play host to just two distilleries by the early 1980s. As demonstrated in the last chapter, recently the sector has shown signs of a phoenix-like recovery and Irish Whiskey is now the fastest growing premium spirit category in the world. As society becomes ever more gastro-aware, advertisements can successfully portray the unique sense of both place and story that will allow the Irish Whiskey category to regain the global distinction that it once held at the turn of the twentieth century.

€15000', *The Irish Times*, 29 March 2016, p. 3.

2   Ibid.

3   Irish Whiskey Association, *Vision for Irish Whiskey: A Strategy to Underpin the Sustainable Growth of the Sector in Ireland*, 2015, p. 7. Available at: <http://www.abfi.ie/Sectors/ABFI/ABFI.nsf/vPagesSpirits/Home/$File/Vision+for+Irish+Whiskey+May+2015.pdf> (Accessed 2 December 2015).

Using a case study approach this chapter suggests that the uniquely Irish concept that is Irish Single Pot Still Whiskey can fulfil the enhanced gastronomic identity demands of future drinkers. It takes the Irish whiskey sector generally and the case of Pernod Ricard in particular, and investigates how modern distillers are beginning to use strong story elements particularly around place and method to advertise their premium ranges. Following the lead of other internationally recognised place-based drinks such as Cognac, Single Malt Scotch and Champagne, it can be argued that Irish whiskey needs to rise above the notion of its generic national nomenclature to claim a more unique *terroir*-based identity in an increasingly competitive premium drinks market.

In the past, Irish food and drink was limited both in terms of choice and opportunity. Religion was a key determinant in how and when people ate and drank. Most Irish people above the age of 40 can remember the necessity for abstinence during the Lenten period. Pre-Celtic Tiger entertaining outside the home was relatively limited. It often involved just the immediate family visiting a local hotel to celebrate an event such as a communion or a wedding. In his 1970s guidebook to the capital *The Essential Dublin*, Kelleher offered a bleak description of food and drink in Ireland at the time. He suggested that there were 'too few [restaurants] for a cosmopolitan city' and described a pub meal experience at the time as follows:

> Two pieces of yesterday's lightly margarine bread wilting at the edges, enveloping a tiny piece of ham or processed cheese, and served with a cup of something only distantly related to coffee, is served at lunchtime to the mainly male clientele.[4]

Ireland has now moved on from the impoverished fare described by Kelleher. The increasing number of Irish Michelin awards and celebrity chefs attest to this. The country has shown demonstrable expertise in the exportation of food and drink which is now worth in the region of €13 billion to the Irish economy.[5] There is also an ever-increasing presence

4   Terry Kelleher, Maurice Craig and Bernard Share, *The Essential Dublin* (Dublin: Gill and MacMillan, 1972), p. 64.
5   Bord Bia, 'Why Ireland'. Available at: <https://www.irishfoodanddrink.com/> (Accessed 25 October 2021).

of artisanal food and drink businesses here. There are currently over 125 microbrewing companies operating in the Republic of Ireland [6] and by the end of 2020 the number of operational Irish whiskey distilleries had increased to thirty-eight and the map of the Irish whiskey landscape had been radically redrawn.[7]

Previous chapters have described how a returning diaspora during the Celtic Tiger period coupled with increased foreign travel led to the social conditions necessary for a gastronomic culture to develop in Ireland. Both domestically and internationally the Irish nation has arrived at a place where gastronomic expectations are now very high. Advertisers are aware that modern consumers seek Irish products that express what Trubek describes as an 'integrity of somewhereness'.[8] Her definition suggests that many modern consumers are no longer impressed by products that lack provenance. On the international stage the country is already synonymous with iconic drinks such as Guinness and Irish Whiskey. The notion of 'integrity of somewhereness' is dependent on context and to export markets, such drinks already offer a sense of the 'local'. The designation 'Irish Whiskey' is prominently displayed on the majority of whiskeys produced here today. As international spirit shelves become congested, however, product identity becomes more important. Irish spirits may now require the enhanced elements of place-integrity that have long been attributed to others such as Cognac and Single Malt Scotch. Tomás Clancy advocated such an approach for many years and referred to it as his 'Irish AC proposal':

> It would allow a generation of Irish people to reconnect with the variety, diversity and generosity of our own soils, our lands … Many consumers, in the EU and across Ireland, can tell you about Parma Ham, the slopes of Burgundy and the AC cheeses of Northern Italy, but do not comprehend the complexity of Meath, Kilkenny or

6   Bernard Feeney, *Craft Beer and Independent Microbreweries in Ireland 2018* (Bord Bia, 2018), p. 8.
7   Irish Whiskey Association, Drinks Ireland. Available at: <https://www.ibec.ie/drinksireland/irish-whiskey/our-industry/economic-contribution> (Accessed 18 September 2021).
8   Amy Trubek, *The Taste of Place: A Cultural Journey into Terroir* (London: University of California Press, 2008), p. 115.

Wexford soils, slopes or produce. Yet it is there to taste in unprotected products from Gubbeen Cheese to Air Dried Connemara Lamb.[9]

In recent years, several whiskey companies have shown interest in exploiting heritage links to place and story to help premiumise and thus distinguish their product from more proprietary brands. We have had the 2009 advertising campaign from Johnnie Walker fronted by actor Robert Carlyle entitled: *The man who walked around the world*. Part of this campaign involved a six-minute short film, shot in one continuous take, and depicted Carlyle recounting the history of the Johnnie Walker brand while walking through the highlands of Scotland.[10] Others such as the 2013 Tullamore Dew *Parting Glass* campaign used music, in the form of the traditional Irish song *The Parting Glass* and story in the guise of a mock Irish wake, to evoke a sense of authentic heritage around their product.[11] By introducing irreverent humour into the mix, brands that have been traditionally focused on an older demographic can attract a younger audience. In the Tullamore Dew campaign, what appeared to be a very sombre traditional wake scene emerges as an illustration of a stag party scene where the future groom is humorously bidding farewell to his single life and single friends before his wedding day. The Jameson's *Legendary tales of John Jameson* advertising campaign illustrates a similar use of humour, story and heritage to enhance premiumisation. The campaign uses significant historical events to create a fictional period tale detailing the heroic exploits of its protagonist, John Jameson. According to Passariello and Colchester (2011):

> Alcoholic-drink makers have traditionally used their ads to convey a party vibe, as in the Budweiser tag line 'King of Good Times'. But to peddle premium spirits to a younger, hipper crowd, some brands have thrown tradition into the mix, oscillating

9   Tomás Clancy, 'An Irish AC proposal'. Available at: <http://tomasclancy.wordpr ess.com/the-irish-ac-proposal/> (Accessed 7 February 2020).

10   Johnny Walker, 'The man who walked around the world' Advert (2009). Available at: <https://www.youtube.com/watch?v=fZ6aiVg2qVk> (Accessed 20 November 2021).

11   Tullamore Dew, 'The parting glass' Advert (2013). Available at: <https://www.yout ube.com/watch?v=RL9yB0ne67A> (Accessed 2 December 2021).

between humour and a message focused more on heritage. A case in point is the Jameson Tall Tales campaign.[12]

Much like the Tullamore Dew *Parting Glass* campaign, the article goes on to cite Mark Figliulo who is keen to emphasise the importance of striking a balance between history and humour to attract a younger demographic. The very name of the campaign series suggests that Jameson was keen to downplay the history aspect of the campaign and adopt a more fun approach.

> 'The risk of being too much in heritage is boring the hell out of people,' says Mark Figliulo, chairman and chief creative officer of TBWA\Chiat\Day New York, a unit of Omnicom Group Inc., which created the new Jameson commercial. 'We don't want to say our whiskey is for sitting around and discussing the problems of the world.' Playing up history is one of the techniques marketers use to enhance a brand's aura and justify premium prices.[13]

The Story of Irish Pot Still Whiskey: An Advertising Opportunity

Many believe that the origin of whiskey lies buried deep in the soil and history of Ireland. Old Celtic ruins near Cashel in Tipperary include what are reputed to be the remnants of Bronze Age distillation equipment and 'around the end of the 12th century, when the English invaded Ireland, apparently they discovered the inhabitants drinking uisge beatha .... which became corrupted to a more anglicised 'whiskybae' eventually shortened to "uishigi" or "whiski"'.[14] In 1823, Ireland had no less than

---

12   Christina Passariello and Mac Colchester, 'Jameson Pours Out Tall Tale to Lure younger drinkers, whiskey uses shot of invention to stress its Irish roots', *The Wall Street Journal* [online], 17 February 2011. Available at: <http://www.wsj.com/articles/SB10001424052748703373404576148323588693058> (Accessed 12 December 2020).

13   Ibid.

14   Neil Ridley and Gavin Smith, *Let Me Tell You about Whiskey* (London: Pavillion Books, 2014), pp. 12–13.

eighty-six distilleries in operation.[15] However, a number of factors led to the demise of the sector. Chief among these was a refusal on the part of Irish whiskey distillers to adopt the newly patented continuous distillation method introduced by former tax inspector turned distiller, Aeneas Coffey, in 1830, which efficiently produced substantial amounts of raw neutrally flavoured spirit at minimal cost. Ireland's major traditional pot distillers claimed that the Coffey Still whiskey lacked the character and depth that Irish Whiskey had become renowned for throughout the world. This original pot still style of whiskey was made by a uniquely Irish process that used both raw and malted barley in the mash bill to provide a dense flavour profile dominated by a unique creamy mouthfeel and spicy flavour. The main distillers in Dublin at the time, John Jameson, William Jameson, John Power and George Roe rejected the neutral spirits proposed by Coffey. They referred to the output of these continuous stills using the pejorative term 'silent spirits', meaning lacking in taste and character. Coffey's new technology, on the other hand, was embraced by the Scottish and was a contributing factor in their later international success.[16] Other factors that contributed to the decline in Irish whiskey included the diversion of raw materials to support the Allies during World War 1, prohibition in the United States 1919–1933, and a devastating 1932 trade war with our former landlords and trading partners, Great Britain, which led to our exclusion from 25% of world markets. By 1953 there were only six distilleries operating. This was ultimately reduced further when Jameson, Powers and Cork Distilleries merged to form Irish Distillers in 1966 and all production was centralised in the Midleton plant in Cork. This ultimately left just two distilleries operating on the island, New Midleton and Bushmills. The 1975 modernisation of the Midleton distillery by Irish Distillers and its 1988 takeover by French giant Pernod Ricard was a key turning point and led to heavy investment in Irish spirits once more and a new renaissance in Irish whiskey has since emerged. This time however, the focus moved away from the original Irish pot still style of whiskey to

15 Department of Agriculture, *Irish Whiskey Technical File*. Available at: <https://www.agriculture.gov.ie/.../IrishWhiskeytechnicalfile141114.pdf> (Accessed 4 December 2015).

16 Peter Mulryan, *The Whiskeys of Ireland* (Dublin: The O'Brien Press, 2002).

the more neutral smooth lightly flavoured profile of Jameson. It could be argued that because of the limited number of players involved in production over much of the last thirty years that Irish Whiskey, though very successful, was always destined to lack a certain amount of individuality.

The Jameson brand is owned by Pernod Ricard. This multi-billion-euro international drinks company was founded in 1975 by Paul Ricard and Jean Hémard. It has over 18,000 employees and operates in 85 countries with annual sales of more than 8 billion euro.[17] In 1988, the company acquired Irish Distillers Ltd and it was then that the push for Irish Whiskey's rebirth truly began. Strong advertising campaigns down through the years such as *Rush Hour* in 2000 and *Beyond the Obvious* in 2005 proved very successful and led to a situation where Jameson's sales increased from 500,000 cases in 1996 to 5 million cases in 2015.[18] Until relatively recently, Pernod Ricard has focused on the idea of selling Irish Whiskey as a drink that was almost the opposite of Single Malt Scotch. This was essentially its point of differentiation, as pointed out by O'Connor:

> After their 1988 purchase of IDL Pernod Ricard launched a massive campaign to put bottles of Jameson on global bar shelves with a very simple message about what made Irish different to Scotch: It's unpeated. It's triple distilled. It's sweet, it's beguiling and all the intimidating parts have been removed.[19]

O' Connor claims that such a campaign was factually incorrect in its description of Jameson whiskey in that it's not truly triple distilled, and that it is, in fact, a blended product and therefore not a pure Irish pot still. He admits, nonetheless, Pernod Ricard's undoubted success in ultimately saving the Irish whiskey category from extinction. However, this chapter contends that for the continued success of the Irish Whiskey category

---

17   Businesswire.com, 'Pernod Ricard: FY20 full-year sales and results'. Available at: Pernod Ricard: FY20 Full-year Sales and Results (Accessed 3 December 2021).

18   'Irish Distillers celebrates major Jameson global sales milestone', *Hotel and Restaurant Times* [online] 2015. Available at: <http://hotelandrestauranttimes.ie/ irish-distillers-celebrates-5m-cases-jameson-milestone-opens-new-microdistillery-midleton/> (Accessed 11 January 2016).

19   Fionnán O' Connor, *A Glass Apart: Irish Single Pot Whiskey* (Victoria: The Images Publishing Group Pty Ltd, 2015), p. 214.

to be secured, the product needs to both enhance and convey, through advertising, a new set of more *terroir*-based attributes based upon the revival of the Irish pot still style that once dominated world markets.

Previously mentioned examples such as the Johnnie Walker *Man who Walked around the World* campaign, the Tullamore Dew *Parting Glass* campaign and the Jameson *Legendary Tales* campaign all point to a successful blend of history and storytelling that allows considerable differentiation in a crowded premium spirits' market, while maintaining the bedrock of authenticity that the whiskey drinker demands. Despite the obvious success of these campaigns, consideration must now be given to more authentic points of differentiation as consumers demand further elements of premiumisation. The Irish Single Pot Still Whiskey story offers an interesting opportunity in this context. While it fulfils the existing requirement for providing unique place-based points of differentiation it also introduces the story of its traditional method of production. This uniquely Irish method of using both malted and un-malted barley gives the whiskey a sensorial profile that can be clearly identified among competitor products. Champagne is another product category that has similar method points of differentiation. By designation it can only be made using the traditional *Méthode Champenoise* process. As with Irish Pot Still whiskey this method imparts to the final wine a unique taste and flavour profile that has contributed to the product being clearly defined among other international sparkling wine drinks. In the case of Champagne this unique process is formally linked to place and enshrined in European *appellation contrôlée* law. In 2014, after much work by the newly formed Irish Whiskey Association, the concept of Irish Pot Still Whiskey was also given substantial protection under EU policies with the submission by the Department of Agriculture in October 2014 of a technical file setting Irish whiskey specifications. Those specifications include the following explanation of Irish Pot Still Whiskey:

> 'Pot Still Irish Whiskey/Irish Pot Still Whiskey' is made from natural raw materials, currently non-peated malted barley and includes un-malted barley and other un-malted cereals, water and yeast. Other natural enzymes may also be used at the brewing and fermentation stages. The un-malted barley is an essential ingredient of 'Pot Still Irish Whiskey/Irish Pot Still Whiskey' as it gives both a distinctive spicy

flavour to the whiskey and influences the texture by giving the whiskey a distinct creamy mouth feel.[20]

Promoting a Single Point of Origin Advantage

For many gastronomic goods, a relatively narrowly defined single point of origin goes hand in hand with the concept of *terroir* and helps provide an indication of quality. This has not been the case for Irish Whiskey up until now because the product's identity has been based on country of origin rather than a specific region. The idea of single point of origin finds a more natural bedfellow in Scottish Single Malt where individual whiskies are associated not only with Scotland, the nation, but also with regions within Scotland such as The Highlands, Islay or Speyside and more definitively with single distilleries located in these areas. The same is true of other well-known drinks categories such as Cognac and the previously mentioned Champagne, where both specific sites and methods are held out as key points of authenticity and differentiation. It is this combination of unique location and defined process that offers such potential from an advertising perspective. Once such points of differentiation are clearly established, the possibilities for exploitation through story are clear. The notion of a premium drink being tied to a single *terroir*, a term which as we have seen earlier can encompass both place and method, is common in quality drinks categories. We have high quality Single Quinta wines from Portugal, Einzellage wines from Germany and site-specific Grand Champagne Cognacs as well as numerous individually designated sites in French wine regions such as the Premier Cru vineyards of Bordeaux or the Grand Cru sites in Burgundy. One of the most notable casualties of Irish whiskey identity in previous years was its loss of uniqueness due to the previously mentioned structure of the industry. In fact, because of the

20   Department of Agriculture, *Irish Whiskey Technical File 2014*. Available at: <https://www.agriculture.gov.ie/.../IrishWhiskeytechnicalfile141114.pdf> (Accessed 4 December 2020).

legal requirement for Irish whiskey to be aged for a minimum of 3 years, up until quite recently many independent brands were distillates from just one distillery – Cooley. According to Fionnán O' Connor:

> This is an unspoken truth of the modern Irish Whiskey market. Despite shelves groaning with the weight of new independent whiskey brands over the past few years, (a recently announced) Dingle bottling will be the first genuinely new single malt made in Ireland in the past 25 years.[21]

Considerable advertising opportunities now exist for the promotion of a category of Irish whiskey based upon both its single point of origin and its traditional pot still production methods. With the recent emphasis on the promotion of its own Irish Single Pot Still range, Pernod Ricard are already moving in this direction and it is likely that others will follow. Campaigns based on the concept of Irish Single Pot Still Whiskey offer several key points of differentiation that make the product attractive to the whiskey consumer seeking a premium product. Firstly, they offer the idea of authentic exclusivity because the product comes from a single defined location. Secondly, they introduce a product that is manufactured in a uniquely Irish way by using a proportion of un-malted green barley to impart a unique creamy mouthfeel and spicy taste. Finally, they introduce heritage attributes because the product reflects the authentic revival of a uniquely Irish style of whiskey that once dominated world markets. Through a range of recent advertisements Pernod Ricard have led the way in ensuring key points of place and method differentiation continue to be emphasised in the competitive ultra-premium spirit's market. This is best captured in one of their recent press campaigns where both place and method elements are clearly emphasised through four handwritten notes printed in the advert that point to the Midleton Single Pot Still Logo. These notes can be categorised as unique determinants of both, as demonstrated below. As such the advertising campaign helps emphasise

21   Gary Quinn, 'Why Dingle Distillery's new single malt marks a turning point for Irish whiskey', *The Irish Times* [online], 18 December 2015. Available at: <http://www.irishtimes.com/life-and-style/food-and-drink/why-dingle-distillery-s-new-single-malt-marks-a-turning-point-for-irish-whiskey-1.2471404> (Accessed 11 January 2016).

Irish Single Pot Still Whiskey's fulfilment of the requirements of our more gastro-aware society.

Place examples in the ad campaign:

> From grain to glass in one distillery.
>
> A tradition preserved at a single address.
>
> A whiskey making style practised only in Ireland for over 300 years.

Method examples in the ad campaign:

> Triple distilled in copper pot stills for smoothness.
>
> A unique combination of malted and un-malted barley adds the spiciness and creamy mouthfeel.

It is because of these unique qualities that Irish Single Pot Still Whiskey offers such advertising potential in terms of attributes like authenticity, history, story, process integrity, legal authentication, exclusivity and provenance. Promoting the story of place and method will also encourage a halo effect when it comes to Ireland's more successful generic blended products such as Jameson. These whiskeys continue to be the mainstay of the sector and make up the lion's share of Irish whiskey consumption both domestically and abroad. However, in the same way that the Scottish Single Malt whiskey category supports the image of the more dominant and successful blended Scotch offering, there also needs to be room for *terroir* focused whiskies in Ireland. It is likely that other future whiskey producers will also start advertising campaigns based around place and method attributes in competition with Pernod Ricard's Irish Single Pot Still Whiskey range. Because of Irish whiskey's three-year maturation rule the new wave of independent distillers, for the most part, still depend on others to produce their current saleable stock. As they switch to producing and promoting their own unique spirits many of these same distilleries will soon be free to express a more intimate relationship with their own individual *terroir*. This might be reflected in the choice of water used, the provenance of their barley or even more innovative *terroir* aspects such as using local turf in the malting process. Thus, according to Fionnán O' Connor, 'the real boom in Irish Whiskey is yet to come'.[22]

Conclusion

In recent years, the lion's share of Irish whiskey sales has fallen to more generic Irish whiskey products such as Jameson. However, a newly emerged gastro-aware consumer now seeks a more complex whiskey that offers a truly defined sense of place-integrity. The Irish Whiskey Technical file of 2014 has allowed the key points of differentiation of place and method to become legally established, thus paving the way for future exploitation. Pernod Ricard's enthusiastic promotion of their own Irish Single Pot Still Whiskey range provides an excellent example of how these place and method requirements are being met and bodes very well for the future of *terroir*-based Irish whiskeys generally. Once the sector recognises the premiumisation benefits that can come from the exploitation of place and method through story, it is very likely that more of them will consider advertising campaigns that incorporate other *terroir* aspects such as sourcing local barley, water and barrels that will further enhance the product's place and process story. The late Tomás Clancy suggested in 2016:

> Pretty soon those that are selling their own (whiskey) are going to start shouting about it. My prediction is the minute distilleries are selling their own whiskey produced in their own locality, from their own water and so forth, we will see *terroir* talk begin.[23]

When the changes predicted by O' Connor and Clancy begin to emerge it will then be up to the advertisers to decide how best to express the originality of Irish *terroir* to their audiences. Pernod Ricard has provided us with an important example of how a unique place and method specific gastro identity might be used to best effect. They appear to be the first

22 Ibid.
23 Tomás Clancy, 'Coming our way in wine this year,' *The Sunday Business Post Magazine*, 10 January 2016, pp. 28–29.

major force in the exploitation of such a story in Ireland. There will undoubtedly be others. These newer distilleries will face the considerable
challenge of developing innovative ways of transmitting that unique *terroir* message while still maintaining the strong links with heritage and
story that the Irish Whiskey category demands. The benefits of such an
approach are clear and will ultimately allow the Irish Single Pot Still category, which lay dormant for so much of the last century, to once again
play a major role in how Irish whiskey is perceived by drinkers in the new
millennium.

CHAPTER 9

Cognac, Scotch and Irish: Lessons in Gastronomic Identity

I embarked on my first real food and drink job during the summer of 1986 when a good friend and I started working in The Belgravia Sheraton's fine dining restaurant in London's Knightsbridge. We were employed as (very inexperienced) waiters in this small exclusive restaurant. I often wonder whether my career would have taken a different turn if it hadn't been for that first job. I remember being struck by the unique reverence in which certain wines and spirits were held. It was also the first time I encountered a full-time sommelier. The exclusivity and expense associated with not only rare wines, but expensive cognacs and whiskies fascinated me. When I returned to London three years later, I went on to manage The Wine Press Wine Bar & Restaurant near Regent's Park. It was there that I embarked on a formal wines and spirits education journey that would ultimately culminate in a Diploma in Wines and Spirits in 2002. Thirty-seven years after that first job, I have poured a lot of drinks in numerous different settings and the fascination with the products discussed in this chapter has remained with me since those early experiences in 1986.

This chapter expands on the previous chapter's focus on Irish whiskey and delves into other well-known beverages such as cognac and scotch. It demonstrates why drinks like these have achieved iconic status and how much of that recognition stems from the fact that they are firmly anchored to the places they come from. As such, these drinks play a key role in attracting tourists to their region thus enhancing their gastronomic identity even further. The chapter suggests that up until recently Irish whiskey has not been identified with those same place anchors and is therefore at a disadvantage, as global spirits markets move towards premiumisation.

Tourism has become a truly global business in recent years. According to the United Nations World Tourism Organisation, 1.4 billion tourists travelled abroad in 2018. Up until the recent pandemic there had been a continuing rise in those figures since the 2009 economic crisis.[1] There are myriad reasons why people travel to destinations. They travel for business or to visit friends and relatives, to enhance their knowledge and to learn. In recent years food and drink has become an essential ingredient in that motivational mix and increasingly it is proving to be an important reason for travel. According to Taleb Rifai, UNWTO Secretary General 'For many of the world's billions of tourists, returning to familiar destinations to enjoy tried and tested recipes, or travelling further afield in search of new cuisine, gastronomy has become a central part of the tourism experience.[2] As competition among destinations increases, it is often the quality of the food and beverage experience that acts as a differentiating factor when tourists are choosing their destination. By examining the beverage-place relationship of individual drinks we can posit that some place-specific relationships, through regional identity, are superior to others. Such superiority enhances the potential for food tourism development in a market increasingly demanding premiumisation.

There has always been a very strong relationship between food and identity. Within their gastronomic DNA, many countries also carry elements of their past and present beverage cultures, ones that are uniquely identified with their nation. Here we focus on a trilogy of historic beverages that relate very specifically to three separate countries, France, Scotland and Ireland. We explore cognac's relationship with the Charente region of southwest France, single malt whisky and its relationship with the regions of Scotland and finally Irish whiskey's relationship with Ireland. The Irish whiskey sector has potential to benefit from the gastro-tourism sector if its nascent revival can take cognisance of the necessity for delimited place-based relationships between the product and its associated provenance. Richards states that 'with the disintegration of established structure of meaning, people are searching for new sources of identity that provide some

---

1   Our World in Data, 'International arrivals by world region'. Available at: <https://ourworldindata.org/tourism> (Accessed 7 November 2021).

2   United Nations World Tourism Organisation AM Report Vol. 4 'Global Report on Food Tourism,' p. 4. Available at: <https://www.e-unwto.org/doi/book/10.18111/9789284414819> (Accessed 2 February 2015).

security in an increasingly turbulent world'.[3] He goes on to cite Hewison noting that 'heritage and nostalgia have provided a rich source of identity, particularly in tourism'. Irish whiskey has the potential to provide for this desire for heritage and nostalgia. Because of their unique history and the place-based nature of their beverages, both cognac and scotch offer a good template for positioning Irish Whiskey in the gastro-tourist's mind, as a beverage based on provenance and place.

Cognac

Cognac has been made in the Charente region of France for 300 years. Its reputation as one of the world's best-known grape spirits is beyond repute and has led many to extol its virtues. Victor Hugo referred to it as 'the liquor of the gods'.[4] But cognac is much more than just a well-regarded name or brand. Over three centuries it has become rooted in a very specific place identity. The success of cognac reflects a deeper understanding of *terroir* than one might typically associate with beverage products. The Cognac region covers mainly two French Departments, Charente-Maritime and Charente which plays host to the town of Cognac itself. Like many French drinks, cognac is first and foremost tied by name to its physical place. There are many other examples of this as anyone who enjoys a glass of Bordeaux, Champagne or Burgundy can attest to. This crucial emphasis bestowed on a place's food and drink offering is very important when it comes to making a food tourism location attractive. The other players in our beverage trilogy don't have that same place advantage; there is no town called 'Irish Whiskey', no region called 'single malt'. Such

3   Greg Richards, 'Gastronomy: An essential ingredient in tourism production and consumption?' in Anne-Mette Hjalager and Greg Richards (eds), *Tourism and Gastronomy* (New York: Routledge, 2002), p. 4.

4   France 24, 'Cognac Liquor of the gods'. Available at: <https://www.france24.com/en/20150227-you-are-here-cognac-liquor-of-the-gods-france-gastronomy-charentes> (Accessed 12 December 2020).

place associations are written large across the cognac drinks category. It is divided into six districts: Grande Champagne, Petite Champagne, Borderies, Fins Bois, Bons Bois and Bois Ordinaires. Each of these districts is strongly associated with slightly different styles of cognac as is often the case in place-based food and drink products. The best are from the three districts that immediately surround the town of Cognac itself.[5] Cognacs are all blended from a minimum of 2 year-old grape spirit and even the moderately good tend to be aged considerably longer. This drink has three grades of quality. The fact that the acronyms associated with each grade are in English indicate a strong Anglo-Saxon association. They are, VS (Very Special), a blend of a minimum of 2 years in age, VSOP (Very Special Old Pale), a minimum of 4 years aging in wood, and finally XO (Extra Old), the very best, which are aged for a minimum of 6 years in oak. Because of this very defined identity, the town of Cognac and its surrounding districts have acted as important tourism sites in recent years. As with other famous beverage tourism destinations such as Bordeaux, a very strong association between the place and key family names has enhanced that gastro-tourism potential. Visitors can experience the cellars of world-famous cognac houses such as Hennessy, Martell and Otard. They can learn the history of these great Charentais families, visit where they lived and experience through taste, the brandies they have brought to the epicurean world throughout 300 years of beverage history.

The integrity of cognac's association with place is guaranteed through its strict *Appellation d'Origine Contrôlée* (AOC) rules and regulations. Delimited as far back as 1909 and subsequently named an AOC in 1936, producers of cognac must adhere to a strict set of regulations that are overseen by the *Institut national de l'origine et de la qualité*. These are all contained, as with other *appellation* products, in strict regulations as determined by the *Institut* in cognac's comprehensive *Cahier des Charges* which lays down enforced regulations that cover areas such as definition of origin, methods of production and key characteristics that ensure the product is entitled to the classification.

---

5   Christopher Fielden, *Exploring the World of Wines and Spirits* (London: Wine and Spirit Education Trust, 2005), p. 196.

Another important aspect that ties this beverage to its place comes in the form of the *Bureau National Interprofessionnel du Cognac* (BNIC). The BNIC has an important role in both protecting the cognac name and promoting the interests of producers. Comparisons can be drawn between its role and that of the very protectionist *Comité Interprofessionnel du vin de Champagne* (CIVC) in Champagne which has been prominent in protecting the coveted identity of champagne down through the years. Like the CIVC the BNIC's' mission is 'to develop and promote cognac, representing the best interests of all Cognac professionals including growers, merchants and members of other activities related to the cognac trade'.[6] It is involved in organising the structure of the region, promoting the appellation's identity and facilitating market access. The BNIC is the mechanism that all cognac parties use to promote and protect cognac's regional identity. As we shall see later, Scottish whisky has the Scottish Whisky Association which performs a similar role in Scotland and the recently formed Irish Whiskey Association performs a similar function in an Irish whiskey context.

Modern Markets Tied to Place through Historical Story

In recent years cognac has also developed a following among a younger Afro-American audience. It is rare that the growing demands of a market can be tied down to particular events but the release of Busta Rhymes's song *Pass the Courvoisier Part 2* triggered a boom in sales of Courvoisier and other cognacs and opened the floodgates to references to 'yak' in hundreds of hip hop numbers.[7] And yet even this much more modern

---

6   Bureau National Interprofessionnel du Cognac. Available at: <http://www.bnic. fr/cognac/_en/4_pro/index.aspx?page=missions>_(Accessed 1 April 2015).

7   Wayne Curtis, 'Cognac's identity crisis: How the liquor's marketing success among both rappers and codgers has blinded consumers to its subtler pleasures', *The Atlantic Magazine*, June 2012[online]. Available at: <http://www.theatlantic. com/magazine/archive/2012/06/cognacs-identity-crisis/308982/> (Accessed 4 February 2015).

aspect of cognac's identity can be traced back to an historical association with place. Several authors note the connection between cognac's history and Afro-American culture. According to Mitenbuler, the recent attention garnered through the Busta Rhymes hip hop hit hides the fact that cognac's relationship with African Americans stems back to when black soldiers were stationed in Southwest France during both world wars. This relationship was most likely bolstered by the arrival onto the Paris jazz and blues club scene, between the wars, of black artists and musicians like Josephine Baker.[8] Mulcahy notes that Hennessy cognac held a special place in the heart of African-American markets. She cites Maurice Hennessy:

> He also explains one of the reasons why rappers like cognac. Or at least why they favour Hennessy cognac. In 1951, he says, Hennessy was the first spirit to advertise in *Ebony* magazine, while in the late 1960s, the brand made the bold move of promoting African American Herbert Douglas (bronze winner at the 1948 Olympic Games in London), to vice president, making him one of the first African American VPs in corporate America.[9]

Place-Specific Touristic Events

Such a strong regional identity in the Southwest of France allows cognac to leverage gastro-tourism elements to the mutual benefit of both local tourism and the drinks industry. Cognac's identity is rooted in history and nostalgia which undoubtedly provides a unique selling point when it comes to attracting tourists to the region. Such a sense of *patrimoine* can be exploited in several touristic ways from museums to cognac house

---

8   Reid Mitenbuler, 'Pass the Courvoisier: The decades-long love affair between French cognac producers and African-American consumers'. Available at: <http:// www.slate.com/articles/life/drink/2013/12/cognac_in_african_american_cul-ture_the_long_history_of_black_consumption.single.html?print> (Accessed 3 April 2015).

9   Orna Mulcahy, 'Roll out the Barrels', *The Irish Times Magazine*, 18 April 2015, p. 33.

tours, from vineyard walks and trails to cognac-themed music festivals. The annual three-day *Fête du Cognac* festival is a case in point and typifies the French passion for celebrating their unique food history through place specific cultural events. *Fêtes du Champagne* and the *Beaujolais Nouveau* celebrations offer other examples of drinks products being linked to cultural events. These events would not be taking place if the drinks in question were not firmly rooted through history and law to very defined places. As we shall see this celebration of the association between place and particular drinks is not unique to France.

Single Malt

There are strong similarities between cognac and scotch when it comes to understanding their regional place identity. Scotch is a very dominant player on world markets. The industry contributes approximately 5 billion pounds to the UK economy 'making it bigger than the UK's iron and steel, textiles, ship building and computing industries'.[10] Though not immediately obvious to the everyday drinker, Scotland's whisky industry is made up of two quite different products. Firstly, we have blended scotch which is by far the biggest selling variant of scotch whisky on world markets which is typified by strong export brands like Johnnie Walker and Ballantine's. Blended Scotch is much less place-specific then the other main scotch variant, single malt. Single malt is a high-end whisky made from 100% malted barley whisky from a single distillery location. Figures in 2015 indicated that 'the value of single malts increased by 4.5% .... and it has enjoyed a massive 190% growth over the past decade'.[11] The strong

10   Lauren Eads, 'Scotch industry "bigger than iron and steel"'. *The Drinks Business* [online]. Available at: <http://www.thedrinksbusiness.com/2015/01/scotch-indus try-bigger-than-iron-and-steel/> (Accessed 20 April 2015).

11   Becky Paskin, 'The top ten scotch whiskey brands', *The Drinks Business* (2013) [online]. Available at: <http://www.thedrinksbusiness.com/2013/09/the-top-10-scotch-whisky-brands/> (Accessed 4 May 2015).

place-relationship with single malt helps drive the demand for blended scotch and even though sales are more limited the association with place is more defined and much stronger. As mentioned in the previous chapter, a halo effect exists between the two products.

Single malt whisky trades very heavily in terms of its *terroir* distinction. Like cognac it has a strong association with place and possesses a very specific sense of regional gastronomic identity. The international prominence of single malt has contributed to scotch becoming one of the world's most successful spirits. Also, just like cognac, its rich gastro-tourism potential helps bolster its position as an attractive destination through a unique *terroir*-based identity. Tomás Clancy described Speyside, Scotland's most prominent whisky appellation, as follows:

> Here was a region of the world with similar soils, landscape, even weather to our own, but which had held onto a rich, beautiful tradition of whisky making and now offered excitement like that of visiting Bordeaux or Burgundy as you passed each small very beautiful distillery with its pagoda topped malting towers and a name that leaped from the signpost.[12]

It is this powerful sense of place as described by Clancy that has allowed Scottish whisky tourism to flourish. There are many examples of single malt Scottish distilleries exploiting these place-based associations. Indeed fifty-two Scotch whisky visitor centres and distilleries play host to approximately 1.1 million visitors each year.[13] In general, beverage attractions in Scotland have always compared very favourably with other tourist attractions:

> Data also reveals that distilleries, breweries, and wineries also attracted the greatest proportion of overseas visitors of any other visitor attraction throughout 2013. Figures from the Visitor Attractions Barometer also indicate that distilleries, breweries, and wineries also generate the highest average spend per trip by visitors, with £12.60, significantly higher than other visitor attraction types. Distilleries, breweries, and

---

12   Tomás Clancy, 'Scotland the brave and wise', *The Sunday Business Post Magazine*, 1 June 2014, p. 10.

13   VisitScotland, *Whisky Tourism – Facts and Insights March 2015*, p. 1. [online] Available at:_<www.visitscotland.org/.../ Whisky%20Tourism%20%20Facts%20 and%20Insights2.pdf> (Accessed 10 February 2015).

wineries also generate the highest figure for average total retail per attraction, with £624,161 in 2013.[14]

At a regional level gastro-tourism benefits diverse rural areas and helps consumers form relationships with individual whisky brands based on their place-association. As with the six districts of cognac, such place-based relationships form an integral part of the spirit's brand identity and encourage sales. *The Scotch Whisky and Tourism Report 2011* posed an interesting question in this regard. Does Scotch whisky drive tourism or does tourism drive Scotch whisky?

> It may not matter. The tourist who visits Speyside to watch the wildlife and visit a distillery may take a bottle home. Having a reminder of Scotland sat on the shelf may encourage them, or friends and family, to return in future years. In this sense Scotch whisky and tourism are a perfect blend and likely to complement one another.[15]

Scotland has five key whisky regions. They include Highland, Speyside, Islay, Lowland and Campeltown. Each region produces whiskies of a defined style with certain common characteristics. Speyside offers the gastro-tourist a unique insight into its place-based identity with over half of all single malt distilleries in Scotland situated there. The region is home to the Speyside Malt Whisky Trail, a gastro-tourism initiative that allows tourists to experience seven of Speyside's finest distilleries in an organised and coherent manner. Advertised as the only Malt Whisky Trail in the world, the initiative has proved very successful in the promotion of Scottish whisky among tourists. Speyside mimics cognac's *Fête de Cognac* with its 'Spirit of Speyside Festival' which since 1999 has taken place in Speyside. This three-day festival celebrates the region's whisky heritage through a variety of whisky-themed events that most recently included The Great Speyside Bake Off and The Sound of Aberlour event which involved

---

14   Ibid., p. 5.
15   VisitScotland, *Scotch Whisky and Tourism 2011* [online]. Available at: <www.sco tch-whisky.org.uk/.../scotchwhiskyandtourismreport.pdf> (Accessed 10 February 2015), p. 5.

> Cask Strength boys Joel Harrison and Neil Ridley deliver a tasting with a difference, matching five distinctly different expressions of Aberlour with five different pieces of music, each expressing a story or style all of its own.[16]

As with cognac, legislatively, Scottish whiskey is heavily anchored to its own place of origin. Its production is governed by the Scottish Whisky Act 2009 which clearly lays down production methods, defines individual places of origin and protects the terms single malt and blended malt. This comprehensive piece of legislation regulates Scottish whisky in a similar way to the AOC legislation in Cognac. Although some producers find it somewhat restrictive it protects the identity of Scottish whisky and ensures its authenticity in an increasingly homogenous drinkscape.

The Scottish Whisky Association report, mentioned above, heavily emphasised the crucial link that exists between the promotion of Scottish whisky and the promotion of tourism in Scotland. It coined the term 'the distillery effect' where

> clusters of tourism and culture related activities have developed around whisky distilleries across Scotland. The 'distillery effect' was found to support an additional 60 jobs in the local community in sports, recreational and cultural industries and an additional 70 jobs in accommodation around each distillery. This suggests on average an additional 130 jobs clustered around each distillery.[17]

Highlighting the link between Scotch whisky and overseas tourism the report cites two separate research examples from the wine sector noting the positive impact wine tourism can have on the price of a bottle of wine and that tourism can provide a vehicle for smaller producers to add value to their product.[18]

It is quite evident that there is a strong and positive relationship between exports of Scotch whisky to individual countries and tourism activity from those countries. Though considerably more advanced, the link between this iconic product and tourism can help point the way for the

---

16   Spiritofspeyside.com, Available at: <http://www.spiritofspeyside.com/best_new_event> (Accessed 1 May 2015).
17   VisitScotland, *Scotch Whisky and Tourism 2011*, p. 3.
18   Ibid., p. 18.

Irish whiskey tourism model. It is very clear that what differentiates both single malt whisky and cognac from others is that they both provide strong regional anchors to the land in terms of their individual identity. Each of these place anchors has a story to tell, a story about people, the regional flavour profile, a specific soil type or indeed the story of the ingredients and processes that go to make up that individual drink.

Irish Whiskey

It is the unique place-specificity mentioned above that can provide the last member of our beverage-trilogy, with some possible direction. According to Bord Bia, Irish Whiskey is now the fastest growing subsection of the entire whiskey category globally. Jameson is indisputably the main engine behind this.[19] As with cognac and single malt, Irish whiskey is also strongly linked to our cultural identity. Of course, some of Ireland's associations with alcohol are negative and much has been made of that in recent years but it is very important to also consider the positive aspects of this ancient Irish product. We always had a strong reputation for our whiskey and in 1823 Ireland had no less than 86 distilleries in operation.[20] However, several factors led to the demise of the sector. These are described in more detail in the previous chapter but included the impact of World War 1, prohibition in the US along with tax disadvantages imposed after independence from Great Britain.

People's gastronomic horizons have broadened in recent years, as has our desire for more interesting food and drink experiences. Ireland's burgeoning restaurant scene attests to this. Words like 'artisan', 'place' and 'story' now pepper our food narrative but when it comes to whiskey Ireland is

19   Bord Bia, *The Future of Irish Whiskey Report 2013.* Available at: <www.bordbia.ie/.../ bbreports/.../The%20Future%20Of%20Whiskey.pdf> (Accessed 11 March 2015).

20   Department of Agriculture, *Irish Whiskey Technical File.* Available at: <https:// www.agriculture.gov.ie/.../IrishWhiskeytechnicalfile141114.pdf> (Accessed 4 March 2015).

sometimes found lacking in this regard. In a recent article, David Havelin epitomises this lacuna by referencing an interesting quote from a rather obscure source:

> Irish whiskey has a perception problem. And not just among our foreign comrades. Here's Bono, doing a bit of soul-searching over U2's last album: '... the album should have had more of the energy of the musicians and those who inspired it ... a bit more anarchy, a bit more punk. We didn't want a pastiche of the era so we put all those seventies and early eighties influence in the juicer and a blend emerged ... more like an Irish whiskey than a single malt.'
>
> Like many whiskey drinkers in Ireland and elsewhere, Bono is using *single malt* as a synonym for both *scotch* and *quality whiskey*, and as an antonym for *Irish whiskey*. I'm not singling out Bono; this usage is common in Ireland. The news has yet to trickle out that we produce our own quality single malts, along with single pot stills that can stand toe-to-toe with anything from Scotland.[21]

The dominance of a small number of large distilleries until relatively recently has undoubtedly helped Irish whiskey develop a strong presence on the world stage. Jameson's whiskey alone is responsible for 3.4 million of the 5 million cases exported.[22] However such great success has led to a regional identity deficit among international consumers. It can be argued that Ireland is perceived among external markets as being one single region when it comes to whiskey production and that in order to future proof the sector there needs to be much more identifiable regional depth in terms of Irish whiskey's authenticity and story. This lacuna in whiskey's regional identity could become a problem as consumers continually seek out new paths to premiumisation. Having a regional identity is key in a locavore driven market and one might look to the model of cognac and scotch above to help illustrate the point. Both products express strong local identities that prove very attractive to the global spirits enthusiast.

---

21   David Havelin, 'The curse of accessibility', *Liquid Irish* [online]. Available at: <http://www.liquidirish.com/2015/03/the-curse-of-accessibilty.html> (Accessed 2 April 2015).

22   Bord Bia, *The Future of Irish Whiskey Report 2013*. p. 17 Available at: <www.bord bia.ie/.../bbreports/.../The%20Future%20Of%20Whiskey.pdf> (Accessed 11 March 2015).

As the global market moves towards premiumisation there are increasing demands for a depth of local regionality that Irish whiskey simply doesn't have at present. These regional differences offer specific place identities that are expressed through soil types, production methods, types of cask, raw ingredients and of course strict *appellation contrôlée*-style laws. Once determined, such identities can then be re-enforced through other means and gastro-tourism has an important role to play in this regard. Scotland is a 'country which saw from the 1770s onwards but particularly from the early 19ᵗʰ century a massive increase in tourism both domestic and external'.[23] They are therefore an appropriate example.

> Scottish whiskey was not a new product, not created by or for tourism, but much promoted through tourism and the marketing of Scotland; the hand of welcome held out by the Highlander on the railway poster should have had a glass in it, perhaps from the Royal Lochnagar distillery. Blackpool rock (or indeed Ferguson's Edinburgh rock) was a souvenir; Scotch whisky became a taste. The regional – indeed regional even within Scotland – became national and international and while there were other mechanisms of diffusion, tourism played some part in this.[24]

Gastro-tourism in Ireland has a similarly important role to play in addressing Irish whiskey's regional identity issues. It can help tell the Irish whiskey story. As with cognac and single malt these stories must be individual and unique to a certain region. This is where small individual distilleries have a very important role to play just as they did in Scotland. This point is captured in the Bord Bia report entitled *The Future of Irish Whiskey*.

> Emerging consumers associate whiskey with aspirational value. The high social cachet around Scotch single malt has fuelled its global demand to such an extent that demand is now outstripping supply in some markets.[25]

23   Alister Durie, 'The periphery fights back: Tourism and culture in Scotland to 2014', *International Journal of Regional and Local Studies*, 5 (2), 2009, pp. 30–47, p. 31.
24   Ibid., p. 30.
25   Bord Bia, *The Future of Irish Whiskey Report 2013*. p. 6 Available at: <www.bord bia.ie/.../bbreports/.../The%20Future%20Of%20Whiskey.pdf> (Accessed   11 March 2015).

Irish Whiskey: The New Australian Chardonnay?

Comparison can be drawn between Irish Whiskey today and Australian wine. Throughout the 1990s and early noughties Australian wine was quite the marketing success story. The Australians unlocked the complexity of wine for a new generation introducing simple varietal wines, with clear and informative labels and branding. They broke the chains of complex *appellation contrôlée* style regulation often associated with Old World wine. However, perhaps more attention should have been paid at the time to the fact that these chains were also the ties that also gave Old World wines their sense of place. Despite all their faults and restrictions such place-anchors offered a very strong sense of regional identity. Australian wine triumphed in subsequent decades and the beverage world fell in love with varietals like Chardonnay and Shiraz. Much of this dominance was achieved by non-place-specific branding. However, in more recent years the Australian wine sector has recognised that the market is becoming more quality driven. They have begun to question an approach that eschews the idea of *terroir*.

> Historically, many Australian winemakers have derided the French approach to making wine, especially the idea that the finest wines come only from a *terroir* – the union of climate and soil characteristic of each place. Australian producers instead pride themselves on what they regard as a less snooty and more democratic approach: blending grapes from different regions to achieve a consistent wine. But some are now asking whether marketing an Australian wine's locality, as much as its grape variety, might not work better.[26]

In previous chapters we noted how David Aylward recognised the growing demand among wine consumers for a wine product that possessed value-added qualities. He suggested that Australian wine lacked what he defined as a cultural economy. This cultural economy could 'weave individual and community values, passion, care, identity, and terroir together

---

26   *The Economist* (2008), 'From quantity to quality'. Available at: <http://www.economist.com/node/10926392> (Accessed 7 May 2015).

with the more tangible aspects of production, distribution, price points and marketing'.[27] Aylward stresses the point that because of wine education, the proliferation of wine critics, writers and the influence of changing consumer demands, trends that were once about simple product differentiation were now about 'developing into a quest for product story, a wine experience, and an appreciation for its cultural qualities'.[28] Parallels can be drawn between Aylward's thesis and one possible future that the Irish whiskey industry might have. If more regional identity and differentiation can be introduced into our Irish whiskey repertoire then gastro-tourism is one of the vehicles that can affirm that regional identity by fulfilling the whiskey consumer's quest for product story.

Conclusion

Modern Ireland has a rapidly growing whiskey sector that has, up until recently, been dominated by a single player. We now have numerous distilleries emerging, phoenix- like, from the ashes of a once prominent distilling sector. Many of these distilleries are independent and located throughout the country in places such as Meath, Kerry, Dublin and Carlow. Most of them understand that gastro-tourism is an important ingredient in helping contribute to their product's identity. Throughout this chapter we have noted that, due to their strong sense of place-integrity, both cognac and scotch have been well positioned to benefit from recent upsurges in gastro-tourism and there is good potential for further exploitation. We have also posited that there has been something of a lacuna in Irish whiskey's own *terroir*-based identity, at a regional level. The Irish whiskey sector needs to learn from the authentic place-based identity of its liquid cousins, cognac and scotch, so that its own unique gastronomic identity can be enhanced. As an industry it must find a way

27   David Aylward, 'Towards a cultural economy paradigm for the Australian wine industry', *Prometheus*, 26 (4), 2008, pp. 373–385, p. 373.
28   Ibid., p. 374.

to capture the regionality and uniqueness of the Irish whiskey product. Among the many whiskey styles produced across the island we must begin a process of clear differentiation. By doing this, Irish whiskey will be better positioned to take its own rightful share of an increased global interest in gastro-tourism. As a synergistic consequence this approach will also help position Irish whiskey firmly in the mind of the international consumer. In truth, the sector has already made substantial progress. In October 2014 the Department of Agriculture published a technical file setting out the specifications with which Irish whiskey must comply. This is a very important step in allowing Irish whiskey to be unique among a growing range of spirit products and gives it important GI (Geographical Indicator) status at European level. The 2014 technical file also defines the production of a uniquely Irish style of whiskey 'Pot Stilled Whiskey' as discussed in the previous chapter. This is a style that has a strong association with Ireland and offers great potential as a key point of differentiation among other spirit styles. We have also had the development of the Irish Whiskey Association. Like the BNIC in Cognac and the Scottish Whiskey Association in Scotland, this organisation is key in developing a cohesive strategy for Irish whiskey in the coming years. Existing distilleries like Midleton already have a very strong whiskey tourism product and have recently announced their intention to invest a further 13 million euro in their already successful tourism experience.[29] In fact, as tourism destinations, attractions like Midleton and the Jameson Experience regularly feature in Fáilte Ireland's list of the most popular of all tourist attractions in the country. We can see that the newly developing distilleries also recognise the importance of gastro-tourism in promoting their product's identity as many are already investing heavily in on-site visitor centres. However, one key element seems to be lacking. This chapter suggests that Irish whiskey would greatly benefit from being developed along more regional lines in a similar way to cognac and single malt. These regional lines should be affirmed by regulation akin to AOC laws. A failure to

29   Eoin Burke Kennedy, 'Midleton Distillery experience to get €13m revamp', *The Irish Times* [online], 29 November 2021. Available at: <https://www.irishtimes.com/business/agribusiness-and-food/midleton-distillery-experience-to-get-13m-revamp-1.4741615> (Accessed 3 December 2021).

do this may limit Irish whiskey in the mind of the consumer who seeks a level of connoisseurship that we haven't witnessed in markets before. Irish whiskey may be travelling down the path of the Australian wine products of the noughties, providing a good quality product as demanded by the market, yet ultimately lacking in place authenticity as the consumer slowly moves along the route to premiumisation. It is at this early stage of development that the sector should come together and begin to tease out regional differences that can be enhanced in the coming years. Once developed, gastro-tourism will play a strong role in highlighting those regional identities. The promotion of premium regionally identified whiskeys will also help with the success of more generic Irish whiskey just as the exclusivity of single malt whisky in Scotland has aided the worldwide success of blended scotch. By learning the place specificity lessons of cognac and scotch and exposing Irish whiskey to a more regional identity we will encourage regionally specific gastro-tourism events, whiskey trails, cultural celebrations and festivals, thus broadening and deepening potential markets.

Irish whiskey has been more than a thousand of years in evolution. It has lived, breathed and matured through many difficult periods of our history. It has survived temperance and prohibition, international take-overs, two world wars and an oppressive taxation regime that stymied its development on global markets. Throughout all this time it has always remained authentically Irish. For too long it has not held its rightful place among the world's great beverages. Because of a near mono-structure down through the years it has become too generic, too rooted in a national rather than a regional identity. Its core perception in export markets still relates to the island of Ireland as evidenced by the dominance of Jameson. Unlike cognac and single malt, it doesn't have any clear regional differentiation between, for example, Western Irish whiskey and Southern Irish whiskey or perhaps Dublin whiskey and Dingle whiskey, where each regional style and taste is anchored to a place. Methods of differentiation between styles could include the local barley used, water content, tradition or story. If emphasised, these place-based styles will enhance the potential development of both the Irish whiskey sector and its associated gastro-tourism elements in a world that is continually seeking out new layers of authenticity and provenance.

Gastro-tourism can both help sell that *goût de terroir* and define it among a cohort of increasingly knowledgeable consumers. It can help position our national beverage in a way that allows the modern food tourist to clearly identify its place-specificity. Only then will this ancient Irish drink possess a true integrity of somewhereness.

CHAPTER 10

French Wine: Exporting Gastronomic Identity Beyond Borders

In 2007, I jumped at the chance to spend a week in the beautiful Rhone Valley region in France as an industry guest of Inter-Rhone, a representative body for wine merchants and growers. I was participating in what this chapter later refers to as the Inter-Rhone Wine Educators Annual Programme; an example of how a gastronomic identity can be exported beyond national borders. During the week-long trip I had many opportunities to engage on a personal level with the people and places of the region. One night in particular stands out in my mind. We were invited to a meal in a local village hall, hosted by several vignerons and their families. One of the vignerons had studied in Ireland and therefore had a strong connection with the small Irish contingent on the trip. Late in the evening he beckoned us upstairs and led us out into the darkness of the Rhone Valley skies to point out the barely visible lights of nearby wine villages in the distance. To this day Southern Rhone wines like Gigondas, Vacqueyras and Rasteau are among my favourites and every encounter brings to mind the warmth of the people and places I encountered on that trip.

In other chapters throughout this book we have highlighted Ireland's long association with Irish Whiskey and the Irish pub. The German nation has strong associations with beer. Scotland has established associations with scotch whisky, haggis, shortbread and salmon.[1] But of all modern cultures France is portrayed as having the strongest gastronomic identity and it is wine that most readily springs to mind when we discuss the beverage culture of France. This chapter explores innovative ways in which France exports its oenological sense of place beyond recognised boundaries. It

---

1   Andrew Jones and Ian Jenkins, 'A taste of Wales-Blas Ar Gymru: Institutional malaise in promoting Welsh food tourism products', in A. Hjalager A. and G. Richards (eds), *Tourism and Gastronomy* (Oxon: Routledge, 2002), p. 125.

examines the important role that story can play in developing positive relationships with geographically delimited French wine products. It argues that if successful, the exportation of such regional gastronomic identity can represent a form of Tourism without Travel [2] and can enhance the relationship between wine consumers and the wine's regional identity. Munoz and Wood suggested that themed locations act as 'cultural ambassadors' outside their home countries.[3] A similar interaction between the consumer and the product offers the potential to experience both the story and the sense of place associated with a specific region's wine. This in turn may help form a beneficial bond between the drinker and the defined region in question and can help places like Ireland to consider the importance of their own regional differences when it comes to food and drink.

Wine means different things to different audiences. Some are interested purely in the drink itself, as a social product that performs the same role as any other libation. Others view the taste of the drink as just one aspect of a complex gastronomic experience. For the latter, it is the story of the wine that allows for such complexity. That story can include many things; the place it comes from, the people who made it, the weather conditions of the harvest that year, the history of the wine itself, the packaging of the bottle, the adherence to specific regional legislation and even the events at the time the wine was produced, bottled and sealed. In his book *Liquid Memory*, Jonathan Nossiter suggests that 'wine is among the most singular repositories of memory known to man'.[4] The author compares this repository to things like museums, and novels and how they capture and share specific memories and moments in time. However, according to Nossiter, 'wine is unique because it is the only animate vessel of both

2   Mark McGovern, 'The cracked pint glass of the servant: The Irish pub, Irish identity and the tourist eye', in Michael Cronin and Barbera O' Connor (eds), *Irish Tourism: Image, Culture and Identity* (Clevedon: Channel View Publications, 2003), p. 94.

3   Caroline Munoz and Natalie Wood, 'No rules, just right, or is it? The role of themed restaurants as cultural ambassadors', *Tourism and Hospitality Research*, 7 (3–4), June–September 2007, p. 243.

4   Jonathan Nossiter, *Liquid Memory* (Canada: D&M Publishers Inc., 2009), p. 13.

personal memory – that of the drinker (or maker) and the subjectivity of his experience and the memory of that subjectivity – and communal memory. That is, it is communal to the extent that a wine is also the memory of the *terroir*.[5] A specific wine is an unusual product in that it has within it, the power to tell the story of a place and, to be the story of that particular place. One might liken it to a book that describes a place, experience or time. Having offered the reader an insight into what that place, experience or period entails, the book can then be consumed. Through its consumption the story of that place is enhanced. If we continue the analogy, the book (in this case a bottle of wine) offers the reader (the drinker) the added benefit of having been written, published, printed and then sealed at the very time being described in that place and you, the drinker, are privileged to break that time seal, open that book and consume the story of that place as intended by the original wine-author. The suggestion is that wine has the power to hold within the confines of its bottle, memories, feelings and emotions that reflect its surrounding natural environment. Philosopher Roger Scruton's description of Burgundy presents an eloquent description of this unique animation.

> To appreciate Burgundy as it really is you must leave it to mature for at least five years, after which time a strange transformation occurs in the bottle. The grape gradually retreats, leaving first the village, then the vineyard and finally the soil itself in the foreground. Historical associations come alive as tastes and scents, ancestral traits appear like submerged family features and that peculiar Burgundy nose, as distinctive as the nose of Cleopatra, sits at the rim of the glass like a presiding god.[6]

It is important to state from the outset that for the purposes of this chapter the wines referred to exclude much of the modern branded wine that offers a relatively limited reflection of *terroir*. Many of these wines purport to tell a story of sorts, but they are a poor representation of the type of wine alluded to by Scruton above. Wine is a product, more than any other, that reflects its association with a particular place. The place story encompasses not only the factors already mentioned, which are internal to the

5   Ibid., pp. 13–14.
6   Roger Scruton, *I Drink Therefore I Am: A Philosopher's Guide to Wine* (London: Continuum International Publishing Group, 2009), p. 37.

wine, but also factors that are external to the product. Here we can include the vignerons' own story and other elements that we may associate with the wine such as traditionally linked foods, practices and events. Among many consumers, there is a desire to hear that story and it is its communication that poses a challenge for winemakers. In some instances, New World producers have led the way in terms of pursuing their own exportation of an oenological sense of place. As a category they have been using the story of tradition to imply a long wine heritage and in some cases an association with the traditions of historic wine nations like France. Their story of place has also included a cultural dimension that has become evident in recent years. In previous chapters we mentioned Aylward's concept of cultural economy. Using the cultural economy that forms part of that story, can encourage real connections between consumers of wine and the product itself. Beginning in the 1980s, the Australian wine industry grew from relatively modest levels to become the fourth largest exporter in the world of wine.[7] They marketed their product as fruit-driven value-for-money drinks. Brands such as Jacobs Creek and Thomas Hardy became very popular, especially in Irish markets. However, in time, New World producers began to recognise that world markets were becoming less satisfied with these wines and a more sophisticated consumer was emerging. There were increasing demands for a more complex product that offered more than a varietally labelled fruit drink in a glass. Such demands stem from a more food aware consumer who has engaged with TV food programmes, magazine articles and other influences such as foreign travel, wine clubs, enhanced opportunities for dining out etc. The Australian reaction to these new consumption demands took many forms including the development of a new general strategy entitled *Directions to 2025* which introduced new categories of Australian wines, which, mirrored the categorisation that the French already use through their *appellation contrôlée* laws. Wine Australia developed several promotional initiatives that encouraged a relationship between it and consumers on a cultural level. Aylward describes this as the 'way in which wine's cultural and economic qualities can be woven into a

---

7   David Aylward, 'Towards a cultural economy paradigm for the Australian wine industry', *Prometheus*, 26(4), 2008, p. 373.

much more enriched fabric'.[8] Examples of Wine Australia linking wine to other cultural spheres include the organisation of events such as *The Wine Australia University Wine Championships*[9] and *The Young Wine Writer of the Year* competition. They also engaged with sporting culture by organising wine themed rugby events to co-inside with international matches.[10] At a brand level individual Australian wines have also been keen to associate their wines with cultural events. Jacobs Creek's organised a series of outdoor Hollywood movies shown on their visitor centre lawns. In 2015 the same wine company was involved in developing a series of documentary films based on the lives of well-known tennis stars. According to coverage at the time:

> The 'Made By' film series forms part of the new Jacob's Creek 'Made By' global campaign which agency Cummins and Partners says celebrates the people, places and passions that go into crafting every bottle of Jacob's Creek wine.[11]

These examples help demonstrate that the New World wine sector now values the importance of having a cultural economy attached to their wine. Such an approach is not unique to wine products. Neville, suggests that Guinness has used a similar approach in French advertisements by linking stout to Ireland's leading literary figures in advertisement campaigns, thus inferring that in some way the product has cultural parity with great Irish writers. She uses the example of a French advertisement for Guinness to illustrate:

8   Ibid.
9   Gemma McKenna, 'Oxford triumphs in University Wine Championships', *Harpers Wine and Spirits Trade Review*, 30 January 2012 [online]. Available at: <http://www.harpers.co.uk/news/news-headlines/11650-oxford-triumphs-in-university-wine-championship.html> (Accessed 2 May 2012).
10 Jean Smullen, *Wine Diary 2011* [online]. Available at: <http://www.jeansmullen.com/index.php?option=com_eventlist&Itemid=27&func=details&did=645> (Accessed 18 April 2012).
11 Sarah Aquilina, 'Jacob's Creek branded content shows an unseen side of Novak Djokovic', *Marketing Magazine* [online]. Available at: <https://www.marketingmag.com.au/news-c/jacobs-creek-branded-content-shows-unseen-side-novak-djokovic/> (Accessed 15 October 2021).

Dublin, an idyllic city in which to absorb writers like Joyce, Yeats, Beckett, Shaw and Behan. Dublin, the historical home of Guinness. Seamus Heaney, Roddy Doyle, Paul Durcan, you have such an embarrassment of choice. And to be honest, if you arrived in the city as an ordinary weekend tourist, you might well not have sufficient time to appreciate all these riches properly. So why not just lump them all together: Heaney, Yeats, Guinness, Beckett, Joyce.[12]

The above are successful examples of the beverage world's active involvement in developing their product's cultural economy. But this is only part of their strategy. The true essence of a wine's sense of place lies in its story and the communication of this story as previously described must be part of that same strategy. Aylward refers to this story as 'the fabric of culture that is attached not to buildings, icons or performances, but to community interaction, collective and individual belief systems, a products anthropological value, or the sense of place and purpose that becomes inherently bound within that products development'.[13] It can prove even more difficult to export the sense of place associated with a wine but again the New World has attempted this through a variety of programmes. Examples include the Wine Australia's Regional Heroes Series[14] and their Wine Ambassadors Initiative.[15] By developing strategies that seek to expose potential markets to the story of a wine's place, one can achieve, at least partially, a feeling of 'Tourism without Travel' [16] thus exposing the consumer to the story of the place without the necessity for being physically present. Although

12   Grace Neville, 'The commodification of Irish culture in France and beyond,' in Eamon Maher and Eugene O'Brien (eds), *France and the Struggle against Globalization: Bilingual Essays on the Role of France in the World* (Lewiston: Edwin Mellen Press, 2007), pp. 151–152.

13   Aylward, 'Towards a cultural economy paradigm', p. 380.

14   'Wine Australia calls on independents to back Regional Heroes campaign', *Harpers. co.uk* [online], 5 November 2009. Available at: <https://harpers.co.uk/news/fullst ory.php/aid/7614/Wine_Australia_calls_on_independents_to_back_Regional_ Heroes_campaign.html> (Accessed 20 March 2020).

15   'Six new Australian wine ambassadors to be unveiled in Japan this evening', Wine Titles Media [online], 3 May 2014. Available at: <https://winetitles.com.au/ six-new-australian-wine-ambassadors-to-be-unveiled-in-japan-this-evening/> (Accessed 20 March 2020).

16   McGovern, 'The cracked pint glass', p. 91.

McGovern' original concept of Tourism without Travel was referring to the influence of the Irish pub in an emerging global culture, comparisons can be drawn with Wine Australia's attempt to use the story of place to influence that same global market. McGovern suggests in a separate article that one of the characteristics of late capitalism is that commodities possess an exchange value that is based on their cultural associations[17] and it seems clear that by telling the story of a wine's place New World producers have allowed this cultural association to become an important part of the wine's make up. It therefore helps differentiate it from products that may not possess those same cultural attributes.

Just as the New World has drawn greatly from the Old World in terms of its wine-making origins, perhaps the Old World has something to learn from countries like Australia when it comes to commodifying gastronomic culture to help compete in a globalised marketplace. There is little doubt that countries like France are playing catch-up in this regard but there are several innovative examples that show how the French wine industry has started to value and commodify its own the story of place.

The concept of Tourism without Travel mentioned above, suggests that there are opportunities for consumers to experience a place through means other than a physical visit. These can include things like stories and associations that help commodify the wine's culture and allow it to metaphorically travel. It was mentioned earlier how Munoz and Wood suggested that themed locations act as cultural ambassadors outside their home countries. In their study, they explored the influence of themed restaurants on a host nation's cultural perception of the themed country. The following examples show how French wine stories can also travel into communities beyond the wine region itself and like Munoz and Wood's themed restaurants, act as cultural ambassadors.

17   Mark McGovern, 'The Craic market: Irish theme bars and the commodification of Irishness in contemporary Britain', *Irish Journal of Sociology*, 11(2), 2002, p. 80.

Cahors Malbec: From the Vineyard to the Town

Cahors is a region in Southwest France with a long history of wine-making. There are records of Cahors being sold in London in the thirteenth century.[18] Due to its deep colour its wines were historically referred to as the 'Black wines of Cahors' but the region was more famous for the hue and longevity of its wines in the Middle Ages than it is today.[19] Since the mid-2000s Cahors has worked hard to develop and promote its own story. It is likely that this has been, in part, a response to the Argentinean association with Cahor's original malbec grape and its recent success in key markets such as the UK and the US. The main strategist behind the Cahors marketing campaign since 2006 has been UIVC Marketing Director Jérémy Arnaud (Fiorina, 2010).[20] A conference was held in 2007 entitled 'Black Paradox' where the influence of the wine's association with the colour black was discussed not only by wine experts but also by a sociology Professor from the Sorbonne and a writer accomplished in exploring emotional responses to colour. That first conference encouraged the development of several key initiatives that anchor the wine to its oenological sense of place. The Cahors strategy reflected the use of the culture and story surrounding their wine as much as the quality of the product itself. It included the launching of a Cahors blog: www.blackisphere.fr, with a striking presentation and layout which was heavily themed to reflect the wine's historical association with colour. Although it's no longer in existence, at the time the blog was considered innovative and provided a forum for the communication of events and topics of interest that related to the wines of Cahors. Cahors also developed CahorsMalbec.com, an English language website that directly targeted

18   Jancis Robinson and Julia Harding, *The Oxford Companion to Wine* (Oxford: Oxford University Press, 2015), p. 127.
19   Hugh Johnson and Jancis Robinson, The *World Atlas of Wine*, 8th edn (London: Octopus Publishing, 2019), p. 113.
20   Tom Fiorina, 'Black is back: Cahors Malbec returns to the world stage', *The Vine Route*, 21 March, 2010. Available at: <http://www.thevineroute.com/southwest/black-is-back-cahors-malbec/> (Accessed 16 April 2020).

the US and UK market while at the same time re-enforcing the message that Cahors was the true home of malbec and the history of the place and that grape are very much intertwined.

Another innovative approach to exporting the story of Cahors wines involved the development of the Cahors wine glass. An original glass design was commissioned and was promoted in the hope that people would associate that glass with the story of Cahors. The glass design initiative is interesting in that it facilitated the exportation of an oenological sense of place that allowed the story of Cahors malbec to be transported outside the region itself by visitors to that region. By allowing drinkers to take away the unique glass design that was associated with the region the story of the unique wine travelled beyond Cahors.

One final initiative undertaken involved the development of the Cahors Malbec Lounge, in the heart of Cahors town itself, which opened in the revamped *Maison du Vin*. The design of the lounge reflected the deep malbec grape colour and the distinctive Cahors glass. Of particular interest was the fact that the Malbec Lounge not only catered for tastings and tours but also opened itself to a range of cultural and community events such as music concerts and events themed with Cahors such as the Malbec In Love *soirée* which included a Speed Wine Dating event, and an event entitled 'Malbec Black Jack'.[21] There is a comparison to be drawn here between events such as these and the previous Australian examples where attempts were made to develop the wine's cultural economy. Cahors continues to have some success in exporting the story of its wine beyond the town and beyond the Southwest region itself. Through its story, its glass, its blog, its website and the Cahors Malbec Lounge people have been able to experience Cahor's sense of place well beyond the vineyard.

21 *French Wine News* [online], 'Cahors rejuvenates wine tourism'. Available at: <http://www.frenchwinenews.com/cahors-rejuvenates-wine-tourism/> (Accessed 6 April 2012).

Muscadet Zenith: From the Vineyard to the Concert Hall

Cahors was not alone in its efforts to export elements of its gastronomic identity beyond its vineyard's borders. The development of the
Bar Muscadet au Zenith at the Zenith Nantes Metropole Concert Hall
provided another example of both the exportation of place and the enhancement of cultural attributes that one might associate with a wine.
Muscadet is a flagship wine from the Loire region. In 2011 a project was
initiated by the trade organisation *Interprofession des Vins de Loire*. The
initiative involved exposing up to 80,000 concert goers to several ambassador vintners who operated in the Bar Muscadet au Zenith during a
range of cultural events. Attendees at music concerts from diverse acts like
Motorhead, James Blunt and Lenny Kravitz were exposed to the vintner
ambassadors from the Loire. According to *French Wine News* at the time:

> ...this initiative represents an unprecedented example of a communication and wine-
> tasting campaign which is aimed at promoting the rediscovery of the wines of Nantes
> and its flagship appellation, Muscadet, by associating its image with major cultural
> events that are both high-quality and innovative.[22]

What makes this example unique is the involvement of the ambassadors
from the Loire regions and the use of their own wines during the campaign. The sixteen ambassadors acted not only as sales representatives but
also as networkers who developed a bond between event goers and the
physical place that is the Loire Muscadet region. Two distinct outcomes
were achieved. Firstly, the story of the wine's sense of place was told to
a wide variety of audiences and secondly the wine benefited in terms of
its cultural economy, in that it was associated with range of unique cultural events in the mind of the consumer. The thirty events that made up
the 2012 contract included not only concerts but also musicals, modern
circus acts and even political debates.

---

22   *French Wine News* [online], 'Muscadet at Its Zenith'. Available at: <http://www.fre
     nchwinenews.com/muscadet-at-its-zenith/> (Accessed 16 March 2012).

Inter-Rhone: From the Vineyard to Other Countries

Inter-Rhone is the organisation that represents all wine merchants and growers in the Rhone valley. It has responsibility for the promotional, economic and technical needs regarding the wines of the region.[23] Inter-Rhone offered another key example of how to export its regional gastronomic identity beyond national borders through its *Wine Educators Annual Programme.* Up until the recent Covid 19 crisis, each year, Inter-Rhone invited several key influencers to a five-day educational trip in the Rhone valley. Three or four people who held influencing roles in the wine trade in several different countries were usually hosted. These people worked as wine educators, journalists, sommeliers and promoters. This trip not only offered participants an opportunity to taste the Rhone's wines but also instilled in them the unique sense of place associated with the region itself. As well as the more obvious exposure to the region's wines, the influencers had the opportunity to meet with the vignerons themselves, to interact with their communities and families and to walk the vineyards in their company. They were exposed to the typography, the people, the soil and the stories of the local areas. Inter-Rhone's ambition was that these influencers would then go on to promote the Rhone regions wines among their own communities thus exporting that sense of place outside the region and outside of France.

The Beaujolais Nouveau Story: From the Vineyard to the Rest of the World

One of the most successful examples of exporting an oenological sense of place beyond national boundaries is the worldwide success that has

---

23   Inter-Rhone, Available at: <https://www.vins-rhone.com/en/inter-rhone/prese ntation> (Accessed 20 September 2020).

been Beaujolais Nouveau Day. Beaujolais is a wine region in the South of Burgundy. Although it produces a range of excellent wines, principally from the Gamay grape, it is best known worldwide because of the success over the years of its Beaujolais Nouveau wine. Originally this wine started out as vin *de primeur*, a wine drunk in the year it was made. It was sold in towns near the Beaujolais region and brought in much needed cash funds thus allowing the vignerons to concentrate on their more complex wine production. In 1951, Beaujolais Nouveau was officially recognised through a set of regulations enforced by the *Union Interprofessionnelle des Vins du Beaujolais* (UIVB). Its official release date was set on November 15. Over time the local tradition of drinking the first Beaujolais of the season made its way to Paris and fans of Beaujolais began competing to be the first to bring the Beaujolais Nouveau to town following its annual official release at a minute past midnight on the 15th of November. This date was officially changed to the third Thursday in November in 1985, thus maximising the winemaker's sales by guaranteeing the race for Beaujolais Nouveau always began in the run up to a weekend.[24] The Beaujolais Nouveau story offers us a final example of how the tradition and heritage associated with a particular place can be used to export that sense of place and indeed its story throughout the world. In 2021 the tradition of Beaujolais Nouveau celebrated its seventieth year and, although recently less popular in some markets, it still accounts for around 50 million bottles being distributed. Of these, only around half are destined for the French market while the rest are exported. Despite declining sales due to market premiumisation it is still exported to 110 different countries, worldwide.[25]

While the above examples show the benefits of exporting a regional gastronomic identity, there have been some instances that demonstrate how associating products with a sense of place can go spectacularly wrong.

24   Intowine.com, 'Beaujolais Nouveau: History behind the third Thursday in November'. Available at: <http://www.intowine.com/beaujolais2.html> (Accessed 10 March 2019).

25   Alex Ledsom, 'Everything you need to know about Beaujolais Nouveau Day', *Forbes* [online], 21 November 2019. Available at: <https://www.forbes.com/sites/alexledsom/2019/11/21/everything-you-need-to-know-about-beaujolais-nouveau-day/?sh=2eb0afc724fe> (Accessed 15 September 2021).

Nike's 2012 St Patrick's Day branding of a style of running shoe is a case in point. As a tribute to what they believed was a well-known Irish beverage, Nike branded their new trainers as Black and Tans. They were correct in assuming that a Black and Tan was indeed a drink made from mixing Guinness and ale but they failed to notice that many young modern Irish would not be familiar with this traditional Irish drink and more importantly that the name Black and Tans was embedded in Irish culture as the British paramilitary unit that was involved in violent action against civilians in the 1920s. The nickname has been immortalised in Irish folklore through its use in various anti-British songs such as *Come out ye Black and Tans*. The use of this term for a brand of trainer caused a media uproar and led to substantial negative press for Nike.[26] The intention of the campaign was clear. Nike were attempting to link their products to Ireland by using a traditional drink identified with that particular place. Unfortunately, as the media at the time put it, not only was the link tenuous in that the Black and Tan drink is not popular in Ireland but also the story associated with the history of that drink is a very negative one. Nike paid a considerable price for their mistake.

Conclusion

In the introduction to this chapter, it was suggested that that exportation of a regional gastronomic identity can represent a form of Tourism without Travel and can enhance the relationship between wine consumers and a wine's regional identity outside its own natural borders. Bruwer and Alant suggest that an important outcome of the tourism experience can, among other things, be a greater consumer affinity with a

---

26   Jennifer Wholley, 'Nike sorry over "Black and Tan" Shoe', *The Irish Times*, 16 March 2012 [online]. Available at: <https://www.irishtimes.com/news/nike-sorry-over-black-and-tan-shoe-1.704563> (Accessed 18 March 2020).

wine product.[27] Although they are referring to physical travel to achieve such affinity, if it is enshrined in the story of place, the wine itself may in some ways act as a cultural envoy. As such it has the power to enhance the relationship between the consumer and the wine's place of origin. There has been considerable research in recent years around the importance and value of visiting a wine region when it comes to developing an affinity between a wine and the consumer. Because wine is a product that is so tied to a particular place, it is the story of that place that cements the emotional bond between product and drinker and 'winery visits are amongst the most significant sources of brand awareness and wine purchase decisions, due to the connection made by the visitor to a winery's brand story'.[28] This connection will be most successful if it is not only based on concrete links, but when there is also an emotional dimension.[29] We have seen throughout this chapter that many strategies can be used to create this. Wine Australia have demonstrated that they value these emotional bonds and indeed have been successful in using them to change how their products are perceived. We have also seen that, despite being steeped in tradition, French wine regions have also begun developing strategies that help form bonds between products and consumers. These bonds apply to drinkers who haven't had the opportunity to physically visit the region in question. The examples in this chapter show how the unique sense of place associated with a region can be exported beyond the vineyard. Firstly to the local town as in the case of Cahors and secondly from the vineyard to the city as in the case of the Muscadet Bar at the Zenith Nantes Metropole. The region's identity can also be exported to another country as demonstrated by Inter-Rhone and finally to the rest of the world as shown by the historic success of Beaujolais Nouveau. These examples suggest that a wine's story can be removed from the vineyard and

27   John Bruwer and Karin Alant, 'The hedonic nature of wine tourism consumption: An experiential view', *International Journal of Wine Business Research*, 21 (3), 2009, p. 236.

28   Joanna Fountain, Nicola Fish and Steve Charters, 'Making a connection: Tasting rooms and brand loyalty', *International Journal of Wine Business Research*, 20 (1), 2008, p. 9.

29   Ibid., p. 8.

placed somewhere else. The advent of new communication technologies makes this approach even more feasible and the next chapter will explore further opportunities in this regard. By using the wine's entire story to build an emotional affinity between the drinker and the wine, producers can leverage their own sense of place as demonstrated by the examples in this chapter. As markets move towards premiumisation consumers will continue to demand not only better quality when it comes to the liquid in the glass but also a stronger gastronomic identity and all the story, history, place and cultural aspects that such an identity entails. By considering the approaches explored here, wine regions and individual producers will hopefully be in a better position to meet these new demands.

PART IV

Emerging Phenomena

CHAPTER II

Traditional Wine versus New Technology

Throughout my career, I never really considered gastronomy and technology as natural bedfellows. Much of my own food and drink background is rooted in history and bound by concepts like tradition and authenticity. I often look to the past for guidance on recipes, classic techniques and approaches to food and drink service. To a certain extent this approach still governs my gastronomic view. The recent pandemic has been important in showing us that people can rapidly adapt to new technologies, not just regarding how food stories are told but also when it comes to our places of consumption. The crisis has made even culinary luddites like me, more familiar with food delivery apps, QR codes for ordering in situ, temperature scanners, cashless transactions and Covid passes held in digital wallets. In the last two years technology has infiltrated the fine dining experience like never before, as all levels of food business 'pivoted' to survive. What follows recognises how the industry is shifting and suggests that developing technologies can change how food stories reach new audiences, and how, as practitioners, we must be willing to embrace such changes to survive.

This chapter examines how wine stories can be told in different ways. It explores how the methods we use to tell those stories have changed due to the arrival of new media and how the nature of the traditional drinks industry can sometimes inhibit the benefits that technology can bring to the storytelling experience. The chapter argues that in some cases a reluctance to fully embrace social media technology is rooted in strong associations with tradition and authenticity. As we shall see, it has the potential to put more traditional producers at a disadvantage, when compared to the progress both New World wines and the ultra-traditional whiskey industry have made in exploiting new ways of telling their own beverage story.

Archaeological evidence suggests that wine was in existence at least as far back as 4000 BC.[30] This ancient beverage hasn't dramatically changed over recent centuries. It is still predominantly a drink made from the natural fermentation of grapes and is fundamentally defined by its association with specific places. Because of its somewhat unique association with place, the story of that place has taken on particular relevance in the wine world. Some more traditional winemakers appear reluctant to fully embrace new technological ways of telling that story. They still rely on the traditional methods of encouraging consumer engagement with their wines. These methods include expensive experiential visits and complex place-based wine regulation. But new technology is rapidly changing the storytelling narrative and newer generations now imbibe their stories through platforms like TikTok, Facebook, Twitter, YouTube and Instagram rather than through traditional channels. With access to so many rich and authentic stories French winemakers should be leading the charge when it comes to using emerging technologies to get their message across. To date, data suggests that they have been quite slow in this regard. The sector places a laudable emphasis on tradition, heritage and concepts such as *terroir*, perhaps to the detriment of consumer engagement. Historically access to wine knowledge was the preserve of the better off in society and wine was considered a beverage of the upper classes. Such class barriers have been broken down in recent years as wine has become more democratised and younger, less class-bound drinkers are accessing the story of wine in many non-traditional ways. It would be naive of the more traditional wine sector to deny the power and future potential of new media in telling the story of wine. Such a quixotic approach may negatively impact on how younger wine drinkers perceive the product.

30   Tom Standage, *A History of the World in Six Glasses* (New York: Walker Publishing Company Inc., 2005), p. 47.

Story and Technology: A Powerful Combination

One of the most potent examples in popular culture of both the power of story and the way it can be enhanced through technology comes from an unusual source. In his 2009 *Irish Times* article entitled 'Hit and Myth', Brian Boyd emphasises the important role that story plays in encouraging an emotional relationship between a product and its millennial audience and how technology is used as a mechanism to deliver this story. In this case, singer and *X Factor* sensation of the time, Susan Boyle, is Boyd's rather unique example. He suggests that Boyle's story mimics that of the hero in Joseph Campbell's influential 1949 book, *The Hero with a Thousand Faces*. In the book, Campbell emphasises the key elements of story that one might associate with the classic hero:

> The hero starts in the ordinary world; they then receive a call to enter a strange world; the hero must face tasks and trials and survive a severe challenge. If the hero survives, they will receive a great gift.[31]

Boyd's implication is that even though Susan Boyle has obvious musical talent, it is the power of the hero's story that has catapulted her to international acclaim. He emphasises the ubiquitous power of Campbell's hero process, what he called the monomyth, a term borrowed from Joyce's *Finnegans Wake*. He notes that film-maker George Lucas freely admits to using the same story elements in the successful *Star Wars* movie franchise. One might reasonably ask at this juncture what any of this has to do with wine. This use of story is crucial in developing an emotional response among consumers to any product, but a beverage as culturally charged as wine is particularly suited to the influence of story power. James Twitchell puts it well when he says that 'stories often carry emotions as meaning. In a sense, we learn how to think and feel by hearing stories'.[32] Twitchell

---

31   Brian Boyd, 'Hit and myth', *The Irish Times* (*Weekend Review*), 21 November 2009, p. 9.

32   James Twitchell, 'An English teacher looks at branding', *Journal of Consumer Research*, 2004, pp. 484–49.

applies the story concept to marketing and goes on to suggest that a brand can also be interpreted as a cultural story, but society has been very slow to accept an actual culture based on commercial storytelling:

> Essentially what has happened to stories is that they have jumped loose of individual story tellers and become part of a cacophony used to distinguish machine made products.[33]

Both Boyd and Twitchell suggest that many classic elements of story are dominant in how business creates an emotional link between products and consumers. By emphasising story in relation to wine, links such as those mentioned above can be emulated. The dominant orthodoxy in French wine culture suggests that the story of a wine's place is key to understanding the wine itself. That story is constructed in different ways. In France it includes elements that are tied up in the history of French wines, complex *appellation contrôlée* laws, varied classification systems based on regional differences and the close relationship French wines have with their sense of place. French wines are perceived as being heavily codified and in the past that story was only understood and available to an elite few, who possessed the necessary cultural capital and had the resources to access and appreciate both the wines and the regions they came from. Often the best way to understand French wine was through an experiential visit. With the advent of new technologies, place can now be viewed through a different, more technological lens. Using a range of new media, we can enhance the story of a wine's place to such a degree that it can be experienced by the drinker at a substantial remove from the product's physical origins.

The second important element in the Susan Boyle example relates to the fact that technology was so crucial in allowing her story to reach such enormous audiences. It is impossible to imagine a similar success story existing in a 'YouTube-less' world.

---

33   Ibid., p. 485.

An estimated 300 million people had watched the now famous YouTube clip of the 48-year-old Scottish singer making her debut on *Britain's Got Talent* on April 11[th.] The video was a seven-minute hop, skip and jump into global recognition.[34]

Susan Boyle shows us that technology has dramatically changed the way our stories are told. We used to rely on print media, film or radio to help tell the story of our products. All these elements were controlled to a large extent by media gatekeepers who held a lot of power in determining how stories were recounted. To develop a product's story, one had to feed relevant copy to journalists or indeed place and pay for specific stories to appear in the form of advertisements, product placement and so on. The explosion of social media has changed the storytelling narrative. According to Roach:

> Today a story about a company history can be posted on a website, it can also be told in pictures on Facebook or Pinterest. Blogs by employees can expand and continue the story, and the blogs can be enhanced with tweets. Also, CEOs can follow the lead of Steve Jobs and give corporate culture-defining keynote speeches to live web audiences.[35]

Because of technology the story of traditional French wine in particular is no longer limited to elite groups who may have accessed that story as part of the cultural capital accumulated through a privileged upbringing. Today the world's wine-scape has changed. Developments in the New World have, in the last twenty years, introduced wine to a whole new audience by decodifying its mysteries. It has introduced varietal labelling, the production of simple ready to drink wines with clean up front and readily identifiable flavours. The subsequent explosion in social media has changed the way new wine drinkers hear and interpret the wine story. Up until relatively recently this digital focus tended to be centred predominantly in New World wine areas. The French wine sector, though

---

34 Boyd, 'Hit and myth', p. 9.
35 Thomas J. Roach, 'Telling it like it is', Rock products, 115, 12, 2012, p. 3, 33. Available at: <https://search.ebscohost.com/login.aspx?direct=true&AuthType=ip,shib&db=a9h&AN=84616811&site=ehost-live&scope=site> (Accessed 22 May 2022).

improving, is still at a considerable disadvantage in this regard. 'Most commonly associated with notions such as tradition, authenticity and *terroir*, the French wine industry doesn't instantly jump to mind as a leader in innovation.'[36] A survey by a well-known digital marketing agency, found that even at an early stage 94% of American wineries were on Facebook compared to just 53% of French wineries. Regarding Twitter, only 41% of French wineries had a Twitter account compared to 73% of American wineries.[37] Obviously there have been great improvements since then but such results are indicative of a deficit among some traditional French winemakers in terms of appreciating the potential of these new technologies. Reasons for this lacuna can be suggested but are difficult to verify due to the lack of primary research in the area. It has been suggested that there has been a tendency among some French wine producers to be somewhat elitist in their approach to brand marketing. Makers of the Bordeaux first growths and the exclusive wines of Burgundy have been slow to embrace change and the recent social media revolution will take time to adapt to. Though happy to incorporate technological improvements in terms of how their wine is made, some elite wineries are often reluctant to embrace change that potentially impinges on their reputation for tradition and authenticity. Chateau Margaux is currently investigating the impact that Stelvin screw cap technology will have on the maturation of their wines which have always been traditionally corked. This investigation will take place over twenty-five years before any decision is taken re: changing their bottle closure measure. It is not surprising therefore that an industry so heavily invested in tradition finds it difficult to embrace recent social media changes. They may view the intrusion of social media as a watering down of exclusivity. Pelet and Lecat gave a paper at the Academy of Wine

36   'French vineyards blow dust off the barrels and embrace a digital revolution in wine', *The Conversation* [online], 30 December 2015. Available at: <https://thec onversation.com/french-vineyards-blow-dust-off-the-barrels-and-embrace-a-digi tal-revolution-in-wine-50544> (Accessed 14 November 2021).

37   Lucy Shaw, 'Wineries who shun social media will experience "Digital Darwinism"', 2012, www.drinksbusiness.com. Available at: <http://www.thedrinksbusiness. com/2012/06/wineries-who-shun-social-media-will-experience-digital-darwin ism/> (Accessed 14 March 2013).

Business Research Conference in Bordeaux where they explored, through a series of qualitative interviews, how digital social networks might enhance the selling of Burgundy Wines.[38] The reaction to social media and its usefulness among this small group of well-known Burgundy producers is telling. None of those surveyed would recognise digital social networks as an absolute necessity and some even suggested that selling authenticity over the internet is useless. The very best winemakers of France have always seen demand outstrip supply. They deeply value the direct physical relationship with the consumer when they visit the cellar and perhaps see social media networks as having little to contribute. There are undoubtedly many exceptions to this reluctance on the part of some wine makers but as recently as June 2014 at the Academy of Wine Business Research Annual Conference, Szolnoki et al noted in their findings that 'there is a significant difference between European and overseas countries in the way they use social media and the overseas countries of Australia, US and South Africa use social media more frequently'.[39] Though France appears to perform reasonably well in terms of its interactions with technology, there is insufficient data in the paper to indicate why only 106 survey responses were received in France, the largest producer of wine in the world, compared with multiple times that response rate in countries such as Germany, Austria, Australia, US and Italy. The authors note that one of the reasons for a lack of utilisation of social media may rest in the fact that 'social media tools were developed in overseas countries and that

38   Jean Eric Pelet and Benoit Lecat, 'Can Digital Social Networks enhance the online selling of Burgundy Wine', 6th Academy of Wine Business Research Conference at The Bordeaux Management School, France, 2011. [online]. Available at: <http://academyofwinebusiness.com/wp-content/uploads/2011/09/62-AWBR2011_Pelet_Lecat.pdf> (Accessed 24 November 2014).

39   Gergely Szolnoki, Dimitri Taits, Carsten Hoffmann, Ruth Ludwig, Liz Thach, Rebecca Dolan, Steve Goodman, Cullen Habel, Sharon Forbes, Nicola Marinelli, Damien Wilson, Antonio Mantonakis, Philip Zwanda, Zoltan Szabo, Ildiko Csak, Caroline Ritchie, Su Birch and Siobhan Thompson, 'A cross-cultural comparison of social media usage in the wine business', 8th Academy of Wine Business Research Conference at Hochschule Geisenheim University, Germany 2014 [online]. Available at: <http://academyofwinebusiness.com/wp-content/uploads/2013/04/Szolnoki-Taits-Nagel-Fortunato.pdf> (Accessed 24 November 2014).

the wine industry in Europe has a deep tradition of more than a hundred years which is reflected also in the way of communication between producers and consumers.'[40]

Revealing French Wine's Hidden Code

One notable challenge faced by traditional French wine makers rests in the codified nature of its product. Aside from the obvious language differences, quite complex legislation and labelling systems can often pose problems for consumers when it comes to interpreting a wine fully. Grape varieties are traditionally not mentioned on the label and the complexities of their *appellation contrôlée* systems are often not apparent. Technology has the power to de-codify the French wine story and make it more accessible to the modern consumer. David Moore, co-founder of Moore Brothers Wine Company, a strong promoter of using digital technology, is clear in this regard. He says that technology has great advantages, especially when informing drinkers about lesser-known wines. He cites grape varieties such as *Nebbiolo, Sangiovese* and *Gamay* which can sometimes appear mysterious and difficult to understand for consumers.

> This presents a lot of challenges in marketing (nothing says 'merlot' on it), so over the years we've built a lot of systems to provide contextual information about the wines and the regions to our customers. This current project (QR Coding technology) helps make it easier for our customers when they're not in the store.[41]

Of course, wine may be enjoyed based on taste alone, but because it is such a culturally laden beverage it offers the potential for further levels of enjoyment, mainly through a drinker's interpretation of the wine's story. Without specific knowledge and a deeper understanding they may not

---

40   Szolnoki et al., 'A cross-cultural comparison'.
41   Erica Ogg, 'What food goes well with my Syrah, ask your wine bottle', 2012. Available at: <http://gigaom.com/2012/07/02/what-food-goes-well-with-syrah-ask-your-wine-bottle/> (Accessed 12 March 2013).

appreciate the place the wine comes from or the history and traditions associated with that place. Roger Scruton offers us an excellent example of how wine can be enjoyed through this deeper understanding in a book chapter entitled 'Le Tour de France'. He recounts story after story as he journeys around France's classic wine regions. Each story places specific wines into a historical or literary context. He observes:

> I can champion the local against the global by exploring in my glass, the country which I have adopted as my spiritual home and head for the villages and vineyards of France, which refuse to be anything but a place enshrined in a name.[42]

Scruton's stories of place and their historical/literary context can be viewed as providing a more complex understanding of the product so that the consumer, with the appropriate knowledge, can unlock the rich meaning associated with particular wines. Scruton, through this literary medium, allows the drinker to experience this without the necessity for actual travel. He refers to this when he says: 'Before drinking France at home I used to travel there.'[43]

One way to access and understand wine on a deeper level is through the power of technology and there are several ways it can be used to enhance the wine's story.

Smartphone Applications that Enhance the Story Experience

The explosion of smartphone technology has led to a variety of applications (apps) specifically designed to appeal to wine enthusiasts. Properly designed apps have the power to enhance the oenophile's story experience either when they visit an actual vineyard or through technologies that allow the wine's story to be innovatively enjoyed without the necessity for an experiential visit. A simple Google search based on the term 'wine

42   Roger Scruton, *I Drink Therefore I Am: A Philosopher's Guide to Wine* (London: Continuum International Publishing Group, 2009), p. 31.
43   Ibid.

apps' reveals over 400 million hits. The sector is moving very fast. In 2013 Mehta cited Ylesias who suggested that by 2017 all phones will be smart-phones.[44] With the benefit of hindsight, we can see now how this pre-diction was well exceeded. To illustrate their potential for enhancing the story of wine let us briefly examine how just one these early applications demonstrated the benefits of technology. It shows how engagement with the product is not dependent on the consumer visiting the actual winery or even the associated region/country. The Brancott Estate Vineyard in New Zealand was an early adopter of app technology and in 2012 com-missioned the development of the *World's Most Curious Bottle App*. The app was unique in that it didn't rely on a physical visit to the winery and instead offered an innovative puzzle approach to help develop and tell the story of the wine. It incorporated the tag line 'What if your mobile could take you on a curious journey?' on its publicity material.[45] The app dem-onstrates that this simple bottle of wine has transformed into something that not only challenges and informs but is also heavily connected to the social media world. It worked in conjunction with the labels on bottles of Brancott wine, thus ensuring the application user purchased a bottle. It then offered the drinker several interactive experiences or stories such as using virtual Brancott wine bottles to play music or using the phone's GPS location to pinpoint the actual signposted direction of the Brancott estate in Marlborough, New Zealand. These experiences built upon each other and helped tell and enhance the story of Brancott Estate wine. Though it has now been surpassed by more advanced approaches, this early application offers a good example of how technology can be used to encourage consumers to experience the story of a wine's place without ever actually travelling to that place. It allowed the exportation of the winery's gastronomic identity and for that identity to be consumed at a location other than the vineyard itself through the power of technology.

44   Glenn Mehta, *Infinite Ripple: The Social Media Revolution* (United Kingdom: Xlibris Publishing, 2013), p. 40.

45   World's Most Curious Bottle Application (Version 1.1) [Mobile application soft-ware]. Available at: <http://itunes.apple.com> (Accessed 14 March 2013).

QR /NFC Codes: Unlocking the Wine Story

QR (Quick Response) codes are best described as advanced bar codes that when scanned with a smartphone application introduce the browser to large amounts of information about the product, delivered directly to the user's smartphone. NFC (Near Field Communication) codes operate in a similar fashion with the added advantage that the consumer doesn't have to scan the code using their smart phone and the NFC capability of the phone is sufficient to provide direct access to additional information. The benefit of using such technologies for the traditional winemaker is that it is very unobtrusive and is usually positioned on the wine bottles back label so has limited impact in terms of traditional labelling yet has the power to tell a wine's complex story through a specifically targeted website that communicates in a language the wine consumer understands. According to one industry specialist, 'interactive packaging allows us to tell the story that for years we dreamed of conveying to the consumer'.[46] QR/NFC codes scanned at defined locations also allow more detailed and understandable information about wines and wineries to be communicated to the user. This technology is well suited to enhancing the story of place as part of a visitor experience where wineries can incorporate QR code reference points during their tour to help inform visitors through their smart phones about the tour, offer tasting room trivia and even involve visitors in various competitions. However, a physical visit is not always necessary. Using QR/NFC code-enhanced labels, wine drinkers can potentially rate a wine while they are drinking it and then share that rating in real time with their friends or colleagues through various social media channels. QR/NFC codes are also used to convey wine information through the drinker's smartphone regarding tasting notes or indeed commentary through audio/video from the winemakers themselves.

46 Editor citing John Charles Boisset of the JCB Collection, 'QR codes and NFC chips—The future of wine marketing', Advisor Wine Industry Network, 27 August 2021. Available at: <https://wineindustryadvisor.com/2021/08/27/qr-nfc-wine-marketing> (Accessed 29 September 2021).

Such possibilities are restricted only by the developer's creativity and imagination. This technology has the potential to allow a heavily codified wine bottle to be communicated to the consumer, detailing relevant information about the wine it contains and the story behind the label. Some winemakers however, have taken things a step further in how they use new technology to communicate with their customers.

Augmented Reality

More recently several wine companies have started to use 'Living Label Technology' to enhance their wine's story. Augmented reality labels allow the consumer to download a living wine label app, and when they activate the app, by pointing their mobile device at the wine in question, the label activates an animation to reveal the story on the consumer's phone. That story may involve a picture of a person on the label coming to life and giving a specific narrative or it may involve the image on the label changing or enhancing in some way. It could be described as a combination of the earlier technologies mentioned above. Although this technology is not yet extensively used in the wine sector there are already some interesting examples on wine shelves including the *19 Crimes* range of wines, *The Walking Dead* range and *Matua Wines.*[47]

The Future Is New Media

In an interview with *The Drinks Business* Paul Mabray, a leading digital expert described 'the wine industry as the last to have not succeeded online'. He added:

47   Living Labels.com. Available at: <https://www.livingwinelabels.com/> (Accessed 4 October 2021).

> Social media is one of the most powerful customer interaction channels in the world; more relevant than anything seen in human industry ... those who choose to keep waiting will see their customers migrating to the use of these channels and will experience digital Darwinism.[48]

As we have seen in earlier chapters, it is the concept of story that helps develop the required emotional relationship between a wine and its audience and today's social media phenomenon is all about story. In the first quarter of 2021 Facebook reached 1.908 billion users.[49] These users tell each other stories every day. By channelling wine stories through social media, we can get our product message across to large audiences in a very short period of time. Perhaps it is the story of how the winery was founded, or a more intimate story of winery workers' achievements or family history. Europa Village Wines[50] were an early adopter of technology and began creating a customer bond with their wine story through Twitter and Facebook a full thirteen months before their winery opened. This resulted in 300 enthusiasts signing up to their wine club in advance of the winery's launch. Their current website homepage shows that they now use Facebook, Twitter, YouTube, Instagram, Pinterest and LinkedIn to help tell their story. Europa Village's early use of YouTube is also interesting from a story perspective. They uploaded vineyard stories that encouraged a personal relationship with the product. There were personal interactions with the winery sommelier, the head chef or indeed certain winery tasks such as pruning or hand corking. There were also several uploaded entries that concerned the vineyard dog Bella. These short films were entitled:

Bella girl watching over the winery
Bella checking the grapes for harvest

---

48 Lucy Shaw, 'Wineries who shun social media will experience "Digital Darwinism"' (2012) www.drinksbusiness.com. Available at: <http://www.thedrinksbusiness.com/2012/06/wineries-who-shun-social-media-will-experience-digital-darwinism>/ (Accessed 14 March 2013).

49 Statista.com, 'Number of daily active Facebook users worldwide as of 2nd quarter 2021'. Available at: <https://www.statista.com/statistics/346167/facebook-global-dau/> (Accessed 10 October 2021).

50 Europavillage. Available at: <http://europavillage.com> (Accessed 12 March 2020).

Bella the winery pub greets her public

Focusing on the story of Bella and her antics in the vineyard was a simple story mechanism delivered through YouTube that allowed customers to feel an intimate connection with the vineyard, even from afar. Obviously, they could then look forward to interacting with Bella in real life should they ever visit the actual location.

Locals Telling Local Stories

Delivering product information, though useful, rarely results in the consumer of that information developing a true affinity with the product being discussed. However, there are exceptions to this. The potential for using new media to convey the true story of a defined place was exploited by two previously unemployed filmmakers from Dublin. Their Story Map project enabled both physical and virtual visitors to Dublin to experience a unique flavour of the city through stories told by local inhabitants and linked to defined places in the city. Andy Flaherty and Tom Rowley are two Irish film makers and were the entrepreneurs behind then Story Map project.[51] Having realised that the capital city had been receiving an undue amount of negative publicity, they set about telling the story of Dublin by engaging with local people, usually in the specific Dublin locations where the stories happened. With YouTube as their principal medium, the two filmmakers uploaded a story a week onto Story Map. These stories were accessed either online or by using the Story Map smartphone application. They were location based and accessed through coloured links indicated on street maps. Each story provided an authentic cultural flavour of Dublin city. The project was funded by Dublin City Enterprise Board. A map key on the bottom left of the Story Map was colour coded according to various themes such as Funny, Historic, Literary or Places of Interest. One of the better-known contributors was Roddy Doyle who wrote

---

51   Storymap, Available at: <https://www.youtube.com/user/StorymapDublin/featu red> (Accessed 14 June 2019).

a short piece entitled *The Spire* based on one of Dublin's well-known monuments. The story was read by poet Sarah Maria Griffin and accompanied by a well-produced piece of YouTube footage that plays once you move the cursor over the Spire's location on the map. Much of the Spire's sense of place is captured through sound. The narrator's voice foregrounds the bustling sounds of O' Connell Street as the story's main protagonist awaits her first date's arrival at the Spire, their appointed rendezvous point. The combination of Doyle's effective writing style, Griffin's narration and the excellent sound and image quality 'evokes a small and delicate moment at the monument'[52] and helps capture the very essence of place one might associate with the heart of Dublin.

The Story Map example helped enhance the tourism product in Dublin and endowed it with cultural attributes, thus providing a real-life experience of the city's famous thoroughfares, buildings and watering holes. It is the use of local people and the place-specific nature of the stories that suggest the potential for similar technologies being used to the benefit of the wine sector to establish a bond between their own consumers and their wine's sense of place. The Story Map approach lends itself well to a regional wine setting and could help in expressing a sense of *terroir* through similar mechanisms. The story of this *terroir* might then be accessed by visitors to the site or the app. Stories need to be more than just a transmission of facts and require a local voice that allows the audience to feel that they are interacting with the story in an intimate way. Because of how it carefully chose its story tellers, Story Map managed to convey a sense of local intimacy in the delivery of its message. According to one of its founders, Andy Flaherty:

> We attend pretty much every cultural night going to see if there are any good characters there and tap them up for stories. Any story we get we ask the storyteller to recommend if they know of any other characters or storytellers.[53]

52   Ibid.
53   Richard Fitzpatrick, 'City streets come alive to the sound of spinning yarns', *Irish Examiner* [online]. 16 August 2012. Available at: <http://www.irishexaminer.com/lifestyle/features/humaninterest/city-streets-come-alive-to-the-sound-of-spinning-yarns-204255.html> (Accessed 14 June 2013).

The cultural aspect of the story experience is crucial in developing a permanent bond between the product, in this case Dublin city, and the story consumer.

Scottish Whisky: Steeped in Tradition Yet Adapting to New Technology

There are many similarities between the traditional French wine sector and the whisky industry. Both offer products that are rooted in heritage, tradition and place. Both have elements that are *terroir* driven. Laphroaig is one of Scotland's well-known distilleries. Though owned by global drinks company Suntory, the distillery successfully portrays itself as a unique and independent operator. Laphroaig has embraced the use of new technology in several important ways. It demonstrates how a relatively small distillery can tell its story to a large number of clients. It allows loyal customers the opportunity to interact with the distillery, its products, people and stories without the necessity of visiting the actual place. They do this through two principal mechanisms, namely their Friends of Laphroaig (FOL) platform and Laphroaig Live. Twenty-six years ago, the business introduced the concept of Friends of Laphroaig (FOL) and today they have over 500,000 official Friends of Laphroaig registered on their website. Through the clever use of technology, the FOL achieve a place-affinity with the distillery and it is this place linkage that enables its drinkers to form a strong emotional bond with the whisky. When someone becomes a member of the FOL, they are allocated their own specific plot at the Laphroaig distillery. The FOL section of their website allows registered members to virtually visit their plot. Each plot is individually displayed and members are encouraged to get to know and email their plot neighbours. In addition, a Google maps facility is available that allows the plot to be viewed from the air and its position on the Island in relation to the distillery is clearly highlighted by GPS technology. Many Friends of Laphroaig will never visit their plot but the

technology allows them to do so in a virtual way. As part of their regis-
tration the FOL also receive a Certificate of Lifetime Lease for their own
square foot of Islay. This certificate provides us with an example of how,
according to Hobsbawm 'inventing traditions .... is essentially a process
of formalisation and ritualisation, characterised by reference to the past
if only by imposing repetition'.[54] The virtual plot is linked to the physical
plot in the distillery and should the opportunity arise to visit, FOL members can identify their plot by planting their country's flag. This concept is
heavily promoted on their site and provides a physical place-link between
the FOL and the distillery. In addition to paying a nominal ground rent
of one dram of whisky, mention is made on the certificate of several symbolic commitments that are offered on the part of the distillery for the
lifetime of the leaseholder. These include providing an individual map to
the leaseholder's plot, protective clothing and access to the leaseholder's
cupboard, which contains a tape measure and a pair of designated wel-
lington boots. The actual provision of wellingtons as well as other in-
vented traditions are borne out by tourist guides recounting visits to the
distillery:

> Names and addresses of the first couple of hundred thousand friends were also
> recorded in large leather registers held in the Friends' lounge at the distillery. On
> arrival Friends are given their miniature as rent, plus signed certificates which tell
> them where in the registers they can find their entries and information on where to
> find their plot of land, plus a small flag of the nationality of their choice (and there
> is a wide choice). The plots of land are in a large field on the inland side of the coast
> road near the distillery, and Friends are invited to go and plant their national flag in
> their own personal square foot of land. This field looks as if it can get boggy, which
> is where the racks of Wellington boots come in.[55]

This ritual of FOL visitors' entitlements has gone on since the FOL inception in 1994. Some may perceive it as a somewhat crass portrayal of

---

54 Eric Hobsbawm, 'Introduction: The invention of tradition', in Eric Hobsbawm
    and Terence Ranger (eds), *The Invention of Tradition* (Cambridge: Cambridge
    University Press, 1983), p. 4.
55 Undiscoveredscotland.co.uk. Available at: <http://www.undiscoveredscotland.
    co.uk/islay/laphroaigdistillery/> (Accessed 17 June 2013).

tradition and history but there is no doubting how successful the FOL concept has been. The attractiveness of such a virtual place-association is clear when it comes to some of the comments displayed in the FOL chat room and one can't help but be struck by their apparent sincerity.

> Just wanted to post a quick hello to you all out there, and to say how very nice this site is. Lots to look through and enjoy. What a great idea. Makes the experience of Laphroaig even more enjoyable. My family forefathers left dear old Scotland over 200 years ago, and now at last, I have a small piece of the homeland to claim as 'our own'. Thanks folks. Very nice. Plot No: 502605[56]

Laphroaig was an early adopter when it came to using new technology. In 2007 it began to use live internet broadcastings to help promote their brand. Laphroaig live-London 2007 was streamed online and billed as an interactive whisky tasting. Hosted by Murray Norton, the show featured several panellists and a studio audience and was watched online by considerable numbers of interested whisky lovers. Since its inception in 2007 *Laphroaig Live* has become an annual event and now forms an integral part of Laphroaig's strategy in allowing their clients to interactively experience the story and taste of Laphroaig without the necessity to travel to the distillery. The show has been broadcast from several very different locations: *Laphroaig Live Islay 2008, Laphroaig Live Kentucky 2009, Laphroaig Live Jerez 2010, Laphroaig Live Sydney 2011 and Laphroaig Live Germany 2012*. When one views each webcast, it becomes clear that the places chosen always have some clear *terroir* driven link with the distillery itself. In 2009, the *Laphroaig Live* road show was taken to Maker's Mark Distillery in Kentucky USA where Laphroaig source most of their bourbon barrels used in the aging process. In 2010, they broadcast from Jerez, Spain, because it is the home of the Sherry Butt, a style of barrel that Laphroaig has used since the very early days of production. In 2011, the distillery moved to Sydney where they were joined by descendants of the Johnston brothers who originally started the Laphroaig Distillery before emigrating to Australia in 1836. In 2012 *Laphroaig Live* broadcast

---

56   John Creighton Laphroaig.com/friends/chat. Available at: <http://www.laphro aig.com/friends/chat/Default.aspx?Page=25> (Accessed 18 June 2013).

from the 200 year-old Oktoberfest Fair in Germany, famous for its beer making tradition which has very close ties to the production of whisky. During the global pandemic the distillery continued using the Laphroaig Live Virtual Events model and in June 2021 hosted its second Laphroaig Virtual Fèis Ìle Open Day which featured several virtual tasting and whisky storytelling events.[57] Not only can viewers participate in the live broadcast through social media but they can also experience a sense of Islay by tasting the same whiskies as the tasting panel. When first broadcast, the streaming technology required was both new and cumbersome but in the more recent years the advent of more easily accessible and affordable technologies has improved the quality of virtual events like these. Laphroaig are not unique and there are now many live online tasting events available where subscribers purchase products in advance and then attend the live internet tasting from the comfort of their own home. Like the distillers of Laphroaig many winemakers find themselves located in relatively remote rural locations. This technology allows personal interactions with consumers and even suppliers so that drinkers can, virtually at least, experience the wine, the location and its people without having to physically travel there.

Conclusion

The concept of story has always been important in the promotion of products and in society at large. It has been at the very heart of cultural life down through the centuries. Wine, more than any other drink, has been part of that cultural story since ancient civilisations first discovered its pleasures. Tom Standage tells us that even in ancient Greece, 'politics, poetry, and philosophy were discussed at formal drinking parties, or symposia, in which the participants drank from a sacred bowl of diluted

---

57   'Fèis Ìle 2021: 1st June was a good day with Laphroaig'. Available at: <https://www.laphroaig.com/en/feis-ile-2021> (Accessed 27 October 2021).

wine.'[58] In France, elements of tradition and heritage have dominated the nature of their wine product for centuries. Throughout the recent rise in popularity of New World wines, France has retained its reputation for quality, luxury and *terroir* focused wines. The dominant orthodoxy in French wine culture has determined that the wine's story be communicated through complex and codified *appellation contrôlée* systems and indeed through experiential knowledge of the wine's *terroir* gained usually through a visit to individual wine regions or locations. However, the world is changing and the 'digital Darwinism' referred to earlier in this chapter is a very real threat to all gastronomic products rooted in history, tradition and place. Winemakers need to adapt more quickly to a new media age. The sector is not alone in its suspicion of new technology. According to Mehta, even that most ancient of traditional institutions, the Catholic Church, only relatively recently began to fully embrace a new way of communicating its own story:

> In late 2012, former Pope Benedict XVI took the Vatican firmly into the social media era by launching his @Pontifex Twitter Account, aimed at communicating with the more than one billion Roman Catholics around the world.[59]

The Laphroaig whisky example illustrates the suitability of *terroir* driven products when it comes to bridging the gap between culturally laden drinks and consumers. Their positive approach to new media in a whisky sector dominated by tradition and history can offer a potential path to others. By failing to fully embrace technology some producers are missing out on an opportunity to communicate their authentic gastronomic identity to a wider audience.

It is the contention of this chapter, that the power of French wine's story needs to be further emphasised by new media. The potential for new technology to help communicate that story is boundless. Use of smartphone applications, QR/NFC codes, augmented reality and social media

---

58   Tom Standage, *A History of the World in Six Glasses* (New York: Walker Publishing Company Inc., 2005), p. 3.

59   Glen Mehta, *Infinite Ripple: The Social Media Revolution* (United Kingdom: Xlibris Publishing, 2013), p. 42.

platforms offer French wine an important opportunity, perhaps more than any other beverage, because of its natural association with *terroir*, history, authenticity and tradition. Such attributes are proving to be key differentiating factors as the wine world becomes more globalised. Technology doesn't, as is sometimes feared, dilute such associations in the mind of the wine drinker. As we have demonstrated in this chapter, if properly used, it can enhance them. The place and story focus of examples like Story Map and Laphroaig suggest potential solutions to the age-old problem of some drinkers finding French wine complex and difficult to engage with. New media can be harnessed to help tell the story of wine to more digitally aware audiences whose chosen medium of communication in future will most likely be based on emerging technologies. The more traditional French wine sector should be open to these developments and must proactively engage with them to ensure continued growth in future years.

CHAPTER 12

From Penny Universities to Starbucks

Coffee didn't really feature in my early life. Tea dominated most Irish households during my youth and those who drank coffee usually preferred instant, in my experience. In 1994 I took a job as a manager at Searcy's Loose Box Bar and Restaurant in London's Knightsbridge. This was my first close encounter with an Italian-style espresso coffee machine. This huge chrome embossed machine was busy most of the day hissing and gurgling as it spewed out an array of lattes, cappuccinos and espressos that were popular in London at the time. I think my ongoing espresso addiction began during this period. When I came home to Ireland a few years later, similar espresso coffee machines were everywhere and the dominance of that new coffee culture is reflected in the following discussion.

This chapter explores how gastronomic communities can engage with places and products in new and different ways. It's clear from what follows that the chapter is rooted, to some degree in the past. It examines the emergence of coffee culture in Ireland and how the experience we enjoy today is not a recent cultural import but rather has its origins in a long, sometimes forgotten history. It situates that history as the first of five defined coffee phases in Ireland. These phases have brought us to a situation where café culture has now become integral to our lives.

Much like food, the beverages we drink can often act as key signifiers in social exchanges. Coffee is one drink that has the potential to convey a message about who we are or how we might like to be seen, and Ireland's relationship with coffee culture appears at first glance to be a relatively new one. Passing through the rural village of Leighlinbridge on the banks of the river Barrow in Co. Carlow, passers-by are struck by the picturesque floral frontage that frames a small riverside butcher shop. In addition to its normal offering, the shop also sells coffee for consumption just outside the shop, in a tiny roadside seating area.

Image 8. Cullen's Family Butchers, Leighlinbridge, Co. Carlow.

Picture of Cullen's Family Butchers, Leighlinbridge, Co Carlow (Photo by Brian Murphy 3 August 2021).

In an earlier chapter we explored the potential for traditional butcher shops to express themselves beyond the mercantile nature of their wares. Here we are presented with another example, but with a more pronounced emphasis on encouraging customers to engage and linger a while over a coffee. This rural image helps demonstrate how coffee has become ingrained in Irish society, and it is the coffee tables outside that demonstrate its role as a facilitator of engagement. In the not-too-distant past, the main bastion of Ireland's drink culture was the pub but Cullen's Family Butchers, pictured above, helps demonstrate just how far we have come and how integrated coffee consumption has become in modern Irish life. However, Ireland's coffee story is complex and our more recent experiences of coffee culture are mirrored by an earlier seventeenth- and eighteenth-century engagement with the coffee house. These historic coffee houses were sometimes referred to as Penny Universities[60] because they 'functioned as information exchanges for scientists, businessman writers and politicians'[61]

A recent article by Felix Richter notes that 2021, marked the fiftieth anniversary of the First Starbucks coffee shop in Seattle USA:

> 50 years ago, on March 30, 1971, a store selling freshly roasted coffee beans and coffee equipment opened in Seattle's Pike Place Market. …[Starbucks] has evolved from said little coffee store into a chain of almost 33,000 company-operated and licensed stores, sprawled across more than 80 countries. With a market capitalization of $128 billion, the Starbucks Corporation, still headquartered in Seattle, has grown into the second largest quick-service restaurant chain in the world, trailing only McDonald's in terms of sales, market capitalization and global brand appeal.[62]

It is remarkable to consider how this simple beverage experience has come to dominate social interactions throughout the globe. Whether we are just meeting a friend socially in a café, consuming a coffee at home or using the drink as a stimulus to keep working late into the night, all these experiences revolve around the consumption of a simple hot beverage that doesn't differ a great deal from the drink that emerged many centuries ago. According to Bee Wilson, 'to brew coffee is to do nothing more than mix grounds with hot water and strain out the bits'[63] and yet coffee has come to signify so much more in society. The inventiveness lavished on this substance reflects its status as the 'world's culinary drug of choice'.[64] We have seen the popularisation of barista culture with connoisseurs expressing a wine-like reverence for the many flavours, preparation methods and tasting techniques associated with coffee. Companies

60 Jonathan Morris, *Coffee a Global History* (London: Reaktion Books Ltd., 2019), Chapter 3, para. 12.

61 Tom Standage, *A History of the World in Six Glasses* (New York: Walker Publishing Company Inc., 2006), p. 152.

62 Felix Richter, 'Starbucks at 50: A Sprawling Coffee Empire', Statista.com, 20 March 2021. Available at: <https://www.statista.com/chart/24546/starbucks-stores-worldwide/> (Accessed 10 August 2021).

63 Bee Wilson, *Consider the Fork: A History of How We Cook and Eat* (London: Penguin Group, 2013), p. 363.

64 Ibid.

like Nespresso have come to dominate the home coffee scene and now even offer their valued clients Connoisseur Club courses after their stores close so that the public can gain expert insights into the mystery of coffee from expert Nespresso baristas who train willing devotees in the fine art of tasting and describing a spectrum of flavours.

Many authors have explored the influence of coffee down through the centuries, from its origins in the Arabic world of the fifteenth century, as the wine of Islam[65] through a variety of so-called coffee waves, to its more recent iteration as a beverage that dominates commensal experiences both inside and outside the home. The global history of coffee provides a suitable starting point for our own exploration of coffee as cultural sustenance. This chapter uses authors such as Standage,[66] Morris[67] and Pendergrast [68] to consider this global context. Others including Mac Con Iomaire[69] and Kennedy[70] have examined coffee's history from an Irish perspective and the chapter also looks at their work. It goes on to examine several key coffee phases and in particular, the impact of the Celtic Tiger on this iconic drink. The concept of place also plays a key role and its impact is of central importance in how we engage with coffee.

As is the case with a great many beverages, there are several origin stories that deal with the discovery of coffee as a drink. It mirrors another of the world's great beverages, Champagne, in that foundation myths have impinged on reality somewhat when it comes to records of its original discovery. With Champagne we had an alleged 'eureka-style discovery' by

65   Standage, *A History of the World*, p. 136 and Morris, *Coffee a Global History*, Chapter 2.
66   Standage, *A History of the World in Six Glasses*.
67   Morris, *Coffee a Global History*.
68   Mark Pendergrast, *Uncommon Grounds: The History of Coffee and How It Transformed Our World* (New York: Basic Books, 2019).
69   Mairtin Mac Con Iomaire, 'Coffee culture in Dublin: A brief history', *M/C Journal – A Journal of Media and Culture*, 15. Available at: <http://journal.media-culture.org.au/index.php/mcjournal/article/viewArticle/456> (Accessed 23 May 2020).
70   Máire Kennedy, 'Dublin Coffee Houses'. *Ask About Ireland*, 2011. Available at: <http://www.askaboutireland.ie/reading-room/history-heritage/pages-in-hist ory/dublin-coffee-houses/> (Accessed 25 August 2021).

Dom Perignon.[71] With coffee, the most prominent foundation myth concerns the idea that a ninth-century Ethiopian goatherd named Kaldi noted how his sheep became frisky and agitated having consumed some coffee bean cherries. Kaldi chewed the berries himself and noted their powerful effects.[72] Morris confirms, 'The Kaldi story first appeared in Europe in 1671 as part of a coffee treatise published by Antonio Fausto Naironi, a Maronite Christian from the Levant (today's Lebanon) who had emigrated to Rome. He likely heard it in his homeland.'[73] We can definitively trace the story of coffee from the fifteenth century but just like other drinks such as whiskey, beer and wine, the exact origins of coffee's original discovery cannot be determined and are lost to us.

As coffee developed a reputation as a stimulant, its reach stretched across the sixteenth-century Arabic world. Its diffusion was assisted by pilgrimage practices such as the Hajj. Morris notes that 'the Ottoman conquest of Egypt in 1516–17 facilitated its spread into the Turkish-run empire, reaching Damascus in 1534 and Istanbul in 1554'.[74] The early appeal of the coffee house lay in its ability to provide a legitimate public space that allowed all Muslim men to socialise on an equal footing. A point emphasised by Morris, who noted that it provided a different alternative to the norm of entertaining and socialising in the home which brought inherent inequalities as guests were exposed to the status and wealth of the host. The coffee house provided a much more egalitarian experience:

> Now one could meet peers at a coffee house, and exchange hospitality on a more equal footing through the simple expedient of buying each other cups of coffee. The layout of these early coffee houses facilitated an egalitarian ambience, as patrons were seated according to the order in which they arrived, at long benches or on divans running alongside the walls, rather than by their rank.[75]

71   Brian Murphy, 'Using a 17th century Benedictine monk to convert myth into history in an effort to sell more fizz', in Sylvie Mikowski (ed.), *History and Memory in France and Ireland* (Reims: Epure-Éditions et Presses universitaires de Reims, 2011), p. 295.

72   Pendergrast, *Uncommon Grounds*, Chapter 1: 'Coffee colonises the world', Para. 1.

73   Morris, *Coffee a Global History*, Chapter 2, Para. 2.

74   Ibid., Chapter 2, Para. 15.

75   Ibid., Chapter 2, Para. 20.

The concept of Third Place fits in well with the above quote from Morris. Oldenburg suggests in his book *The Great Good Place* that Third Places are positioned on neutral ground and are also considered a leveller.[76] In fact, Oldenburg presents a specific chapter on classic coffee houses which itself details quite a comprehensive history of the drink and emphasises that beverages such as coffee are key to the idea of Third places suggesting that 'the general rule is that beverages are of such social importance as to become veritable social sacraments'.[77] He goes on to cite Kenneth Davis who observed that 'every social lubricant has its home away from home, its church, as it were, where its effects are celebrated in public ceremonies and ritual conviviality'.[78]

Coffee houses quickly spread from their Arabic home throughout Europe as popular places of social interaction and information hubs that a wide range of society could access. There is considerable variation in the stories that surround the introduction of coffee into Europe. One of the most prominent relates to Vienna. Many consider the Austrian capital as the historical home of the European coffee house although it seems clear that they started to become popular in places like Italy and England before their development there.[79] Nonetheless coffee enthusiasts recognise the Viennese coffee house as being a crucial part of coffee's gastronomic identity.

> The particular culture of the Viennese coffeehouse (*Wiener Kaffeehaus* in German) was designated an 'Intangible Cultural Heritage' in 2011 within the domain of 'social practices' in the Austrian inventory of the 'National Agency for the Intangible

---

76   Ray Oldenburg, *The Great Good Place* (Philadelphia, PA: De Capo Press, 1998), pp. 22–23.

77   Ibid., p. 183.

78   Ibid.

79   Yasmin El-Beih, 'Coffeehouses helped spread modern democracy, spur the Enlightenment and birth periodical literature. So why did King Charles II's cronies try to ban them?' 19 November 2019. Article adapted from the *In Our Time* BBC Radio 4 programme episode on Coffee. Available at: <https://www.bbc.com/travel/article/20201119-how-coffee-forever-changed-britain> (Accessed 22 March 2022).

Cultural Heritage', a part of the United Nations Educational, Scientific and Cultural Organization'[80]

As a place, the Viennese coffee house presents several unique historical features that are still visible today and were always associated with its traditional coffee offering. These include its traditional décor, its style of coffee service, the fact that coffee is always accompanied by a class of water, access to daily newspapers and the recognised quality of allowing customers plenty of time to sit and relax. Although the Austrian association with coffee emerged after other countries, the reputation of the Viennese coffee house is legendary. Oldenburg suggests that

> it is part of Viennese legend that the world's first coffee house was hers; the myth is all the more cherished because of its association with Vienna's finest hour, the Austrians' victory in the Second Turkish Siege. One myth regarding the origin of the coffee house, I have found is likely to be followed by another. A seasoned and cosmopolitan writer recently admitted to having believed and promulgated the Viennese version. The first coffeehouse he explained did not appear in Vienna in 1664 but in Constantinople in 1540. From there, he went on to clarify, the institution spread to Europe, then to England.[81]

Morris confirms Oldenburg's premise that coffee houses were important in seventeenth-century Vienna indicating the coffee trade 'was dominated by Armenians, such as Johannes Diodato, who in 1685 was awarded the first licence for preparing and selling coffee – that is, operating a coffee house'.[82] In addition, both Oldenburg and Morris agree that England was an important location in terms of the evolution of European coffee house culture following the importation of the idea from older Arabian origins. It's also from its original home in England that it began to spread to other nearby regions.

---

80 Yeong-Shyang Chen and Shou-Tsung Wu, 'Social networking practices of Viennese coffeehouse culture and intangible heritage tourism', *Journal of Tourism and Cultural Change*, 17 (2), 2017, pp. 186–207. DOI: 10.1080/14766825.2017.1400037 citing the Austrian Commission for UNESCO, 2015.

81 Oldenburg, *The Great Good Place*, p. 192.

82 Morris, *Coffee a Global History*, Chapter 3, Para.5.

Far from being limited to London, the coffeehouse was an institution that quickly spread to the provinces, as well as to Scotland and Ireland. The eighteenth-century provincial coffeehouse so carefully described by John Brewer had its origins in the reign of Charles the second. John Row opened the first coffeehouse in Edinburgh near the Parliament House in 1673. That same year Colonel Walter Whiteford established a coffeehouse in Glasgow. Lionel Newman had already opened a coffeehouse in Dublin by 1664.[83]

Pincus indicates that the first recorded coffee house in England was 'about the year 1650'.[84] Others [85] are more specific, suggesting that Oxford was home to the first coffee shop in England and a Jewish operator remembered only as Jacob was responsible for its opening in 1650. London followed soon after in 1652, with the opening of its first coffee house. Morris[86] casts some doubt on the exact Oxford date claim but nonetheless broadly agrees with others regarding the prominent role London played in the emergence of coffee house culture. He confirms the commonly held view that

a Jewish manservant from the Levant named Jacob has sometimes been credited with opening a coffee house in the same city [Oxford] in 1650, but, if he existed, he probably served, rather than sold, coffee to his master's companions. There is no doubt, however, that Pasqua Rosée, an ethnic Armenian from the Ottoman city of Smyrna (now Izmir) opened London's, and Europe's, first documented coffee house sometime between 1652 and 1654.[87]

Despite arguments over the exact date 'London did in fact quickly become host to hundreds of coffeehouses. By the late 1650s the Londoner Thomas Rugge claimed that coffee was sold almost in every street. In May 1663 there were over eighty coffeehouses in the city alone.'[88] These coffee

83   Steve Pincus, 'Coffee politicians does create: Coffeehouses and restoration political culture', *The Journal of Modern History*, 67, December 1995, p. 813.
84   Ibid., p. 211.
85   Oldenburg, *The Great Good Place*, p. 185; and Mac Con Iomaire, 'Coffee culture in Dublin: A brief history'.
86   Morris, *Coffee a Global History*, Chapter 3, Para. 7.
87   Ibid.
88   Steve Pincus, 'Coffee politicians does create', p. 812 citing Sachse, 1961 and Latham and W. Matt, 1970–1983.

houses along with their European counterparts became bastions of information, places where people could go if they wanted to hear the latest business news, get information on commodity prices or keep up with business and political gossip all for the price of a cup of coffee.

Penny Universities

The term 'Penny University' is an apt name for a place that performs the diverse set of functions mentioned above and authors such as Oldenburg, Morris and Johnson[89] have used the term to describe seventeenth- and eighteenth-century English coffee houses. Such places became important locations for academic discussion, since anyone could enter and join the discussion for a penny or two, the price of a dish of coffee.[90] After the first recorded European coffee house in Oxford, the proliferation of coffee houses thereafter helped provide several services in terms of information transformation that were crucial to local businesses at the time. They were considered 'the precursor of the daily newspaper'[91] or 'The Coffee Internet' of their time [92] in that they provided a place where businessmen would gather to dispense commercial news of the day. Many early London coffee houses also became associated with specific categories of business dealings: 'Each coffeehouse had a particular clientele, usually defined by occupation, interest or attitude, such as Tories and Whigs, traders and merchants, poets and authors, and men of fashion and leisure.'[93] According to Oldenburg it was customary for patrons to read aloud from newspapers and broadsides so that those who could not

89   Ben Johnson, 'English Coffee Houses, Penny Universities', Historic UK. Available at: <https://www.historic-uk.com/CultureUK/English-Coffeehouses-Penny-Universities/> (Accessed 15 August 2021).
90   Standage, *A History of the World in Six Glasses*, p. 158.
91   Oldenburg, *The Great Good Place*, p. 184.
92   Standage, *A History of the World in Six Glasses*, p. 151.
93   Johnson, 'English Coffee Houses, Penny Universities'.

read would benefit from the daily news. He cites one such broadside's simple proclamation from Aytoun Ellis's book *The Penny Universities*

> So great a Universitie
>
> I think there ne'er was any
>
> In which you may a scholar be
>
> For spending a Penny[94]

It should be noted that some felt that these early Penny Universities not only provided customers with increased access to information and enlightenment but also functioned as bastions of radicalism and political revolution. Indeed, in 1675 King Charles II thought that such exchange of information and political views presented a threat to the monarchy and his:

> ministers attempted to suppress and close down coffeehouses on the grounds of their 'evil and dangerous effects'. The king feared that coffee may provoke instigation or the plotting of violence against the throne and ordered the 'close of coffee-houses altogether', although he later withdrew the ban two days before it was to be put into effect.[95]

As we can see, throughout history the coffee houses served a number of important functions and were an important feature of the international food and drink landscape. However, they also played and continue to play a key role in how Ireland engages with its own food and drink culture.

94   Oldenburg, *The Great Good Place*, p. 185, citing Aytoun Ellis, *The Penny Universities* (London: Secker and Warburg, 1956).
95   Yasmin El-Beih, 'Coffeehouses helped spread modern democracy, spur the Enlightenment and birth periodical literature. So why did King Charles II's cronies try to ban them?' 19 November 2019 citing Brian Cowen in *The Social Life of Coffee: The Emergence of the British Coffeehouse* (Yale University Press, 2005).

Five Irish Coffee Phases

Mac Con Iomaire tells us that 'the earliest reference to coffee houses in Dublin is to the Cock Coffee House in Cook Street during the reign of Charles II (1660–85)'.[96] Like London, coffee houses thrived in Dublin:

> During the second half of the 17th century, Dublin's merchant classes transferred allegiance from taverns to the newly fashionable coffee houses as places to conduct business. By 1698, the fashion had spread to country towns with coffee houses found in Cork, Limerick, Kilkenny, Clonmel, Wexford, and Galway, and slightly later in Belfast and Waterford in the 18th century.[97]

Despite competing well with popular taverns and inns, as places of social engagement, this thriving coffee culture, as described by authors such as Mac Con Iomaire and Kennedy,[98] faced considerable competition throughout the nineteenth and twentieth century from other places such as gentlemen's clubs and the ultimate domination of the Irish pub. Their decline brought Ireland's first coffee phase to a close as the style of coffee house mentioned above all but disappeared in the face of stiff competition.

The latter part of the twentieth century was to bring a new coffee focus in an Ireland that had predominantly developed as a tea drinking nation and the late 1990s saw the introduction of a second major coffee phase. With the emergence of the Celtic Tiger, domestic coffee chains began making early forays into the Irish market. A returning diaspora demanded a coffee culture that many had experienced abroad. In addition, more extensive travel opportunities, made possible by budget airlines, exposed more people to the European coffee cultures of countries like Italy, Spain and France. Irish companies such as Insomnia, which opened its first store in 1997, and Café Sol, which was formed in 1998, joined existing market

---

96   Mac Con Iomaire, 'Coffee culture in Dublin: A brief history'.
97   Ibid.
98   Kennedy, 'Dublin Coffee Houses'.

players like O' Brien's and Bewley's and began to capitalise on an emerging culture that associated coffee drinking with affluence.

As the economy boomed and evidence of ostentation appeared in many areas of Irish life, coffee certainly fitted the bill, as the streets became filled with busy professionals who greeted their long working day with espresso based coffees in hand. For quite a few years, the Irish chains continued to dominate but coffee is a high margin product and it was inevitable that international chains would turn their gaze on Ireland. 2005 was to herald a third phase in Ireland's coffee story. Both Costa and Starbucks entered the market around this time and embarked on developments that would see their stores rapidly expand over a relatively short period. They have made substantial commercial progress since, and 2018 figures from *Hospitality Ireland* suggested they now have 102 stores and 79 stores, respectively, making them the second and third largest players in the country after Insomnia.[99]

The collapse of the Celtic Tiger economy led to another more unexpected fourth phase in Irish coffee culture. The recession brought hardship and many coffee lovers were no longer willing or able to spend precious income on their daily caffeine fix. And yet, they were not prepared to forego their high-end coffee experience. The arrival and popularisation of the Nespresso concept fitted neatly with demands for high quality barista-style coffee that could be prepared more cheaply at home. It chimed well with a nation, who still wanted indulgence, even in a period of decline and uncertainty. Brema Drohan, managing director of Nespresso in Ireland, recognised this at the launch of their flagship store in Dublin in 2014 when she said: 'Then those things stopped. But people still needed treats and there is still discernment and an interest in quality. And people wanted these treats, so they brought them home.'[100]

99   *Hospitality Ireland* citing a report by consultants Allegra, 'Starbucks becomes third largest coffee chain in Ireland'. Available at: <https://www.hospitalityireland.com/restaurant/starbucks-becomes-third-largest-coffee-chain-ireland-53903> (Accessed 14 August 2020).

100 'Smooth operator – Nespresso winning coffee wars', *Independent.ie*. [online], 14 June 2014. Available at: <https://www.independent.ie/business/irish/smooth-operator-nespresso-winning-coffee-wars-30507256.html> (Accessed 20 June 2020).

There is little doubt that the Celtic Tiger period changed our relationship with coffee. Ireland now has a proliferation of coffee chains to choose from, home coffee solutions are everywhere and barista coffee courses and competitions are common. In 2016, Ireland hosted the prestigious World Barista Championship for the first time. However, the Celtic Tiger period has also influenced a fifth and for now final phase in the Irish coffee story. While recent figures from *Hospitality Ireland* suggest that Ireland's top four coffee chains – Insomnia, Costa, Starbucks and O' Brien's – have almost 400 stores between them, we have also recently seen the emergence of the independent coffee house, sometimes unfairly dismissed as part of a fleeting hipster trend. These authentic coffee shops provide a welcome antidote to the branded approach of the larger chains. Coffee houses such as Square in Kildare and Portlaoise and other sustainable independents like PS Coffee Roasters in Clane, founded in 2015, are examples of providers leading the way in a market that increasingly seeks out places that are local and unique. Their proliferation around our cities, towns and more recently rural areas is testament to the fact that, as a nation, we have embraced a modern more European approach to coffee. Independent coffee shops have started to appear in locations that would traditionally have been considered too remote to sustain a viable coffee business but are now thriving in a rural Ireland that is reasserting its own gastronomic identity. Two additional examples help illustrate the point. The first is the Grangecon Kitchen, pictured below, in rural West Wicklow and demonstrates the kind of Sunday morning coffee crowd such an enterprise can draw despite its very rural location and remove from any other facilities.

The second example pictured below is Dilly Dally's Coffee Shop on the rural Grand Canal in South Kildare, owned and run by Linda Sourke. Situated in a picturesque but remote location this unique independent site, which has been developed at the back of Linda's home, provides an important service for walkers, cyclists and indeed the local community. It opened in May 2021 at the height of the Covid crisis.

Our coffee shops provide us with new and alternative opportunities for social engagement in places other than our traditional locales. Through its rise and its demise, the Celtic Tiger economy is in large part responsible

Image 9. Grangecon Kitchen, Grangecon, Co. Wicklow.

Queuing for coffee in rural Ireland at Grangecon Kitchen in Grangecon, Co Wicklow during the pandemic (Picture by Paul Linehan, 21 March 2021).

for that provision and has helped give birth to a new Irish coffee culture that is undoubtedly here to stay.

Coffee Shops as Fourth Spaces

One of the recurring themes discussed throughout this book concerns how places connected to food and drink can be interpreted through a Fourth Space lens. We have seen in previous chapters that whiskey distilleries and even traditional butcher shops can project themselves as such. But the concept can also be used to describe the important engagement

Image 10. Dilly Dally's Coffee Shop in Co. Kildare.
Linda Sourke at Dilly Dally's in Co Kildare (Picture by Brian Murphy 29 August 2021).

that takes place between the coffee drinking public and the coffee places as described in this chapter. Interestingly, the major coffee shop chains such as Insomnia, Starbucks and Costa don't fit comfortably into the Fourth Space model. However, the emergence of a more independent coffee shop focused on the local community, particularly with the advent of Covid, appears much more suited to the concept. Many of the new coffee operations that have sprung up in both urban and rural areas since the pandemic began are now fulfilling the characteristics of that Fourth Space model, as outlined in the introduction. Most of them provide an authentic reflection of their place by being staffed by local people, telling local stories and acting as useful points of contact for tourists and visitors. They provide a personal service that reflects the identity of the area that the place is located in. In addition to the often locally roasted coffee they serve, these places frequently offer a selection of local artisan food. In the case of the Hardware Community Café example which featured in an earlier chapter, food is prepared by a group of local volunteers who gather one night a week to prepare fresh breads and cakes for sale during the week. Often such coffee shops also provide a space to hold community events and classes in the evenings as well as opportunities for local people to gain valuable skills working as volunteers that contribute towards the overall education and training of those volunteers. Because of their some-times remote locations and limited advertising budgets, visibility can be an issue but many exploit social media very effectively through me-diums like Facebook, Instagram, Twitter and TikTok. They depend on such mediums for much of their consumer engagement. In addition, in very rural communities these coffee shops can act as technology hubs and might sometimes be the only local provider of broadband in a rural area. They also provide ancillary functions in that they operate as de facto art spaces, providing opportunities for local arts and crafts people to display their wares. Outside normal trading hours they can provide much needed venues for staging music or drama performances in places that are often lacking in suitable facilities. The previously mentioned independent pro-viders provide some good examples. Square Coffee in Kildare Town and Portlaoise hold comedy nights, live music performances and act as gal-lery spaces while P.S. Coffee Roasters in Clane and Naas also provide live music performances and book launches. Though perhaps less evident and possibly something that might be further exploited in the future, many of these independent coffee shops also position themselves in locations and buildings that have a considerable history and have previously been at the centre of the local community. There are frequent opportunities to ex-plore the historical context of their setting and incorporate aspects of that local history into their offering through booklets, displays or exhibitions thus further embedding themselves in the local community.

Conclusion

This chapter began with an explanation of how coffee culture has become ingrained in Irish life in ways that seemed unimaginable just a few short decades ago. In the *Essential Guide to Dublin*, published in 1972, attitudes to coffee were clear. When describing the capital's premier street, the authors suggest that:

> If you are in the O 'Connell Street area and need a coffee it is more advisable to try one of the self-service restaurants attached to the cinema, such as the Savoy or the Carlton, or one of the pubs nearby. In fact, most Dublin pubs serve coffee, though the quality varies a great deal.[101]

Ireland has taken many years and five coffee phases to reach a situation where its café culture has now become comparable to that of many of its European neighbours. We now take for granted the availability of quality coffee experiences locally. The recent pandemic has led to a situation where many people have stayed close to home and has contributed to a proliferation of independent community focused coffee shops in rural and urban areas. However, these local coffeeshops have in many instances moved beyond the provision of mere refreshment. To varying degrees they have become Fourth Spaces as described above and now fulfil a variety of different roles that have led them to be valued sites of local engagement. They have become a blend of meeting places and workplaces. They offer good coffee, broadband, community, gossip and local news and have in a sense become contemporary versions of the Penny Universities of old discussed earlier in the chapter, although the price of entry now far exceeds the one or two pennies once demanded.

101   Terry Kelleher, Maurice Craig and Bernard Share, *The Essential Guide to Dublin* (Dublin: Gill and Macmillan Limited, 1972), p. 67.

CHAPTER 13

From Soyer to Twenty-First-Century Social Gastronomy

Ten years ago I became a co-founding member of the Dublin Gastronomy Symposium. This conference has grown into a well-recognised international gathering of academics interested in all aspects of food and drink research. When we were designing our second conference programme we included an image of the celebrated Victorian chef, Alexis Soyer. This was the first time I had encountered Soyer and I was fascinated by stories of how he used his culinary skills for social good. More recently, I have become attuned to many examples of how food and drink practitioners can function beyond their economic remit. This chapter helps elucidate Soyer's historical role and the more contemporary importance now placed on social gastronomy today.

The chapters of this book have explored food and drink on many different levels. Much of that exploration has dealt with how consumers engage with places and products and how that engagement is often tied to mercantile gain. This final chapter is important in that it offers an optimistic view of how parts of the food and drink sector have now developed. It suggests that, in some cases, the tribe that I described joining in the book's introduction has developed and nurtured an altruistic function that bodes well for the future. As with the last chapter the ideas discussed here are not new and in fact have roots that can be traced back to Victorian times, but it is their most recent iterations that are most exciting and indeed hopeful.

The term social gastronomy has been with us for several years but has now risen to prominence as an important and well reported part of our food and drink culture. Its purpose was recently defined by one of Ireland's best-known chefs, J. P. McMahon:

> It cultivates local connections and builds long term partnerships around the world, using the power of food as a vehicle for change and development at grassroots level.[1]

The concept provided the theme for the 2021 *Food on the Edge* conference, a leading Irish symposium that draws together many of the world's greatest culinary practitioners and thinkers. The term itself has also been adopted by the eponymous Social Gastronomy Movement (SGM), an organisation that has its origins in the work of chef and social entrepreneur David Hertz. In a 2015 *Ted Talk*[2] Hertz recounts how he overcame many personal social challenges in his early life through culinary achievements before finding his true home in the culinary world. He vowed to give back to local communities by using the tools that helped shape him, hence the founding of his first social enterprise, Gastromotiva in 2006. In 2017 following considerable success in its own right Gastromotiva under Hertz's direction became a co-creator of the Social Gastronomy Movement, which describes itself as 'a global initiative that connects people, projects, companies, universities, international agencies, governments and civil society around the transformative power of food'.[3] Other co-creators of SGM included Nicola Gryczka and Patrick Honauer, now board members of Social Gastronomy Schweiz, and fifty other food systems stakeholders who gathered with the intention to work towards a more inclusive and just food system. It should also be noted that the movement was founded with financial support from the international agricultural company Cargill. Though very much global in approach the organisation points to several best practice examples that demonstrate the considerable impact that social gastronomy can have on our local communities. This chapter explores not only emerging social gastronomists but also

1   'Airfield estate in Dundrum announced as food on the Edge 2021 Venue', 24 June 2021. Available at: <https://foodontheedge.ie/news/> (Accessed 31 August 2021).
2   Patrick D'Arcy, 'How food – Yes, food – Can be a tool for social change', 12 July 2018. Available at: <https://ideas.ted.com/how-food-yes-food-can-be-a-tool-for-social-change/> (Accessed 3 February 2021).
3   Gastromotiva.org. Available at: <https://gastromotiva.org/en/gastromotiva/> (Accessed 12 July 2021).

examples from history that show us that the idea of social gastronomy is not a new one and we have been here before.

We have seen from earlier chapters that there is considerable value in the consumption of food and drink as a commensal experience. The pandemic has taught us how valuable that aspect of food and drink culture is. In a recent article on the impact of the pandemic on the pub, James McCauley puts it best when he says:

> Canadian singer-songwriter Joni Mitchell's 1970s hit 'Big Yellow Taxi' had the immortal lines: 'Don't it always seem to go/That you don't know what you got/'Til it's gone'. With our favourite watering holes absent from our lives since mid-March, and perhaps some not reopening after a five-month hiatus until mid-August, these lyrics may resonate with many in how much we have taken our pubs for granted.[4]

The heightened sense of loss that we feel when our food and drink places are taken away from us helps demonstrate that we are lucky to live, for the most part, in a society that provides such social spaces for our enjoyment. We shall see from the examples below that in some cases, food and drink culture has developed a function that moves beyond the economic provision of services and products and has reached a stage where social projects have now become more prevalent. The chapter explores examples of how food and drink can be used for the betterment of society. Gastronomy can be born out of many motivations, such as the desire to make a living or the need to create something aesthetically pleasing but it can also reach out into the wider community to help assist the less fortunate, to provide sustenance to those who need it or to give purpose to those who may lack direction. According to Baggini, 'the sharing of meals is one of the simplest and most powerful ways of making someone welcome, signalling an assumption of benevolence rather than mutual suspicion'.[5] The idea of using food and drink in non-profit driven, benevolent ways, has more recently begun to manifest itself in the form of social gastronomy.

4 James McCauley, 'What's next for the Irish Pub', *Brainstorm*. Available at: <https://www.rte.ie/brainstorm/2020/0507/1136959-pubs-ireland-future-coronavirus/> (Accessed 17 October 2020).

5 Julian Baggini, *The Virtues of the Table: How to Eat and Think* (London: Granta publications, 2014), p. 249.

Social Gastronomy in the Past

One of the most interesting early examples of social gastronomy was the fascinating interventions made by the Victorian celebrity chef Alexis Soyer at the height of the great Irish Famine 1845–1849. Because of his exploits at the time, one could argue that Soyer was one of the world's most prominent early social gastronomists. He had a fascinating background as a young French chef who worked his way up to the very highest levels in Victorian England to eventually became head chef at the famous Reform Club. Throughout his well-publicised career Soyer would go on to be considered ahead of his time by branding his products, engaging with partner companies and developing kitchen inventions including a very successful small stove that proved very useful in terms of later wartime exploits. He developed sauces and condiments and put his name to various culinary enterprises. He developed a relationship with Crosse and Blackwell who promoted his products. These included Soyer's Relish and Soyer's Sultanas. Later even Soyer's Nectar lemonade appeared. A prolific author, Soyer's first book *Gastronomic Regenerator* did particularly well. Soon after he published *Charitable Cookery* and later *The Modern Housewife* in 1849 and *The Shilling Cookery Book* in 1854. Soyer had a gregarious nature throughout his life and featured heavily in the media at the time as a man about town. In his later years he went on to assist the war effort in Crimea 1855, enhancing the army kitchens and systems, developing diets for field hospitals as well as training pamphlets for military cooks.

One of his most important contributions was in food and drink innovation and Alexis Soyer was always keen to display his expertise in that regard. The devastating Irish famine provided him with a suitable opportunity.

> The Soup Kitchen Act of 1847 called for food to be distributed under Sir Robert Peel's Relief Commission. But with British taxpayers unwilling to pay for Irish needs, the government was overly dependent on private benevolence. Quaker soup kitchens were rarely productive or efficient enough.[6]

6   Maggie Armstrong, 'Celebrity chef with a recipe for the Famine', *The Irish Times*

Alexis Soyer attempted to assist with the design of a complex soup kitchen mass catering invention. On 5 April 1847 he came to Ireland to demonstrate his innovative design. The showcase event pictured below was attended by various local dignitaries and took place on the esplanade of the Royal Barracks (now the National Museum at Collins Barracks) in Dublin. To considerable local fanfare Soyer had come up with an invention that was allegedly capable of feeding 1,000 diners per hour. At the time Soyer's efforts were widely perceived as part of the British reaction to the famine crisis.[7] The showcase was described in detail by Ruth Cowen in her book as follows:

> At forty-eight feet long by forty wide, the enormous soup kitchen occupied 2,000 square feet. Once inside, the VIPs were suitably impressed with the highly organised, conveyor-belt feeding system that Soyer had created. There was a large door at each end of the room, and in the middle a dais, on which stood a massive thirteen-foot, 300-gallon soup boiler on wheels. Beside it was a bread oven, capable of baking a hundredweight of bread at a time, and both were heated by a single fire contained within a sunken coal pit. Around the boiler eight six-foot-wide iron bain marie used the residual heat to keep a further 1,000 gallons of soup warm, and at each end were a carefully designed array of chopping tables, storage tubs, drawers and shelves. Around the roof pillars were circular tin boxes to house condiments, and in each corner of the huge room ventilation safes doubled as storage areas for the meat, vegetables and grain. Under the eaves, vast water butts held 1,792 gallons of water. Against three of the wall's long tables, eighteen inches wide, were cut with rows of holes, each just big enough to hold a white enamelled bowl, and to each bowl a metal spoon was attached by a fine chain. Tin water boxes, placed at ten-foot intervals along the trestles, were furnished with sponges for the helpers to rinse out the bowls between each sitting. It was all as carefully thought out as the time and labour-saving techniques Soyer had introduced in the Reform Club kitchens, only simplified and enlarged.[8]

[online], 28 August 2010. Available at: <https://www.irishtimes.com/life-and-style/people/celebrity-chef-with-a-recipe-for-the-famine-1.644034> (Accessed 1 September 2021).

7   Ruth Cowen, 'A broth of a boy', in *The Extraordinary Life of Alexis Soyer, Victorian Celebrity Chef*, Kindle Edition (London: The Orion Publishing Group Ltd., 2010), Chapter 7.

8   Ibid.

Though largely a publicity stunt sponsored by the British Government who wanted to be seen to do something, according to Cowen, Soyer was genuinely trying to help. Although soup kitchens would eventually be set up all over Ireland, they were considered too late, and the recipes used were so variable and removed from Soyer's specific instructions they didn't have the desired effect. Soyer's failure was ultimately criticised by the press, according to Cowen. Although Alexis Soyer's soup kitchen marvel didn't impact in any material way on the many tragic outcomes of Ireland's famine it does demonstrate an early example of the culinary power we have come to associate with more contemporary celebrity chef culture.[9]

Contemporary Celebrity and Social Gastronomy

There are many recent examples of celebrity chefs intervening for the greater societal good. These examples can take several different forms. They can occur at a national policy level, as in the case Jamie Oliver's national campaign to improve school meals in Britain where the well-known celebrity chef launched a media campaign in 2005 to encourage the UK government to improve the quality of the school dinner offering in Britain.[10] Social gastronomic change can also take place in smaller more practical ways as demonstrated by that same chef's restaurant Fifteen. Originally developed as part of an initiative that was broadcast

9   A graphic representation of Alexis Soyer's Soup Kitchen demonstration in Dublin on 5 in April 1847, in *The Illustrated London News, 17 April 1847*. (Digitised by <http://multitext.ucc.ie/>) The article by Donal Fallon, 'Soyer's Soup Kitchen, 1847', is available in *Come Here to me: Dublin Life and Culture* group blog. Available at: <https://comeheretome.com/2014/04/11/soyers-soup-kitchen-1847/> (Accessed 2 September 2021).

10 Daniel Boffey, 'Jamie Oliver's healthy school dinners continue to boost learning, study shows', *The Guardian* [online], 10 April 2011. Available at: <https://www.theguardian.com/education/2011/apr/10/school-dinners-jamie-oliver> (Accessed 7 July 2021).

as a Channel 4 series *Jamie's Kitchen*, it ended with the creation of a restaurant that thrived long after the cameras stopped rolling. Although the restaurant eventually closed in 2019, along with many others due to economic pressures, it achieved considerable success in terms of helping young people in difficulty:

> When in 2002 Jamie Oliver launched Fifteen, a not-for-profit restaurant designed to train up 15 disadvantaged, young, unemployed candidates into chefs, few expected it would be a success. The initiative was broadcast as a Channel 4 series – *Jamie's Kitchen* – and ended with 12 apprentices completing the programme (three dropped out) and a restaurant that remained solidly booked out for months ... Last week, after 17 years and up to 150 graduates, Fifteen London closed its doors, along with the rest of Oliver's restaurant empire in the UK.[11]

Despite its eventual failure, the concept gave 150 disadvantaged young people significant life opportunities through its culinary training programme. Fifteen is just one high profile example of the practical difference social gastronomy can make in the lives of the disadvantaged. There are many other examples where culinary training intervention has changed the lives of other communities such as long-term prisoners,[12] people with disabilities[13] and a variety of other community groups that have benefitted from culinary and hospitality interventions.

---

11 Nosheen Iqbal, 'Jamie Oliver gave us our big break in the kitchen – And he's still our hero', *The Guardian* [online], 26 May 2019. Available at: <https://www.theg uardian.com/food/2019/may/26/jamie-oliver-fifteen-gave-us-big-break-still-our-hero> (Accessed 8 July 2021).

12 Kenya McCullum, 'Prison culinary training programs change lives and provide a second chance', We are Chefs.com. Available at: <https://wearechefs.com/a-rec ipe-for-success-prison-culinary-training-programs-change-lives-and-provide-a-sec ond-chance/> (Accessed 23 August 2021).

13 'An Tearmann Cafe: Service with a smile, coffee shop with a difference', Available at: <https://www.camphill.ie/thebridge/An-Tearmann> (Accessed 21 August 2021).

Social Gastronomy and the Best Restaurant in the World

One of the world's best-known restaurants of recent years has been Noma in Copenhagen. Founded in 2003 the restaurant has led the globe in terms of culinary innovation and was considered the best restaurant in the world on four separate occasions by the *San Pellegrino Best Restaurant Competition*:

> [I]n 2012 *Time Magazine* named René Redzepi as one of the World's 100 Most Influential People, not just for putting Denmark on the world's gastronomic map, but also because his passion for promoting food innovation is influencing a whole new generation of chefs around the world.[14]

In addition to its many accolades, the restaurant has also been feted for its considerable social gastronomy output down through the years. Noma was co-founded by Clause Meyer and René Redzepi and the team behind Noma have been trying to achieve several social gastronomy objectives far beyond the initial ambition of running one of the world's best restaurants. According to Kieran Morris:

> The New Nordic movement heralded another shift in the world of fine dining. In our current era of climate emergency and brutal inequality, celebrity chefs have transformed again, from ruthless kitchen dictators such as Gordon Ramsay and Marco Pierre White, or mad scientists such as Ferran Adrià, into crusaders for a better world. Where once the dream was to cook for presidents, now the aim is to work with them.[15]

Morris suggests that 'Noma is now reaching beyond farms and fine-dining restaurants, and into halls of power, supermarket aisles, canteens and classrooms'.[16] A number of social gastronomic outputs have emerged:

---

14   Available at: <https://www.visitdenmark.com/denmark/things-do/danish-food/restaurant-noma> (Accessed 4 August 2021).

15   Kieran Morris, 'What Noma did next: How the "New Nordic" is reshaping the food world', *The Guardian* [online], 28 February 2020. Available at: <https://www.theguardian.com/food/2020/feb/28/what-noma-did-next-new-nordic-food-rene-redzepi-claus-meyer-locavore-foraging> (Accessed 4 August 2021).

16   Ibid.

> Meyer has also created a food training programme in Denmark's prisons to reduce recidivism ... Meyer has opened restaurants and cooking schools in Bolivia to help revive the nation's hospitality industry. Dan Giusti, the former executive head chef at Noma took a step that many in his profession would find curious, if not professionally suicidal. He left Noma to start a company that would be philanthropic, beneficial on a daily basis to others: to revolutionize the lunches served in schools with fresh ingredients and made from scratch techniques.[17]

There are other Noma chefs of note. In Albania, Fejsal Demiraj, one of Noma's current sous chefs runs a foundation that researches and catalogues the nation's village recipes to give the country a documented culinary history for the first time. Redzepi himself has set up a non-profit organisation called Mad (which means 'food' in Danish) that partnered with the UN to prevent environmental damage of food production in 2019.[18] These examples all help demonstrate a concerted effort on the part of the Noma restaurant community to improve people's lives through food. Noma's activities are mirrored by a multitude of other social gastronomy projects that are happening throughout the world. The previously mentioned Social Gastronomy Movement's website provides a useful interactive map detailing many projects that allow us to consider how food and drink moves beyond the confines of mercantile experiences and into a more social gastronomic realm.

> The SGM Map is a unique systems map that increases the visibility of Social Gastronomy communities around the globe and supports them to connect with each other, share skills, raise funds, and collaborate on areas of common interest across sectors and regions. This public version of the Map allows anyone to search organization and member profiles by geographic region, primary type of activity, keywords, type of Sustainable Development Goal (SDG), and sector.[19]

17   Laurie Werner, 'How a Noma chef is trying to change school lunches', *Forbes* [online], 28 April 2018. Available at: <https://www.forbes.com/sites/lauriewerner/2018/04/28/how-a-noma-chef-is-trying-to-change-school-lunches/?sh=238983891543> (Accessed 16 April 2021).

18   Morris, 'What Noma did next'.

19   Social Gastronomy Movement Map. Available at: <https://www.socialgastronomy.org/about-us#sg> (Accessed 12 August 2021).

The SGM Map provides an important focal point for those committed culinary practitioners who want to reach out to both communities and each other to progress their important social remit.

Another important example of social gastronomy in action concerns the work of José Andréas and the World Central Kitchen (WCK), an organisation he founded in 2010 which 'uses the power of food to nourish communities and strengthen economies through times of crisis and beyond'.[20] The organisation carries out the very complex task of providing food in particularly difficult situations. One of the most recent examples of this concerns the earthquake in Haiti which has had a truly devastating impact on local communities and killed thousands of people. The immediate response of the WCK is recorded in the news section of their website.

> With the help of WCK's Chef Mi-Sol and the culinary students at École des Chefs in Port-au-Prince, we got our first Relief Kitchen up and running within 24 hours of the earthquake. For a week now, both current culinary students and recent graduates have been preparing thousands of sandwiches and cooking local dishes for first responders and neighbours in need.[21]

The most recent global crisis in Ukraine offers another example of World Central Kitchens rapid response.

> Working at a 24-hour pedestrian border crossing in southern Poland, WCK began serving hot, nourishing meals within hours of the initial invasion, and we are now serving round-the-clock dishes at eight border crossings across the country. Additionally, we are supporting local restaurants preparing meals in 12 Ukrainian cities including in Odessa, Lviv, and Kyiv. WCK teams are also on the ground serving thousands of meals every day in Romania, Moldova, and Hungary.[22]

20   World Central Kitchen, Available at: <https://wck.org/mission> (Accessed 20 July 2021).
21   World Central Kitchen, 'One week after the earthquake: #ChefsForHaiti update'. Available at: <https://wck.org/news/wck-haiti-earthquake-update> (Accessed 20 August 2021).
22   World Central Kitchen, 'Fearing for their safety, thousands of families flee Ukraine'. Available at: <https://wck.org/relief/activation-chefs-for-ukraine> (Accessed 21 March 2022).

Social Gastronomy and Education

The education community have always been engaged in social gastronomy projects and there are many examples of students and lecturers using their culinary skills to assist the community beyond the confines of the classroom. However there has recently been a more formal approach to social gastronomy in terms of classroom delivery and Annette Sweeney, Senior Lecturer in Culinary Arts and the team in TU Dublin have been at the forefront of that engagement with the development and piloting of a new innovative module as part of their level six culinary training programmes entitled Creativity and Social Gastronomy. The module is part of the Mindful Kitchen Project that encourages the development of unique modules that consider food and drink beyond its normal interpretation. It was the result of a co-created process that involved Annette, lecturing colleagues and substantial input from culinary students themselves:

> The module design uses the application of a mindful approach to module learning outcomes, for example – to their own lives, understanding character strengths, the role of positive emotions, and the potential of kindness and compassion. It also seeks to heighten awareness with regard to the lives of others, for example, food producers, to really understand and respect produce, and to those they will encounter as part of social gastronomy activity. Mindful creativity is explored through practical challenges. The tag line for the activity of the module is: Interconnections – Nourishing Lives – Making a Difference.[23]

As part of the programme students have been formally engaging with the local community to develop initiatives that help feed local disadvantaged groups. They have also developed a programme of cookery demonstrations that are designed to assist community groups to improve their own skills so that their families can benefit from better nutrition. According to Annette, 'the module itself is grounded in the concept of mindfulness

---

23   TU Dublin Impact, 'The mindful kitchen: Creativity and social gastronomy.' Available at: <https://tudublinimpact.wordpress.com/2021/05/13/the-mindful-kitchen-creativity-and-social-gastronomy/> (Accessed 23 August 2021).

and selfcare that must now make up the profile of any successful culinary practitioner'.[24]

Social Gastronomy and the Community Pub

In an earlier chapter the social value that the pub can bring to an area was emphasised. Although the term community pub is not one that is frequently used, many have regarded their local pub as such. Rick Muir, citing Boston, describes the essence of a community pub in his 2012 report entitled *Pubs and Places: The social value of the community pub*:

> Community pubs have two distinct but intrinsically related functions. One is as a retail outlet to sell alcoholic drinks and the other is as a place for social interaction. The drink and the socialising of course go hand in hand: after a few alcoholic drinks, the often-random social encounters that occur in pubs become much easier as people shed their inhibitions. A pub without drink would not be a pub.[25]

While there can be considerable confusion over the definition of what a pub is and whether it might be better described as a bar, tavern or inn there is no doubting the clear function of these places, particularly in a social context. Much of the provision detailed in Muir's report centres around the idea that the pub provides additional functions beyond the mere provision of drink. As we have seen, earlier authors such Share,[26] Scarborough[27] and Murphy[28] have been keen to emphasise that the Irish

---

24   Interview with Annette Sweeney on 23 August 2021.
25   Rick Muir, *Pubs and Places: The Social Value of the Community Pub* (Dublin: Institute of Public Policy Research, 2012), p. 5.
26   Perry Share, 'A genuine "third place"? Towards an understanding of the pub in contemporary Irish society' (Sociological Association Ireland Conference, Cavan, 2003).
27   Gwen Scarborough, *The Irish Pub as a 'Third Place': A Sociological Exploration of People, Place and Identity* (PhD Thesis, Institute of Technology Sligo, 2008).
28   Brian Murphy, 'The Irish pub abroad: Lessons in the commodification of gastronomic culture', in Máirtín Mac Con Iomaire and Eamon Maher (eds), '*Tickling the*

pub fulfils many of Oldenburg's place attributes. The United Kingdom has quite a long tradition of supporting the community pub and there are many instances where UK pubs have provided a range of ancillary social services to local communities such as libraries, shops and playgrounds. Until very recently Ireland has been lacking in this regard. It could be argued that the fact that so many Irish pubs have traditionally been family owned has led to a situation where the local pub already forms an integral part of the community. A recent report from Loughborough University in England explored, in detail, the role of the pub in alleviating loneliness. One stakeholder interviewed in the report notes: 'We've seen kind of a big decrease over the last ten years in places like community centres, parish halls, even churches, and pubs quite often, especially in rural areas, are the last place that's almost a public meeting space for people.'[29] The pub has the potential to combat the decline in availability of places, in both rural and urban communities, where local people can meet each other and talk. The ban on bar counter service due to the Covid crisis was particularly cruel in this regard. Bar seating areas in pubs are largely dominated by people (usually, older men) who visit the premises on their own rather than as part of a group, which would normally gravitate towards the tables. As another stakeholder in the Loughborough study notes: 'People don't visit a pub just for the alcohol, it's the social interaction quite often … If they sit near the bar, then usually they want a bit of social interaction, you know, they want to be spoken to, you know, really, that's how I see it.'[30]

Palate': Gastronomy in Irish Literature and Culture (Oxford: Peter Lang, 2014), pp. 191–205.

29 Thomas Thurnell-Read, 'Open arms: The role of pubs in tackling loneliness'. Loughborough University, p. 25. Available at: <https://hdl.handle.net/2134/13663 715.V1> (Accessed 28 August 2021).

30 Ibid., p. 15.

Two Types of Community Pub

There are two distinct types of community pub. The first are pubs that
are purchased by the community for the benefit of that community.
This is quite a common occurrence in the UK, much less so in Ireland.
According to the Plunkett Foundation, a registered charity that supports
the UK community pub sector, there were 119 known community pubs
in the UK in 2019.[31] These pubs are described in the organisations most
recent report as follows:

> Community pubs are owned by members (also known as shareholders) and are run
> democratically on the basis of one-member-one-vote. Membership is voluntary,
> affordable, and open to all in a community, and is the mechanism for ensuring the
> community has a genuine say in how the business is run. This is what gives com-
> munity pubs longevity, as member control and input ensures the pub business is
> continually adapting and serving the needs of its members and wider community.[32]

The prevalence of community pubs in the UK has helped develop local
areas and provides much needed services that otherwise might be removed. It is a model that has grown consistently from the latest data available before the recent Covid 19 pandemic; however, the impact of the
pandemic on the sector remains to be seen although according to Helen
Aldis, Vice Chair of the Plunkett Foundation:

> The months ahead will doubtless be daunting for pubs – and this should never be
> underestimated. But because community pubs so often are more than a pub – offering
> services that may include post offices, cafés, convenience stores, farmers' markets,
> community garden and allotments, affordable housing and renewable energy – they
> are uniquely rooted in community needs. This special connection with the commu-
> nity is what makes community pubs such valuable and unique assets – and what also
> gives them increased financial resilience.[33]

31   *Community Pubs: A Better Form of Business 2020*, report by The Plunkett
     Foundation (2020), p. 2.
32   Ibid.
33   Ibid., p. 3.

Image 11. Maudies, Rathgormack Co. Waterford.

Conor Kane, 'Waterford residents unite to save local pub', *RTÉ News* [online], 9 September 2021. Available at: <https://www.rte.ie/news/regional/2021/0909/1245616-waterford-pub/> (Accessed 9 September 2021).

Up until recently Ireland has not had any community pubs as defined by the Plunkett Foundation but very recently one rural pub, Maudies, in Rathgormack Co Waterford (pictured below) was saved from closure when a group of nineteen local people moved to ensure that Maudie's would remain at the heart of the local community. 'They put up around €12,000 each to buy the popular spot and have been busy putting their various skills to use in renovating it internally and externally over recent months.'[34]

It's important to note that the stated purpose of the purchase was not for profit and the owners pictured above have a clear social gastronomic objective in mind given the pubs central role in such a small rural community:

34 Caroline Allen, 'Rural pub saved by actions of "Village"' people'. *Agriland* [online], Available at: <https://www.agriland.ie/farming-news/rural-pub-saved-by-actions-of-village-people/> (Accessed 1 August 2021).

It's the heart of the place. This will be my son's local too when I'm dead and buried. Not one of us cares if we make a penny out of it. It's all about keeping this place open and keeping people together.[35]

The second type of community pub, and perhaps more common in an Irish context, are pubs which are privately owned but also provide a considerable community function. Many family-owned Irish pubs fit into this category. They have a long tradition of supporting the local community in many ways. They assist with fund raising, support local sports teams and provide free meeting spaces for a wide variety of community groups and get togethers. They can act as informal hubs for casual job recruitment, can provide support for the lonely and integrate themselves into every aspect of local life. The same is true of many British pubs and the UK is unique in how it supports this second type of community pub. This is done through the work of not-for-profit state organisations such as The Pub is the Hub. Originally inspired and set up by Prince Charles in 2001, according to their own remit, Pub is the Hub,

> act(s) as a guide – an independent sounding board, a source of advice, with a wealth of experience and local knowledge to support rural pubs and communities to reach common goals. We also advise communities considering collective ownership partnerships and give them access to the advice they may need to save or maintain their local services also involving the pub. As well as generating awareness and mobilising communities, we seek to influence regional (and national) policy and practice in rural services and related public sectors. We respond to particular current local and national needs, developing different, flexible and innovative business approaches to supporting the appropriate community services within the pub by a good licensee.[36]

The organisation supports the pubs on its books in developing additional community focused services that can run alongside a successful pub business. There are numerous case study examples on the organisations

35   Michelle Flemming, 'Iconic Irish bar undergoing major changes to make it "lady-friendly" after being bought by regulars', *The Irish Mirror* [online], 25 July 2021. Available at: <https://www.irishmirror.ie/lifestyle/iconic-irish-bar-undergoing-major-24611775> (Accessed 12 August 2021).

36   Pubisthehub.org. Available at: <https://www.pubisthehub.org.uk/about/> (Accessed 1 September 2021).

website and ancillary services offered and supported by *The Pub is the Hub* include community playgrounds, community gardens, allotments, book clubs/libraries, heritage and history centres and many more.

Conclusion

This chapter demonstrates that the food and drink sector can provide for the needs of local communities well beyond the provision of food and drink products and services. We have seen both historical and contemporary examples of chefs, restaurants and food businesses gathering together to support social gastronomy projects. We have noted how the culinary education sector in Ireland is making advances in developing curriculum that informs an awareness of the importance of social gastronomy among future chefs. Food and drink places, in their many guises, are increasingly seen by local communities as places where they might congregate, support each other, work remotely and provide distribution points for much needed local services, many of which have deteriorated down through the years. One of the important traits of the Fourth Space engagement model mentioned throughout this book centres around the ultimate motivation of a food and drink business. Social gastronomy is a way for food and drink businesses to demonstrate their function beyond pure mercantile gain. Although it doesn't apply to all business there are sufficient examples emerging to provide considerable hope that the food and drink sector is well positioned in terms of its social ambitions thus proving that, from the heyday of Alexis Soyer to more recent well-meaning community interventions, social gastronomy will continue to function at the very heart of Ireland's food and drink culture.

Afterword

The introduction to this book expressed a desire that this work would seek to bring together several food and drink themes and explore how they might relate to our past, present and future lives. By exploring these areas, something perhaps more personal and reflective than originally envisaged has emerged. Many of the themes discussed have been mirrored by a lifetime of engagement with the food and drink world. Using the lens of that personal experience, the book incorporates the work of many well-known writers in the field, throughout its various sections. The hope is that it offers a new perspective on our traditional understanding of the food and drink studies area. One that provides a focal point for further academic discussion and encourages that discourse to move well beyond the consideration of food as a mere source of sustenance, as alluded to in the book's title.

The content has considered the fact that, up until recently, the area of food and drink studies has struggled somewhat to establish itself as a valid academic domain. This is clearly demonstrated both in the introduction and in other chapters in the work. As someone who is borne out of a food community, it can be difficult to fathom why this is so. Perhaps the nature of food and drink pathways down through the centuries became overly intertwined with servility rather than service. As a subject area attached to what were once considered the lower senses, it may not have been considered worthy of academic interest in the same way that other areas have been. It's also true that, as a nation, the Irish have sometimes lacked confidence in terms of expressing their own unique food identity in the same way that other nations have. In an article reviewing Dr JP McMahon's recent publication *The Irish Cookbook*, Chloe King cites the well-known chef who says:

> A tendency to downplay the quality of Irish food has been and is still, to a degree, commonplace. 'It's a complex issue and it is a historical issue,' he says. 'I think it's a legacy of colonisation and a legacy of the famine where we are not as confident as

other cultures who possibly in the 19th Century were building their food cultures from scratch, and unfortunately that wasn't what happened in Ireland ...[37]

And yet, a newfound confidence in our food culture is reflected in how we as a nation now think about food and drink. The ideas expressed within the chapters of this book reflect this. Chapter 2 demonstrated how Ireland's food and drink culture has developed rapidly in recent years and how we have changed the way we engage with food and drink products and places. Such changes have been complemented by new avenues of research that are emerging from within the wider gastronomic community itself. Chapter 4 alludes to this, particularly in terms of the beverage studies area.

The developments in our food and drink culture have also opened food and drink discussion to many other academic fields and indeed one of the great strengths of the area is its ability to facilitate multidisciplinary research. We now see a great deal of food related research output from academics who come from the fields of history, literature, art, language and others. Many are referenced in this work. These academics increasingly view food and drink studies as a viable area of research and one that frequently intersects with their own specialisms. Their contributions are welcome and further position food and drink studies as an attractive area of academic discourse. Chapter 3 of the book helps demonstrate how such different cultural fields intersect and the potential for continued collaboration.

This book also speaks to the food and drink practitioners and the academic contribution they too have been making. Many chapters serve to recognise the importance of practical expertise not only in terms of the delivery of food and drink services but also in understanding the sector. As new centres of food studies begin to emerge, the input of those with hands-on experience becomes ever more prominent. New researchers are entering the academic space with increasingly recognisable university level qualifications in food and drink domains. They combine practical competence

---

37   Chloe King ' The rise of Irish food: A world class cuisine getting the recognition it deserves', Great British Chefs.com [online], 10 November 2021. Available at: <https://www.greatbritishchefs.com/features/rise-of-modern-irish-food> (Accessed 25 April 2022).

with academic ambition. The nature of these qualifications allows these graduates to collaborate in multidisciplinary ways. Such collaborations are suited to newer more non-traditional educational models and they have a great deal to offer in terms of how a future focused Ireland will continue to interpret its food and drink culture.

The newfound food confidence mentioned above also allows Ireland the ability to be more critical when its gaze turns outwards for inspiration. Many of the chapters here demonstrate the importance of the gastronomic experience in other countries. France is still the natural home of food and drink culture and links between our two nations are strong. Indeed, we have traditionally looked to the French nation for culinary guidance or even validation. But even in this respect, Ireland's food and drink culture is changing. We still take on board aspects of French gastronomy and incorporate them into our new food settings but now we value our own food identity in equal measure. Chapters 9 and 10 reflect this as does the incorporation of the *terroir* concept into the Fourth Space model which is used throughout the book.

Finally, recent history has reminded us of the necessity to adapt to new situations and of the fact that we as a nation are capable of considerable innovation and change. Chapter 11, 12 and 13 offer practical examples of emerging phenomenon that demonstrate this but also emphasise that in order to make a leap forward it is sometimes important to take a look back. History can help a great deal in interpreting how best to advance in the future and that's exactly what this book tries to do. It tries to learn from the past and to use both what's learned, and what's been missed to help inform future food and drink engagement. The work foregrounds the tremendous food and drink potential in Ireland and highlights the fact that we may be on the cusp of a new approach to our food and drink culture. One that allows us to interpret gastronomy in our own way, without an over reliance on outside influences, while recognising the potential contribution of new research in the field. In that way, we can start to truly consider the value of the foods we eat and the drinks we imbibe, beyond their ability to sate a hunger or quench a thirst, thus conferring Ireland's food and drink culture with the credit it has always deserved.

Bibliography

Allen, Caroline, 'Rural pub saved by actions of "Village" people', *Agriland* [online]. Available at: <https://www.agriland.ie/farming-news/rural-pub-saved-by-actions-of-village-people/> (Accessed 1 August 2021).

Amine, Lyn Suzanne, 'Country of origin animosity and consumer response: Marketing implications of anti-Americanism and Francophobia', *International Business Review*, 17, 2008, pp. 402–422.

Anon, 'After rating thousands of Ireland's hotels, restaurants and galleries, Lonely Planet advises tourists: Go to the pub!' *Daily Mail* [online], 12 January 2012. Available at: <https://www.dailymail.co.uk/news/article-2085612/Lonely-Planet-travel-guide-Ireland-advises-tourists-Go-pub.html> (Accessed 12 February 2019).

Anon, 'Airfield estate in Dundrum announced as food on The Edge 2021 Venue', 24 June 2021. Available at: <https://foodontheedge.ie/news/ (Accessed 31 August 2021).

Anon, 'An Tearmann Café: Service with a smile, coffee shop with a difference'. Available at: <https://www.camphill.ie/thebridge/An-Tearmann> (Accessed 21 August 2021).

Anon, 'Au revoir freedom fries', *The New York Times*, 4 August 2006, p. 16.

Anon, 'Beaujolais Nouveau: History behind the third Thursday in November'. Intowine.com. Available at: <http://www.intowine.com/beaujolais2.html> (Accessed 10 March 2019).

Anon, 'Cahors rejuvenates wine tourism'. *French Wine News* [online]. Available at: <http://www.frenchwinenews.com/cahors-rejuvenates-wine-tourism/> (Accessed 6 April 2012).

Anon, 'Dublin Airport passengers offered tours of Walsh Whiskey Distillery – virtually', *Sips and Stories*. Available at: <https://www.walshwhiskey.com/1277/dublin-airport-virtual-walsh-whiskey-distillery-tours/> (Accessed 9 October 2021).

Anon, 'Fearing for their safety, thousands of families flee Ukraine'. World Central Kitchen. Available at: <https://wck.org/relief/activation-chefs-for-ukraine> (Accessed 21 March 2022).

Anon, 'Fèis Ìle 2021: 1st June was a good day with Laphroaig'. Available at: <https://www.laphroaig.com/en/feis-ile-2021> (Accessed 27 October 2021).

Anon, 'French vineyards blow dust off the barrels and embrace a digital revolution in wine', The Conversation, [online] 30 December 2015. Available at: <https://theconversation.com/french-vineyards-blow-dust-off-the-barrels-and-embrace-a-digital-revolution-in-wine-50544> (Accessed 14 November 2021).

Anon, 'From quantity to quality'. *The Economist*. Available at: <http://www.economist.com/node/10926392> (Accessed 7 May 2015).

Anon, 'In 2015 is it an Irish pub or a pub from Ireland?' The Irish Pub Global Federation, 2015. Available at: <https://www.irishpubsglobal.com/irish-pub-company-2015-irish-pub-pub-ireland/> (Accessed 31 January 2020).

Anon, 'International arrivals by world region'. Our World in Data. Available at: <https://ourworldindata.org/tourism> (Accessed 7 November 2021).

Anon, 'Irish whiskey sector back on track with further success in sight', *Irish Times* [online], 9 September 2021. Available at: <https://www.irishtimes.com/business/agribusiness-and-food/irish-whiskey-sector-back-on-track-with-further-success-in-sight-1.4668585> (Accessed 27 November 2021).

Anon, 'IrishWhiskey360° the Irish Whiskey initiative unveiled', Irish Whiskey Magazine [online], 10 September 2019. Available at: <https://www.irishwhiskeymagazine.com/news/latest-news/irishwhiskey360-the-irish-whiskey-initiative-unveiled/> (Accessed 3 September 2021).

Anon, 'Made with care – Coffee artists'. Available at: <https://www.nespresso.com/ie/en/commitments/coffee-farmers?> (Accessed 4 October 2021).

Anon, 'Michelin guide 2020: Full list of Irish restaurants and what the judges said', *Irish Times* [online], 8 October 2019. Available at: <https://www.irishtimes.com/life-and-style/food-and-drink/michelin-guide-2020-full-list-of-irish-restaurants-and-what-the-judges-said-1.4043663> (Accessed 31 January 2020).

Anon, 'Muscadet at its Zenith', *French Wine News* [online]. Available at: <http://www.frenchwinenews.com/muscadet-at-its-zenith/> (Accessed 16 March 2012).

Anon, 'One for the road', Independent.ie, 7 May 2008. Available at: <http://www.independent.ie/irish-news/one-for-the-road-26500016.html> (Accessed 14 May 2019).

Anon, 'One week after the earthquake: #ChefsForHaiti update'. World Central Kitchen. Available at: <https://wck.org/news/wck-haiti-earthquake-update> (Accessed 20 August 2021).

Anon, 'Pernod Ricard: FY20 full-year sales and results'. Businesswire.com Available at: <https://www.businesswire.com/news/home/20200901006151/en/Pernod-Ricard-FY20-Full-year-Sales-and-Results> (Accessed 3 December 2021).

Anon, 'Prince Philip eyes Guinness during bar visit', 15 December 2011. Available at: <http://www.abc.net.au/news/2011-05-19/prince-philip-eyes-guinness/2719622> (Accessed 14 May 2019).

Anon, 'Report finds every county in Ireland has fewer pubs than in 2005', *Irish Examiner* [online], 5 September 2018. Available at: <https://www.irishexami ner.com/news/arid-30866864.html> (Accessed 27 November 2021).

Anon, 'Six new Australian wine ambassadors to be unveiled in Japan this evening', Wine Titles Media [online] 3 May 2014. Available at: <https://winetitles.com. au/six-new-australian-wine-ambassadors-to-be-unveiled-in-japan-this-even ing/> (Accessed 20 March 2020).

Anon, 'Smooth operator - Nespresso winning coffee wars', Independent.ie. [online] 14 June 2014. Available at: <https://www.independent.ie/business/irish/smo oth-operator-nespresso-winning-coffee-wars-30507256.html> (Accessed 20 June 2020).

Anon, 'Starbucks becomes third largest coffee chain in Ireland'. Available at: <https:// www.hospitalityireland.com/restaurant/starbucks-becomes-third-largest-cof fee-chain-ireland-53903> (Accessed 14 August 2020).

Anon, 'The Waiting Game', *The Irish Times*, 29 December 1998 [online]. Available at: <https://www.irishtimes.com/culture/the-waiting-game-1.229340> (Accessed 26 June 2020).

Anon, 'Visiting Irish pub "essential" to 80% of tourists', Drink Industry Ireland [online]. Available at: <https://www.drinksindustryireland.ie/visiting-irish-pub-essential-to-80-of-tourists/> (Accessed 31 January 2020).

Anon, 'Whiskey and food pairing: The fine art for beginners'. Available at: <https:// thewhiskeywash.com/american-whiskey/whiskey-and- food-pairing-the-fine-art-for-beginners/> (Accessed 20 June 2017).

Anon, 'Wine Australia calls on independents to back Regional Heroes campaign'. Harpers.co.uk [online] 5 November 2009. Available at: <https://harpers. co.uk/news/fullstory.php/aid/7614/Wine_Australia_calls_on_independ-ents_to_back_Regional_Heroes_campaign.html> (Accessed 20 March 2020).

Anon, '21 pubs in Ireland you must visit before you die', The Daily Edge.ie [online], 30 November 2013, Available at: <https://www.dailyedge.ie/must-visit-pubs-ireland-1194401-Nov2013/> (Accessed 24 March 2022).

Appadurai Arjun, 'Gastro - politics in Hindu South Asia', *American Ethnologist*, 8 (3), p. 494. Available at: <https://doi.org/10.1525/ae.1981.8.3.02a00050> (Accessed 7 July 2022).

Aquilina, Sarah, 'Jacob's Creek branded content shows an unseen side of Novak Djokovic', Marketing [online]. Available at: <https://www.marketingmag. com.au/news-c/jacobs-creek-branded-content-shows-unseen-side-novak-djokovic/> (Accessed 15 October 2021).

Armstrong, Maggie, 'Celebrity chef with a recipe for the Famine', *The Irish Times* [online], 28 August 2010. Available at: <https://www.irishtimes.com/

life-and-style/people/celebrity-chef-with-a-recipe-for-the-famine-1.644034>
(Accessed 1 September 2021).

Aylward, David, 'Towards a cultural economy paradigm for the Australian wine industry', *Prometheus*, 26 (4), 2008, pp. 373–385.

Bacon, Peter, 'Over-Capacity in the Irish hotel industry and required elements of a recovery programme' (Peter Bacon and Associates, Wexford, 2009).

Baggini, Julian, The *Virtues of the Table: How to Eat and Think* (London: Granta Publications, 2014).

Ballestrini, Pierre, and Paul Gamble, 'Country of origin effects on Chinese wine consumers', *British Food Journal*, 108 (6), 2006, pp. 396–412.

Barich, Bill, *A Pint of Plain: Tradition, Change, and the Fate of the Irish Pub* (New York: Bloomsbury Publishing USA, 2009).

Belasco, Warren, *Food: The Key Concepts* (New York: Berg, 2008).

Bielenberg, Kim, 'Guinness is good for tourism', *The Irish Independent*, 17 December 2011. Available at: <http://www.independent.ie/lifestyle/guinness-is-good-for-tourism-2966533.html> (Accessed 23 January 2015).

Bilkey, Warren and Eric Nes, 'Country of origin effects on product evaluations', *Journal of International Business Studies*, Vol 13 (1), Spring/Summer 1982, pp. 89–100.

Blake Grey, W., 'Music to drink wine by: Vintner insists music can change wines flavours', *San Francisco Chronicle* [online]. Available at: <http://www.sfgate.com/wine/article/Music-to-drink-wine-by-Vintner-insists-music-can-3235602.php> (Accessed 24 April 2014).

Boffey, Daniel, 'Jamie Oliver's healthy school dinners continue to boost learning, study shows', *The Guardian* [online] 10 April 2011. Available at: <https://www.theguardian.com/education/2011/apr/10/school-dinners-jamie-oliver> (Accessed 7 July 2021).

Bohmrich, Roger, 'Terroir: Competing perspectives on the roles of soil, climate and people', *Journal of Wine Research*, 7 (1), 1996, pp. 33–34.

Bord Bia, *The Future of Irish Whiskey Report 2013*. Available at: <www.bordbia.ie/.../bbreports/.../The%20Future%20Of%20Whiskey.pdf> (Accessed 11 March 2015).

Bord Bia, 'Why Ireland'. Available at: <https://www.irishfoodanddrink.com/> (Accessed 25 October 2021).

Bourdieu, Pierre, *Distinction: A Social Critique of the Judgements of Taste*, translated by Richard Niece (Abingdon, Oxon: Routledge Classics, 2010).

Bourdieu, Pierre, 'The forms of capital', in *Handbook of Theory and Research for the Sociology of Education*, edited by J. Richardson (New York: Greenwood Press, 1986).

Boyd, Brian, 'Hit and myth', *The Irish Times* (*Weekend Review*), 21 November 2009, p. 9.

Bramhill, Nick, 'Irish chefs best in world', *Sunday Independent*, 9 January 2011 [online]. Available at: <http://www.independent.ie/national-news/irish-chefs-best-in-world-2489465.html?service=Print> (Accessed 6 October 2012).

Bruwer John and Karin Alant, 'The hedonic nature of wine tourism consumption: An experiential view', *International Journal of Wine Business Research*, 21 (3), 2009, pp. 235–257.

Burke Kennedy, Eoin, 'Midleton Distillery experience to get €13m revamp'. *Irish Times* [online], 29 November 2021. Available at: <https://www.irishtimes.com/business/agribusiness-and-food/midleton-distillery-experience-to-get-13m-revamp-1.4741615> (Accessed 3 December 2021).

Byrne, Brendan, citing Pat Whelan, 'Pat Whelan-building a legacy brand in butchering', www.Think Business.ie, n.d. <https://www.thinkbusiness.ie/articles/pat-whelan-butcher/> (Accessed 5 January 2018).

Carrigy, Aoife, 'Powerful puzzles: Mapping the symbiosis between two great signifiers of Irishness, the writer and the pub'. Available at: <https://arrow.tudublin.ie/dgs/2018/may30/11/> (Accessed 6 September 2020).

Carroll, Rory, '"Ireland is changing": Booze-free bar opens in Dublin', *The Guardian*, 8 May 2019. Available at: <https://www.theguardian.com/world/2019/may/08/ireland-is-changing-booze-free-bar-opens-in-dublin> (Accessed 18 May 2020).

Cawley, Diarmuid, 'A nose for wine: All you need to know about sommeliers'. Available at: <https://www.rte.ie/brainstorm/2019/0314/1036356-a-nose-for-wine-all-you-need-to-know-about-sommeliers/ 14 March, 2019> (Accessed 16 September 2020).

Cawley, Diarmuid, 'All you ever wanted to know about natural wines'. Available at: <https://www.rte.ie/brainstorm/2018/0814/985019-guide-to-natural-wines/ 15 August, 2018> (Accessed 16 September 2020).

Cawley, Diarmuid, 'The power of wine language – Critics, labels and sexism'. Available at: <https://arrow.tudublin.ie/dgs/2018/may30/12/> (Accessed 7 October 2020).

Central Statistics Office, 'Ireland trade in goods 2018'. Available at: <https://www.cso.ie/en/releasesandpublications/ep/p-ti/irelandstradeingoods2018/meatexportsandimports2018/> (Accessed 10 September 2021).

Chaney, Isabella M., 'A comparative analysis of wine reviews', *British Food Journal*, 102 (7), 2000, pp. 472–480.

Chao, Paul and Gupta, Pola, 'Information search and efficiency of consumer choices of new cars, country of origin effects', *International Marketing Review*, 12 (6), 1995, pp. 47–59.

Charters, Steve and Pettigrew, Simone, 'Is wine consumption an aesthetic experience?' *Journal of Wine Research*, 16 (2), 2005, pp.121–136.

Chateau Chunder: When Australian Wine Changed the World, BBC4 Television (2012). Available at: <https://www.bbc.co.uk/programmes/po111zzq> (Accessed 15 March 2020).

Chen, Yeong-Shyang and Wu, Shou-Tsung, 'Social networking practices of Viennese coffeehouse culture and intangible heritage tourism', *Journal of Tourism and Cultural Change*, 17 (2), 2017, pp. 186–207.

CHL Consulting, *CERT Employment Survey of the Tourism Industry in Ireland 2000* (Dublin: CERT Limited, 2000).

Clancy, Tomás, 'An Irish AC proposal'. Available at: <http://tomasclancy.wordpress.com/the-irish-ac-proposal/> (Accessed 7 February 2020).

Clancy, Tomás, 'Around the world with pinot noir'. *The Sunday Business Post*, 8 March 2009. Available at: <http://archives.tcm.ie/businesspost/2009/03/08/story40007.asp> (Accessed 15 July 2018).

Clancy, Tomás, 'Coming our way in wine this year', *The Sunday Business Post Magazine*, 10 January 2016, pp. 28–29.

Clancy, Tomás, 'Scotland the brave and wise', *The Sunday Business Post Magazine*, 1 June 2014, p.10.

Clarke, Donald, 'St Patrick's Day stimulates the nation's need to be twinkly, drunk and sentimental', *Irish Times*, 16 March 2013 [online]. Available at: <http://www.irishtimes.com/culture/heritage/st-patrick-s-day-stimulates-the-nation-s-need-to-be-twinkly-drunk-and-sentimental-1.1327639?page=1> (Accessed 24 June 2021).

Cole, Stroma, 'Beyond authenticity and commodification', *Annals of Tourism Research*, 34 (4), 2007, pp. 943–960.

Community Pubs: A Better Form of Business 2020, The Plunkett Foundation (2020). Available at: <https://icstudies.org.uk/repository/community-pubs-better-form-business-2020> (Accessed 1 August 2021).

Connolly, Robert E., *The Rise and Fall of the Irish Pub* (Dublin: The Liffey Press, 2010).

Cowen, Ruth, 'A broth of a boy', in *The Extraordinary Life of Alexis Soyer, Victorian Celebrity Chef*, Kindle Edition (London: The Orion Publishing Group Ltd, 2010).

Creighton, John, 'Laphroaig friends feedback'. Available at: <http://www.laphroaig.com/friends/chat/Default.aspx?Page=25> (Accessed 18 June 2013).

Curtis, Wayne, 'Cognac's identity crisis: How the liquor's marketing success among both rappers and codgers has blinded consumers to its subtler pleasures', *The Atlantic Magazine*, June 2012[online]. Available at: <http://www.theatlantic.

com/magazine/archive/2012/06/cognacs-identity-crisis/308982/> (Accessed 4 February 2015).

D'Arcy, Patrick, 'How food, yes, food can be a tool for social change', 12 July 2018. Available at: <https://ideas.ted.com/how-food-yes-food-can-be-a-tool-for-soc ial-change/> (Accessed 3 February 2021).

Demoissier, Marion, 'Beyond Terroir: Territorial construction, hegemonic discourses, and French wine culture', *Journal of Royal Anthropological Institute*, 17, 2011, pp. 685–705.

Dervan, Cathal, 'Guinness cash in on Obama's Moneygall visit', Irishcentral.com, 2011, Available at: <http://www.irishcentral.com/news/Guinness-cash-in-on-Obamas-Moneygall-vist--122495959.html> (Accessed 14 June 2018).

Dietler, Michael, 'Feasting and fasting', in *Oxford Handbook on the Archaeology of Ritual and Religion*, edited by Timothy Insoll (Oxford: Oxford University Press, 2012), p. 181.

Digby, Marie Claire, 'Irish butchers beef dripping wins best food product in UK and Ireland', *The Irish Times* [online] 8 September 2015. Available at: <https://www.irishtimes.com/life-and-style/food-and-drink/irish-butcher-s-beef-dripping-wins-best-food-product-in-uk-and-ireland-1.2344248> (Accessed 12 December 2017).

Digby, Marie Claire, 'Waterford Blaa awarded special status by EU', *The Irish Times*, [online] 19 November 2013. Available at: <https://www.irishtimes.com/life-and-style/food-and-drink/waterford-blaa-awarded-special-status-by-eu-1.1599 966> (Accessed 2 January 2018).

Ditterich-Shilakes, Kirsten, 'Muse in a stem glass: Art, wine and philosophy', *Wine and Philosophy: A Symposium on Thinking and Drinking*, edited by Fritz Allhoff (Oxford: Blackwell Publishing, 2008), pp. 44–62.

Doyle, Kevin and Donnelly, Margaret, 'Revealed: The 50 bus routes under new "drink link" plan for rural Ireland', *Independent.ie*, 8 May 2018. Available at: <https://www.independent.ie/business/farming/rural-life/article36885 011.ece> (Accessed 2 February 2020).

Drummond, Gillian, 'New Yorkers shun French restaurants', *Caterer and Hotelkeeper*, 15 May 2003, p. 11.

Durie, Alister, 'The periphery fights back: Tourism and culture in Scotland to 2014', *International Journal of Regional and Local Studies*, 5 (2), 2009, pp. 30–47.

Eads, Lauren, 'Scotch industry "bigger than iron and steel," *The Drinks Business* [online]. Available at: <http://www.thedrinksbusiness.com/2015/01/scotch-industry-bigger-than-iron-and-steel/> (Accessed 20 April 2015).

Egan, Barry, 'I can't see much vertical drinking before Christmas', *The Sunday Independent*, 15 August 2021, p. 11.

El-Beih, Yasmin, 'Coffeehouses helped spread modern democracy, spur the Enlightenment and birth periodical literature. So why did King Charles II's cronies try to ban them?' BBC.com, 19 November 2019. Available at: <https://www.bbc.com/travel/article/20201119-how-coffee-forever-changed-britain> (Accessed 22 March 2022).

Fagan, Honor, 'Globalisation and culture: Placing Ireland', *Annals AAPSS*, 581, 2002, p. 137.

Fáilte Ireland, *Food and Drink Strategy 2018–2023*. Available at: <https://www.failte ireland.ie/FailteIreland/media/WebsiteStructure/Documents/Publications/FI-Food-Strategy-Document.pdf> (Accessed 23 April 2019).

Fáilte Ireland, 'Key tourism facts 2019', 21 March 2021. Available at: <https://www.failteireland.ie/FailteIreland/media/WebsiteStructure/Documents/3_Research_Insights/4_Visitor_Insights/KeyTourismFacts_2019.pdf?ext=.pdf > (Accessed 30 November 2021).

Fáilte Ireland, 'Tourism facts 2005', [online], p. 1. Available at: <http://www.failte ireland.ie/FailteIreland/media/WebsiteStructure/Documents/3_Research_Insights/3_General_SurveysReports/TourismIreland2005.pdf?ext=.pdf> (Accessed 28 September 2012).

Fallon, Donal, 'Soyer's Soup Kitchen, 1847', *Come Here to Me: Dublin Life and Culture*. Available at: <https://comeheretome.com/2014/04/11/soyers-soup-kitchen-1847/> (Accessed 2 September 2021).

Fanning, John, 'Advertising the Black Stuff in Ireland 1959–1999: Through a Guinness glass brightly', *The Irish Times*, 25 July 2020. Available at: <https://www.irishtimes.com/culture/books/advertising-the-black-stuff-in-ireland-1959-1999-through-a-guinness-glass-brightly-1.4306112> (Accessed 10 September 2020).

Fanthom, Órla, Phone Interview carried out by author with former employee of Blake's Restaurant 1982–1885, 6 March 2012.

Feeney, Bernard, *Craft Beer and Independent Microbreweries in Ireland 2018* (Dublin: Bord Bia, 2018).

Fegan, Alex, *The Irish Pub* (Element Pictures Distribution, 2013). Available at: <https://www.imdb.com/title/tt3229518/> (Accessed 3 February 2020).

Felzensztein, Christian, Hubbert, Sally and Vong, Gertrude, 'Is the country of origin the fifth element in the marketing mix of import wine? A critical review of the literature', *Journal of Food Products Marketing*, 10, 2004, pp. 73–84.

Fennel, James and Bunbury, Turtle, *The Irish Pub* (London: Thames and Hudson, 2008).

Ferriter, Diarmuid, 'Drink and society in twentieth-century Ireland', in *Food and Drink in Ireland*, edited by Elisabeth Fitzpatrick and James Kelly (Dublin: The Royal Irish Academy, 2016).

Ferriter, Diarmuid, *Nation of Extremes: Pioneers in Twentieth-century Ireland* (Dublin: Irish Academic Press, 1999).

Fielden, Christopher, *Exploring the World of Wines and Spirits* (London: Wine and Spirit Education Trust, 2005).

Finn, Melanie, 'Almost 350 pubs have closed down since pandemic began'. *Irish Independent*, 17 October 2021 [online]. Available at: <https://www.independ ent.ie/irish-news/almost-350-pubs-have-closed-down-since-pandemic-began-40957271.html> (Accessed 21 November 2021).

Fiorina, Tom, 'Black is back: Cahors Malbec returns to the world stage', *The Vine Route*, 21 March 2010. Available at: <http://www.thevineroute.com/southw est/black-is-back-cahors-malbec/> (Accessed 16 April 2020).

Fitzgerald, Ann, 'After losing five shops, three pubs and the post office, how this rural community is revitalising itself', *Farming Independent* [online], 24 March 2019. Available at: <https://www.independent.ie/business/farming/rural-life/after-losing-five-shops-three-pubs-and-the-post-office-how-this-rural-community-is-revitalising-itself-37926624.html> (Accessed 28 May 2019).

Fitzpatrick, Richard, 'City streets come alive to the sound of spinning yarns', *Irish Examiner*, [online] 16 August 2012. Available at: <http://www.irishexaminer. com/lifestyle/features/humaninterest/city-streets-come-alive-to-the-sound-of-spinning-yarns-204255.html> (Accessed 14 June 2013).

Flemming, Michelle, 'Iconic Irish bar undergoing major changes to make it "lady-friendly" after being bought by regulars', *The Irish Mirror* [online], 25 July 2021. Available at: <https://www.irishmirror.ie/lifestyle/iconic-irish-bar-undergo ing-major-24611775> (Accessed 12 August 2021).

Foley, Anthony, The contribution of the drinks industry to Irish tourism, 2017, 14. Available at: <https://vfipubs.ie/wp-content/uploads/2017/09/DIGI-Tour ism-Report-2017-1.pdf> (Accessed 4 May 2019).

Food Vision 2030. Available at: <https://www.gov.ie/en/publication/c73a3-food-vision-2030-a-world-leader-in-sustainable-food-systems/> (Accessed 1 February 2022).

Fountain, Joanna, Fish, Nicola and Charters, Steve, 'Making a connection: Tasting rooms and brand loyalty', *International Journal of Wine Business Research*, 20 (1), 2008, pp. 8–21.

France 24, 'Cognac Liquor of the gods'. Available at: <https://www.france24.com/ en/20150227-you-are-here-cognac-liquor-of-the-gods-france-gastronomy-charentes> (Accessed 12 December 2020).

Gonzalez, Rosa, 'The unappeasable Hunger for Land in John B Keane's *The Field*', *Revista Alicantina de Estudios Ingleses*, 5, 1992, pp.83–90.

Grantham, Bill, 'Craic in a box: Commodifying and exporting the Irish Pub', *Journal of Media and Cultural Studies*, 23 (2), 2009, pp. 257–267.

Guidera, Anita, 'No smoking Ireland makes history with cigarette ban', *Independent.
ie*, 17 January 2014. Available at: <https://www.independent.ie/lifestyle/no-
smoking-ireland-makes-history-with-cigarette-ban-29926186.html> (Accessed
12 March 2019).

Han, Min C., and Terpstra, Vern, 'Country of origin effects from uni-national and
bi-national products', *Journal of International Business Studies*,19 (2), 1987, pp.
235–255.

Hancock, Ciaran, 'Diageo names Leixlip as site of new Guinness Brewery', *Irish
Times*, 11 September 2008 [online]. Available at: <https://www.irishti
mes.com/news/diageo-names-leixlip-as-site-of-new-guinness-brewery->
(Accessed 8 December 2020).

Havelin, David, 'The curse of accessibility', *Liquid Irish.com* [online] Available
at: <http://www.liquidirish.com/2015/03/the-curse-of-accessibilty.html>
(Accessed 2 April 2015).

Hennessy, Niamh, 'Beamish acquisition boosts sales for Heineken Ireland', *The Irish
Examiner*, 27 August 2009 [online]. Available at: <https://www.irishexami
ner.com/business/arid-20099528.html> (Accessed 7 December 2015).

Hobsbawm, Eric, 'Introduction: The invention of tradition', in *The
Invention of Tradition*, edited by Eric Hobsbawm and Terence Ranger
(Cambridge: Cambridge University Press, 1983).

Holohan, Renagh, *The Irish Chateaux: In Search of the Wild Geese* (Dublin: Lilliput
Press, 1989).

Hotel and Restaurant Times, 'Irish Distillers celebrates major Jameson global sales
milestone' [online] 2015. Available at: <http://hotelandrestauranttimes.ie/
irish-distillers-celebrates-5m-cases-jameson-milestone-opens-new-microdistill
ery-midleton/> (Accessed 11 January 2016).

<http://o-www.irishtimes.com.millennium.it-tallaght.ie/newspaper/finance/
.html> (Accessed 25 June 2021).

Hu, Xiaoling, Leeva, Li, Xie Charlene and Zhou Jun, 'The effects of country of origin
on Chinese consumers' wine purchasing behaviour', *Journal of Technology
Management in China*, 3 (3), 2008, pp. 292–306.

Inglis, Tom, *Global Ireland* (New York: Routledge, 2008).

Iqbal, Nosheen, 'Jamie Oliver gave us our big break in the kitchen – And he's still our
hero', *The Guardian* [online], 26 May 2019. Available at: <https://www.theg
uardian.com/food/2019/may/26/jamie-oliver-fifteen-gave-us-big-break-still-
our-hero> (Accessed 8 July 2021).

Irish Whiskey Association, *Vision for Irish Whiskey: A Strategy to Underpin the
Sustainable Growth of the Sector in Ireland*, 2015. Available at: <http://
www.abfi.ie/Sectors/ABFI/ABFI.nsf/vPagesSpirits/Home/$File/Vis
ion+for+Irish+Whiskey+May+2015.pdf> (Accessed 2 December 2015).

Jaffe, Eugene and Lampert, Schlomo, 'A dynamic approach to country of origin of effect', *European Journal of Marketing*, 32 (1/2), 1998, pp. 61–78.

Jaroff, Leon, 'Days of wine and Muzak', *Time Magazine* [online], V 150, 22 (1997) Available at: <https://content.time.com/time/subscriber/article/0,33009,987 433,00.html> (Accessed 19 May 2022).

JOFIS, Volume 6, special issue on Beverage Studies. Available at: <https://arrow. tudublin.ie/jofis/> (Accessed 10 October 2020).

Johansson, Johnny K., 'Determinants and effects of the use of made in labels', *International Marketing Review*, 6 (1), 1988, pp. 47–58.

Johnson, Ben, 'English Coffee Houses, Penny Universities', Historic UK, Available at: <https://www.historic-uk.com/CultureUK/English-Coffeehouses-Penny-Universities/> (Accessed 15 August 2021).

Johnson, Hugh and Jancis Robinson, *The World Atlas of Wine*, 8th edn (London: Octopus Publishing, 2019).

Jones, Andrew, and Ian Jenkins, 'A taste of Wales-Blas Ar Gymru: Institutional malaise in promoting Welsh food tourism products', in *Tourism and Gastronomy*, edited by A. Hjalager and G. Richards (Oxon: Routledge, 2002), pp. 129–145.

Kane, Conor, 'Waterford residents unite to save local pub'. *RTÉ News* [online], 9 September 2021. Available at: <https://www.rte.ie/news/regional/2021/ 0909/1245616-waterford-pub/> (Accessed 9 September 2021).

Kearns, Kevin, *Dublin Pub Life and Lore: An Oral History* (Dublin: Gill Books, 1996).

Keena, Colm, 'Shortage of staff closes successful Dublin restaurant', *The Irish Times*, 23 March 2000 [online]. Available at: <https://www.irishtimes.com/business/ shortage-of-staff-closes-successful-dublin-restaurant-1.258830> (Accessed 15 March 2022).

Kellaghan, Tara, '"Brew as much as possible during the proper season": Beer consumption in Elite households in eighteenth-century Ireland', in *'Tickling the Palate': Gastronomy in Irish Literature and Culture* (Oxford: Peter Lang, 2014), pp. 177–190.

Kelleher, Terry, Maurice Craig, and Bernard Share, *The Essential Guide to Dublin* (Dublin: Gill and Macmillan Limited, 1972).

Kennedy, Máire, 'Dublin Coffee Houses'. *Ask About Ireland*, 2011. Available at: <http://www.askaboutireland.ie/reading-room/history-heritage/pages-in-history/dublin-coffee-houses/> (Accessed 25 August 2021).

Kilcoyne, Clodagh, 'With free beers Trump brothers thank devoted Irish village'. Reuters.com, 2019, Available at: <https://www.reuters.com/news/picture/ with-free-beers-trump-brothers-thank-dev-idUSKCN1T62X2> (Accessed 5 June 2019).

King, Chloe, 'The rise of Irish food: A world class cuisine getting the recognition it deserves'. Great British Chefs.com [online], 10 November 2021. Available at: <https://www.greatbritishchefs.com/features/rise-of-modern-irish-food> (Accessed 25 April 2022).

Laganda, Gernot, '2021 is going to be a bad year for world hunger'. United Nations News. Available at: <https://www.un.org/en/food-systems-summit/news/2021-going-be-bad-year-world-hunger> (Accessed 6 September 2021).

Ledsom, Alex, 'Everything you need to know about Beaujolais Nouveau Day', *Forbes* [online], 21 November 2019. Available at: <https://www.forbes.com/sites/alexledsom/2019/11/21/everything-you-need-to-know-about-beaujolais-nouveau-day/?sh=2eb0afc724fe> (Accessed 15 September 2021).

Lewis, Ross, *CountryWide*. RTÉ Radio interview [online] 2012. Available at: <http://www.rte.ie/radio1/podcast/podcast_countrywide.xml> (Accessed 4 October 2012).

Liu, Fang and Murphy, Jamie, 'A qualitative study of Chinese wine consumption and purchasing, implications for Australian wines', *International Journal of Wine Business Research*, 19 (2), 2007, pp. 98–113.

Mac Con Iomaire, Máirtín, 'Coffee culture in Dublin: A brief history', *M/C Journal - A Journal of Media and Culture*, 15 (2). Available at: <http://journal.media-culture.org.au/index.php/mcjournal/article/viewArticle/456> (Accessed 23 May 2020).

Mac Con Iomaire, Máirtín, *The Emergence, Development and Influence of French Haute Cuisine on Public Dining in Dublin Restaurants 1900–2000: An Oral History* (PhD thesis. Dublin Institute of Technology, 2009).

Malcolm, Elisabeth, 'The rise of the Irish pub: A study in the disciplining of popular culture', in *Irish Popular Culture 1650–1850*, edited by James S. Donnelly and Kerby A. Miller (Dublin: Irish Academic Press, 1998), pp. 50–75.

Manske, Melissa and Cordua, Glenn, 'Understanding the sommelier effect', *International Journal of Contemporary Hospitality Management*,17 (7), 2005,, pp. 569–576.

Martin, Kevin, *Have You No Homes to Go To* (Cork: The Collins Press, 2016).

McCauley, James, 'The death of the Irish rural publican'. Available at: <https://www.rte.ie/brainstorm/2019/0418/1043366-the-death-of-the-irish-rural-publican/> (Accessed 16 October 2020).

McCauley, James, 'What's next for the Irish Pub', *RTE Brainstorm* [online]. Available at: <https://www.rte.ie/brainstorm/2020/0507/1136959-pubs-ireland-future-coronavirus/> (Accessed 17 October 2020).

McCauley, James, 'What's next for the Irish pub?' Available at: <https://www.rte.ie/brainstorm/2020/0507/1136959-pubs-ireland-future-coronavirus/> (Accessed 17 October 2020).

McConnell, Tara, 'Claret: The preferred libation of Georgian Ireland's élite'. Available at: <https://arrow.tudublin.ie/dgs/2012/june612/3/> (Accessed 6 September 2020).

McConnell, Tara, 'The social meaning of Claret in eighteenth century Ireland', in *The Irish Community in Bordeaux in the Eighteenth Century: Contributions and Contexts*, edited by Charles C. Luddington (New Haven, CT: Yale University Press, 2022).

McCullum, Kenya, 'Prison culinary training programs change lives and provide a second chance.' We are Chefs.com. Available at: <https://wearechefs.com/a-recipe-for-success-prison-culinary-training-programs-change-lives-and-prov ide-a-second-chance/> (Accessed 23 August 2021).

McGovern, Mark, 'The cracked pint glass of the servant: The Irish pub, Irish identity and the tourist eye', in *Irish Tourism: Image, Culture and Identity*, edited by Michael Cronin and Barbera O' Connor (Clevedon: Channel View Publications, 2003), pp. 83–103.

McGovern, Mark, 'The craic market: Irish theme bars and the commodification of Irishness in contemporary Britain', *Irish Journal of Sociology*, 1 (2), 2002, pp. 77–78.

McGuinness, Katy and Whelan, Pat, *The Irish Beef Book* (Dublin: Gill and McMillan, 2013).

McKenna, Gemma, 'Oxford triumphs in University wine championships'. *Harpers Wine and Spirits Trade Review*, 30 January 2012 [online]. Available at: <http://www.harpers.co.uk/news/news-headlines/11650-oxford-triumphs-in-univers ity-wine-championship.html> (Accessed 2 May 2012).

Medcalf, Patricia, *Advertising the Black Stuff in Ireland 1959–1999: Increments of Change* (Oxford: Peter Lang, 2020).

Medcalf, Patricia, 'Calling time on alcohol advertising in Ireland', in *Margins and Marginalities in Ireland and France: A Socio-Cultural Perspective*, edited by Catherine Maignant, SylainTondeur and Déborah Vandewoude (Oxford: Peter Lang, 2020), pp. 199–216.

Medcalf, Patricia, 'Guinness and food: Ingredients in an unlikely gastronomic revolution'. Food and Revolution. Dublin Gastronomy Symposium, Dublin, 1st June. Arrow@DIT. Available at: <https://arrow.dit.ie/cgi/viewcontent. cgi?article=1084&context=dgs> (Accessed 22 October 2020).

Medcalf, Patricia, 'Irish cultural heritage through the prism of Guinness's ads in the 1980s', in *Patrimoine/Cultural Heritage in France and Ireland*, edited by Eamon Maher and Eugene O'Brien (Oxford: Peter Lang, 2018), pp. 143–161.

Medcalf, Patricia, 'In search of identity: An exploration of the relationship between Guinness's advertising and Ireland's social and economic evolution between 1959 and 1969', *Irish Communication Review*, 15 (1), p. 3. Available at: <https://

arrow.dit.ie/cgi/viewcontent.cgi?article=1143&context=icr> (Accessed 17 September 2020).

Mehta, Glenn, *Infinite Ripple: The Social Media Revolution* (United Kingdom: Xlibris Publishing, 2013).

Mitenbuler, Reid, 'Pass the Courvoisier: The decades-long love affair between French cognac producers and African-American consumers'. Available at: <http://www.slate.com/articles/life/drink/2013/12/cognac_in_african_american_culture_the_long_history_of_black_consumption.single.html?print> (Accessed 3 April 2015).

Molloy, Cian, *The Story of the Irish Pub* (Dublin: Liffey Press, 2002).

Monaghan, Gabrielle, 'McKillen retreats to crystal palace', *The Sunday Times*, 12 January 2014, p. 3.

Morris, Jonathan, *Coffee a Global History* (London: Reaktion Books Ltd, 2019).

Morris, Kieran, 'What Noma did next: How the 'New Nordic' is reshaping the food world'. *The Guardian* [online], 28 February 2020. Available at: <https://www.theguardian.com/food/2020/feb/28/what-noma-did-next-new-nordic-food-rene-redzepi-claus-meyer-locavore-foraging> (Accessed 4 August 2021).

Morris, Serren, 'Mr Beast Burger locations—Where to get the dream burger', Newsweek.com. 27 April 2021. Available at: <https://www.newsweek.com/mrbeast-burger-locationswhere-get-dream-burger-1586667> (Accessed 8 August 2021).

Muir, Rick, *Pubs and Places: The Social Value of the Community Pub* (Dublin: Institute of Public Policy Research, 2012).

Mulcahy, Orna, 'Roll out the Barrels', *The Irish Times Magazine*, 18 April 2015, p. 33.

Mulryan, Peter, *The Whiskeys of Ireland* (Dublin: The O'Brien Press, 2002).

Munoz, Caroline and Wood, Natalie, 'No rules, just right, or is it? The role of themed restaurants as cultural ambassadors', *Tourism and Hospitality Research*, 7 (3–4), (June–September, 2007), pp. 242–245.

Murphy, Brian, 'Advertising gastronomic identity in an epicurean world: The case for Irish single pot still whiskey', *Irish Communication Review*, 15 (1), Article 7, 2016. Available at: <http://arrow.dit.ie/icr/vol15/iss1/7> (Accessed 18 September 2020).

Murphy, Brian, 'Appellation "Éire" Contrôlée - Heritage links between France's wine heritage and Ireland', in *Franco-Irish Connections in Space and Time: Peregrinations and Ruminations*, edited by Eamon Maher and Catherine Maignant (Oxford: Peter Lang, 2012), pp. 117–132.

Murphy, Brian, *Changing Identities in a Homogenised World: The Role of Place and Story in Modern Perceptions of French Wine Culture* (PhD thesis, 2013). Institute of Technology Tallaght, Dublin, Ireland.

Murphy, Brian, 'Cognac, Scotch and Irish: Lessons in gastronomic identity', in *Voyages between France and Ireland: Culture, Tourism and Sport*, edited by Frank Healy and Brigitte Bastiat (Oxford: Peter Lang, 2017), pp. 237–255.

Murphy, Brian, 'Communicating new definitions of terroir to a millennial audience through the medium of fourth space', in *Kulinarischer Tourismus und Weintourismus*, edited by Daniella Wagner, Michael Mair, Albert Franz Stockl and Axel Dreyer (Wiesbaden: Springer Gabler, 2017), pp. 85–92.

Murphy, Brian, 'The Irish pub Abroad: Lessons in the commodification of gastronomic culture', in *'Tickling the Palate': Gastronomy in Irish Literature and Culture*, edited by Máirtín Mac Con Iomaire and Eamon Maher (Oxford: Peter Lang, 2014), pp. 191–205.

Murphy, Brian, 'The rise of whiskey tourism in Ireland: Developing a terroir engagement template', in a special edition in the *Journal of Gastronomy and Tourism*, 3 (2), 2018, pp. 107–123. Available at: <https://www.cognizantcommunicat ion.com/journal-titles/journal-of-gastronomy-and-tourism> (Accessed 23 September 2020).

Murphy, Brian, 'The role of revolution and rioting in French Wine's relationship with place', in *France, Ireland and Rebellion*, edited by Yann Bévant, Anne Goarzin and Grace Neville (Rennes: Tir, 2011), pp. 149–167.

Murphy, Brian, 'Thinking beyond the Bottle: Traditional French wine versus new media', in *New Critical Perspectives on Franco-Irish Relations*, edited by Anne Goarzin (Oxford: Peter Lang, 2015), pp. 159–180.

Murphy, Brian, 'Using a 17th century Benedictine monk to convert myth into history in an effort to sell more fizz', in *Histoire et Mémoire en France et en Irlande/History and Memory in France and Ireland*, edited by Sylvie Mikowski (Reims: Épure, 2011), pp. 291–308.

Murphy, Brian, 'A Wine Goose Chase reviewed', *Canadian Journal of Irish Studies* 41, 2018, pp. 292–294. Available at: <https://www.jstor.org/stable/e26435 216> (Accessed 23 September 2020).

Murphy, Brian, 'Wine and music: An emerging cultural relationship', in *France and Ireland: Notes and Narratives*, edited by Una Hunt and Mary Pierce (Oxford: Peter Lang, 2015), pp. 143–158.

Murphy, James, *Principles and Practices of Bar and Beverage Management* (Oxford: Goodfellow Publisher, 2013).

Murphy, James, *Principles and Practices of Bar and Beverage Management: The Drinks Handbook* (Oxford: Goodfellow Publisher, 2013).

Murphy, James, 'Shaken not stirred – The evolution of the Cocktail Shaker'. Available at: <https://arrow.tudublin.ie/dgs/2012/june612/4/> (Accessed 6 September 2020).

Murphy, Ted, *A Kingdom of Wine: A Celebration of Ireland's Winegeese* (Cork: Onstream Publications, 2005).

Nagashima, Akira, 'A comparison of Japanese and U.S. attitudes towards foreign products', *Journal of Marketing*, 34, 1970, pp. 68–74.

Neville, Grace, 'The commodification of Irish culture in France and beyond', in *France and the Struggle against Globalization: Bilingual Essays on the Role of France in the World*, edited by Eamon Maher and Eugene O Brien (Lewiston: Edwin Mellen Press, 2007), pp. 143–156.

North, Adrian, 'The effect of background music on the taste of wine', *British Journal of Psychology*, 103, 2012, pp. 293–301.

Nossiter, Jonathan, *Liquid Memory* (Canada: D&M Publishers Inc., 2009).

O Riordan, Sean, 'Last orders: Almost 350 pubs have closed since the start of the Covid 19 pandemic', The Irish Examiner [online], 17 October 2021. Available at: <https://www.irishexaminer.com/news/arid-40723155.html> (Accessed 4 November 2021).

O' Connor, Fionnán, *A Glass Apart: Irish Single Pot Still Whiskey* (Melbourne: The Images Publishing Group, 2015).

O' Halloran, Marie, 'Towns and villages to get €2.8m for "cycle cafes" and outdoor cinemas', *The Irish Times*, 3 August 2020. Available at: <https://www.irishtimes.com/news/politics/towns-and-villages-to-get-2-8m-for-cycle-cafes-and-outdoor-cinemas-1.4320134> (Accessed 21 August 2020).

O'Boyle, Neil, *New Vocabulary Old Ideas: Culture, Irishness and the Advertising Industry* (Oxford: Peter Lang, 2011).

O'Brien, Eugene, *'Kicking Bishop Brennan Up the Arse': Negotiating Text and Contexts in Contemporary Irish Studies* (Oxford: Peter Lang, 2009).

O'Connor Barbara, 'Myths and mirrors: Tourist images and national identity', in *Tourism In Ireland: A Critical Analysis*, Barbara O Connor and Michael Cronin (Cork: Cork University Press, 1993), pp. 68–85.

Ogg, Erica, 'What food goes well with my Syrah, ask your wine bottle'(2012). Available at: <http://gigaom.com/2012/07/02/what-food-goes-well-with-syrah-ask-your-wine-bottle/> (Accessed 12 March 2013).

Overton, John, and Heitger, Jo, 'Maps, markets and merlot: The making of an antipodean wine appellation', *Journal of Rural Studies*, 24 (4), 2008, pp. 440–449.

Parameswaran Ravi, and Pisharodi, Rammohan, 'Facets of country of origin image: An empirical assessment', *Journal of Advertising*, 23 (1), 1994, pp. 43–56.

Parkhurst-Ferguson, Pricilla, 'A cultural field in the making: Gastronomy in 19th century France', in *French Food on the Table, on the Page and in French Culture*, edited by Lawrence Schehr and Alan Weiss (New York: Routledge, 2001).

Paskin, Becky, 'The top ten scotch whiskey brands'. *The Drinks Business* [online]. Available at: <http://www.thedrinksbusiness.com/2013/09/the-top-10-scotch-whisky-brands/> (Accessed 4 May 2015).

Passariello, Christina, and Colchester, Mac, 'Jameson Pours Out Tall Tale to Lure Younger Drinkers, Whiskey Uses Shot of Invention to Stress Its Irish Roots', *The Wall Street Journal* [online] 17 February 2011. Available at: <http://www.wsj.com/articles/SB10001424052748703373404576148323588693058> (Accessed 12 December 2020).

Paul, Mark, citing Pat Whelan, 'Hooking up with Dunnes Stores helps butcher Pat Whelan raise the steaks', *The Irish Times* [online], 13 October 2017. Available at: <https://www.irishtimes.com/business/retail-and-services/hooking-up-with-dunnes-stores-helps-butcher-pat-whelan-raise-the-steaks-1.3252491> (Accessed 3 January 2018).

Peillon, Michel, 'Culture, and state in Ireland's new economy', in *Reinventing Ireland, Culture Society and the Global Economy*, edited by Peadar Kirby, Luke Gibbons and Michael Cronin (London: Pluto Press, 2002).

Pelet, Jean Eric and Lecat, Benoit, 'Can digital social networks enhance the online selling of Burgundy wine'. 6th Academy of Wine Business Research Conference at The Bordeaux Management School, France, 2011. [Online] Available at: <http://academyofwinebusiness.com/wp-content/uploads/2011/09/62-AWBR2011_Pelet_Lecat.pdf> (Accessed 24 November 2014).

Pendergrast, Mark, *Uncommon Grounds: The History of Coffee and How it Transformed our World* (New York: Basic Books, 2019).

Pickard, Christina, 'Judges treated to live music at wine competition', *Decanter* [online]. Available at: <http://www.decanter.com/news/wine-news/530467/judges-treated-to-live-music-at-wine-competition> (Accessed 14 January 2014).

Pincus, Steve, 'Coffee politicians does create: Coffeehouses and restoration political culture', *The Journal of Modern History*, 67, December 1995, pp. 807–834.

Pope, Conor, 'Bottle of Whiskey blessed for spirit of kindness expected to fetch €15000', *The Irish Times*, 29 March 2016, p. 3.

Quinn, Gary, 'Why Dingle Distillery's new single malt marks a turning point for Irish whiskey', *The Irish Times* [online], 18 December 2015. Available at: <http://www.irishtimes.com/life-and-style/food-and-drink/why-dingle-distillery-s-new-single-malt-marks-a-turning-point-for-irish-whiskey-1.2471404> (Accessed 11 January 2016).

Richards, Greg, 'Gastronomy: An essential ingredient in tourism production and consumption?' in *Tourism and Gastronomy*, edited by Anne-Mette Hjalager and Greg Richards (New York: Routledge, 2002).

Richter, Felix, 'Starbucks at 50: A Sprawling Coffee Empire', Statista.com 20 March 2021. Available at: <https://www.statista.com/chart/24546/starbucks-stores-worldwide/> (Accessed 10 August 2021).

Ridley, Neil and Gavin Smith, *Let Me Tell You About Whiskey* (London: Pavillion Books, 2014).

Roach, T. J., 'Telling it like it is', Rock products, 115, 12, 2012, p. 3. *Academic Search Complete*, EBSCOhost [online]. Available at: <http://o-web.ebscohost.com. millennium.it-tallaght.ie/ehost/pdfviewer/pdfviewer?vid=4&sid=13282529-3d32-406a-9281-c4d59c186133%40sessionmgr114&hid=121> (Accessed 26 March 2013).

Robinson, Julia and Harding, Julia (eds), *The Oxford Companion to Wine* (Oxford: Oxford University Press, 2015).

Roseingrave, Louise, 'Beamish Cork site plan gets €150m go-ahead', *Irish Times,* 6 January 2012 [online]. Available at: <http://www.irishtimes.com/> (Accessed 10 January 2015).

Roth, Katharina P., and Diamantopoulos, Adamantious, 'Advancing the country image construct', *Journal of Business Research*, 62 (7), 2009, pp. 726-740.

Ryan, Kelley, 'Pennys' newest addition basically guarantees we're never going to want to leave'. Available at: <https://www.her.ie/food/penneys-newest-addit ion-basically-guarantees-never-going-want-leave-439546> (Accessed 20 October 2020).

Safire, William, *Lend Me Your Ears: Great Speeches in History* (New York: WW Norton & Co, 1997).

Scarborough, Gwen, *The Irish Pub as a 'Third Place': A Sociological Exploration of People, Place and Identity* (PhD Thesis, Institute of Technology Sligo, 2008).

Scotch Whisky and Tourism 2011 [online]. VisitScotland [online]. Available at: <www.scotch-whisky.org.uk/.../scotchwhiskyandtourismreport.pdf> (Accessed 10 February 2015).

Scruton, Roger, *I Drink Therefore I Am: A Philosopher's Guide to Wine* (London: Continuum International Publishing Group, 2009).

Segnit, Niki, *The Flavour Thesaurus* (London: Bloomsbury Press, 2010).

Share, Perry, 'A genuine "third place"? Towards an understanding of the pub in contemporary Irish society' (Sociological Association Ireland Conference, Cavan, 2003). Available at: <https://www.academia.edu/805791/A_genuine_third_ place_Towards_an_understanding_of_the_pub_in_contemporary_Irish_soci ety> (Accessed 2 January 2014).

Shaw, Lucy, 'Wineries who shun social media will experience "Digital Darwinism."' (2012). www.drinksbusiness.com. Available at: <http://www.thedrinksbusin ess.com/2012/06/wineries-who-shun-social-media-will-experience-digital-darwinism/> (Accessed 14 March 2013).

Sheehan, Fionnán, 'Under their influence: FF "gang" killed McDowell's cafe bar idea'. *Independent.ie*, 28 November 2005. Available at: <https://www.independ ent.ie/irish-news/under-their-influence-ff-gang-killed-mcdowells-cafe-bar-idea-25958987.html> (Accessed 31 January 2020).

Sheridan, Kathy, 'Frosty Fáilte', *The Irish Times*, 23 January 1999 [online]. Available at: <http://0-www.irishtimes.com.millennium.it-tallaght.ie/newspaper/week end/1999/0123/99012300184.html> (Accessed 29 June 2012).

Sheridan, Kathy, 'Is smugness going to do for us in the end?', *The Irish Times*, 23 January 1999 [online]. Available at: <http://0-www.irishtimes.com.millenn ium.it-tallaght.ie/newspaper/weekend> (Accessed 29 June 2012).

Sheridan, Kathy, 'It's all smiles as "Ireland of the welcomes" reopens for business', *The Irish Times*, 30 March 2000 [online]. Available at : <https://www.irishti mes.com/opinion/is-smugness-going-to-do-for-us-in-the-end-1.261345> (Accessed 15 December 2021).

Shreeves, Robin, citing John Charles Boisset of the JCB Collection, 'QR codes and NFC chips—The future of wine marketing', Advisor Wine Industry Network, 27 August 2021. Available at: <https://wineindustryadvisor.com/2021/08/27/ qr-nfc-wine-marketing> (Accessed 29 September 2021).

Smith, Clark, *Post Modern Wine Making* (California: University of California Press, 2014).

Smullen, Jean, 'Wine Diary' 2011 [online]. Available at: <http://www.jean smullen.com/index.php?option=com_eventlist&Itemid=27&func=deta ils&did=645> (Accessed 18 April 2012).

Spence, Charles, Liana Richards, Emma Kjellin, Anna-Maria Huhnt, Victoria Daskal, Alexandra Scheybeler, Carlos Velasco, and Ophelia Deroy, 'Looking for crossmodal correspondences between classical music and fine wine', *Flavour*, 2, 2013, 29 [online]. Available at: <http://www.flavourjournal.com/ content/2/1/29> (Accessed 2 May 2014).

Spence, Charles, Mayu U. Shankar, and Heston Blumenthal, '"Sound bites": Auditory contributions to the perception and consumption of food and drink', in *Art and the Senses*, edited by Francesca Bacci and David Melcher (New York: Oxford University Press, 2011), pp.207–238.

Standage, Tom, *A History of the World in Six Glasses* (New York: Walker Publishing Company Inc., 2005).

Statista.com, 'Number of daily active Facebook users worldwide as of 2nd quarter 2021'. Available at: <https://www.statista.com/statistics/346167/facebook-glo bal-dau/> (Accessed 10 October 2021).

Szolnoki, Gergely, Dimitri Taits, Carsten Hoffmann, Ruth Ludwig, Liz Thach, Rebecca Dolan, Steve Goodman, Cullen Habel, Sharon Forbes, Nicola Marinelli, Damien Wilson, Antonio Mantonakis, Philip Zwanda, Zoltan

Szabo, Ildiko Csak, Caroline Ritchie, Su Birch and Siobhan Thompson, 'A cross-cultural comparison of social media usage in the wine business', 8th Academy of Wine Business Research Conference at Hochschule Geisenheim University, Germany 2014. [online] Available at: <http://academyofwineb usiness.com/wp-content/uploads/2013/04/Szolnoki-Taits-Nagel-Fortunato. pdf> (Accessed 24 November 2014).

Taylor, Charlie, 'Last orders: Number of pubs in the republic continues to drop', The Irish Times.com, 22 August 2018. Available at:<https://www.irishtimes.com/ business/agribusiness-and-food/last-orders-number-of-pubs-in-the-republic-continues-to-drop-1.3603452> (Accessed 19 January 2019).

The Irish Wine Association, *The Irish Wine Market 2011*, [online]. Available at: <http://www.abfi.ie/Sectors/ABFI/ABFI.nsf/vPages/Sector_Associati on_-_Irish_Wine_Association~industry-profile/$file/ABFI_Wine%20Fa cts%20Brochure-WEB%202011.pd>f (Accessed 15 September 2012).

Thomas, Cónal, 'The Real Veal: Here's how to tell if your meat is Irish or not'. *The Journal* [online]. Available at: <https://www.thejournal.ie/the-real-veal-heres-how-to-tell-if-your-meat-is-irish-or-not-4477943-Feb2019/> (Accessed 12 September 2021).

Thurnell-Read, Thomas, 'Open arms: The role of pubs in tackling loneliness', Loughborough University. Available at: <https://hdl.handle.net/2134/13663 715.v1> (Accessed 28 August 2021).

Tondeur, Sylvain, 'The Irish whiskey renaissance: A revolution of sorts?' Available at: <https://arrow.tudublin.ie/dgs/2016/June1/7/> (Accessed 6 October 2020).

Tondeur, Sylvain, 'A new phenomenon: Whiskey tourism in Ireland', in *Voyages be-tween France and Ireland: Culture, Tourism and Sport*, edited by Frank Healy and Brigitte Bastiat (Oxford: Peter Lang, 2017), pp. 257–274.

Trubek, Amy, *The Taste of Place: A Cultural Journey into Terroir* (Oakland: University of California Press, 2008).

TU Dublin Impact, 'The mindful kitchen: Creativity and social gastronomy'. Available at: <https://tudublinimpact.wordpress.com/2021/05/13/the-mind ful-kitchen-creativity-and-social-gastronomy/> (Accessed 23 August 2021).

Twitchell, James, 'An English teacher looks at branding', *Journal of Consumer Research*, Vol 31 (2) 2004, pp. 484–489.

United Nations World Tourism Organisation AM Report Vol. 4 'Global Report on Food Tourism'. Available at: <https://www.unwto.org/archive/global/ publication/unwto-am-report-vol-4-global-report-food-tourism> (Accessed 2 February 2015).

Varriano, John, *Wine: A Cultural History* (London: Reaktion Books Ltd, 2010).

Velthius, Sandra, *The Social Value of CLG Na Fianna*. Whitebarn Consulting, 2019. Available at: <http://clgnafianna.com/wp-content/uploads/2019/05/Na_ Fianna_Social_Value_Report_Final_1May2019.pdf> (Accessed 20 May 2022).

Whisky Tourism – Facts and Insights March 2015. VisitScotland [online]. Available at: <www.visitscotland.org/.../ Whisky%20Tourism%20%20Facts%20and%20 Insights2.pdf> (Accessed 10 February 2015).

Werner, Laurie, 'How a Noma chef is trying to change school lunches', Forbes [online] 28 April 2018. Available at: <https://www.forbes.com/sites/lauri ewerner/2018/04/28/how-a-noma-chef-is-trying-to-change-school-lunches/ ?sh=238983891543> (Accessed 16 April 2021).

Whelan, Pat, *An Irish Butcher Shop* (Cork: The Collins Press, 2010).

Whelehan, T. P., *The Irish Wines of Bordeaux* (Dublin: The Vine Press, 1990).

Wholley, Jennifer, 'Nike sorry over "Black and Tan" Shoe', *The Irish Times* [online],16 March 2012. Available at: <https://www.irishtimes.com/news/nike-sorry-over-black-and-tan-shoe-1.704563> (Accessed 18 March 2020).

Willett, Walter, Johan Rockström, Brent Loken, Marco Springmann, Tim Lang, Sonja Vermeulen, Tara Garnett, David Tilman, Fabrice DeClerck, Amanda Wood, Malin Jonell, Michael Clark, Line J. Gordon, Jessica Fanzo, Corinna Hawkes, Rami Zurayk, Juan A. Rivera, Wim De Vries, Lindiwe Majele Sibanda, Ashkan Afshin, Abhishek Chaudhary, Mario Herrero, Rina Agustina, Francesco Branca, Anna Lartey, Shenggen Fan, Beatrice Crona, Elizabeth Fox, Victoria Bignet, Max Troell, Therese Lindahl, Sudhvir Singh, Sarah E. Cornell, K. Srinath Reddy, Sunita Narain, Sania Nishtar, and Christopher J. L. Murray, 'Food in the anthropocene: the EAT–Lancet Commission on healthy diets from sustainable food systems', *The Lancet*, 393 (10170), 2019, pp. 447–492. Available at: <https://www.sciencedirect.com/science/article/pii/S01406 73618317884> (Accessed 23 February 2022).

Wilson, Bee, *Consider the Fork: A History of how we Cook and Eat* (London: Penguin Group, 2013).

'Wine – The Faith', *Wine*, Episode 2. BBC 4 Television, 23 February 2009.

Woods, Killian, 'Take a guided tour of... the billion-dollar tech firm with an Irish pub in its office'. Available at: <https://www.thejournal.ie/office-tour-qualtr ics-dublin-3-3447734-Jun2017/> (Accessed 18 May 2020).

Woods, Killian, 'Why this Tipperary butcher sold his five-decade-old family business to Dunnes', *The Journal.ie*. Available at: <http://www.thejournal.ie/ james-whelan-butchers-dunnes-stores-2-3713094-Nov2017/> (Accessed 20 December 2017).

Websites

A Wine Goose Chase. Available at: <http://awinegoosechase.com/> (Accessed 18 January 2014).

Bureau National Interprofessionnel du Cognac. Available at: <http://www.bnic.fr/cognac/_en/4_pro/index.aspx?page=missions> (Accessed 1 April 2015).

Chapter One Restaurant. Available at: <https://chapteronerestaurant.com/dining/#Chefs_Table> (Accessed 26 August 2021).

Chateau La Coste. Available at: <https://chateau-la-coste.com/en/art-architecture/art-and-architecture-walk.html> (Accessed 4 October 2021).

Department of Agriculture, Food and the Marine. Irish Whiskey Technical File. Available at: <https://www.agriculture.gov.ie/.../IrishWhiskeytechnicalfile141114.pdf> (Accessed 4 December 2015).

Drinks Ireland. Available at: <https://www.drinksireland.ie/> (Accessed 19 May 2019).

Dublin Gastronomy Symposium, Technological University Dublin Institutional Repository. Available at: <https://arrow.tudublin.ie/dgs/> (Accessed 10 October 2020).

EU Geographical Indications Register. Available at: <https://ec.europa.eu/info/food-farming-fisheries/food-safety-and-quality/certification/quality-labels/geographical-indications-register/> (Accessed 12 December 2021).

Gastromotiva. Available at: <https://gastromotiva.org/en/gastromotiva/> (Accessed 12 July 2021).

Inter-Rhone. Available at: <https://www.vins-rhone.com/en/inter-rhone/presentation> (Accessed 20 September 2020).

Irish Communications Review. Available at: <https://arrow.tudublin.ie/icr/vol15/iss1/7/> (Accessed 18 September 2020).

Irish Food and Drink. Available at: <https://www.irishfoodanddrink.com/about-us/> (Accessed 1 September 2021).

Irish Whiskey Association, Drinks Ireland. Available at: <https://www.ibec.ie/drinksireland/irish-whiskey/our-industry/economic-contribution> (Accessed 18 September 2021).

James Whelan Butchers. Available at: <http://www.jameswhelanbutchers.com/info/butchery-demonstrations/> (Accessed 8 February 2018).

Johnny Walker, 'The man who walked around the world' Advert (2009). Available at: <https://www.youtube.com/watch?v=fZ6aiVg2qVk> (Accessed 20 November 2021).

La Cité du Vin. Available at: <https://www.laciteduvin.com/en> (Accessed 4 October 2021).

Living Labels. Available at: <https://www.livingwinelabels.com/> (Accessed 4 October 2021).

Moore's of Grangecon. Available at: <https://www.mooresofgrangecon.com/> (Accessed 28 May 2019).

Mysubwaycareer. Available at: <https://jobs.mysubwaycareer.eu/careers/sandwich-artist.htm> (Accessed 20 September 2021).

Oxford Dictionary.com (n.d.). Available at: <https://en.oxforddictionaries.com/definition/digital_native> (Accessed 20 August 2019).

Postmodern Winemaking. Available at: <http://postmodernwinemaking.com/wine-and-music> (Accessed 6 May 2020).

Pub is the Hub. Available at: <https://www.pubisthehub.org.uk/about/> (Accessed 1 September 2021).

RTÉ – The Seán O Rourke Show. Available at: <http://www.rte.ie/radio1/today-with-sean-o-rourke/programmes/2014/0416/609206-today-with-sean-o-rourke-wednesday-16-april-2014/?clipid=1535470> (Accessed 17 April 2014).

RTÉ. Intermezzo. Available at: <http://www.rte.ie/radio1/podcast/podcast_the-lyric-concert.xml> (Accessed 4 February 2014).

Social Gastronomy Movement Map. Available at: <https://www.socialgastronomy.org/about-us#sg> (Accessed 12 August 2021).

Spirit of Speyside. Available at: <http://www.spiritofspeyside.com/best_new_event> (Accessed 1 May 2015).

Storymap. Available at: <https://www.youtube.com/user/StorymapDublin/featured> (Accessed 14 June 2019).

The Lonely Planet. Available at: <https://www.lonelyplanet.com/ireland/things-to-do/ireland-s-top-pubs> (Accessed 12 March 2019).

The Plunkett Foundation. Available at: <https://plunkett.co.uk/who-we-are/ https://plunkett.co.uk/who-we-are/> (Accessed 1 September 2021).

Tullamore Dew. 'The Parting Glass' Advert (2013) Available at: <https://www.youtube.com/watch?v=RL9yB0ne67A> (Accessed 2 December 2021).

Undiscovered Scotland. Available at: <http://www.undiscoveredscotland.co.uk/islay/laphroaigdistillery/> (Accessed 17 June 2013).

Visit Denmark. Available at: <https://www.visitdenmark.com/denmark/things-do/danish-food/restaurant-noma> (Accessed 4 August 2021).

Wine Anorak. Available at: <http://www.wineanorak.com/clark_smith.html> (Accessed 12 May 2014).

World Central Kitchen. Available at: <https://wck.org/mission> (Accessed 20 July 2021).

WSET Global. Available at: <https://www.wsetglobal.com/> (Accessed 20 September 2021).

Earlier iterations of some of the chapters in this work have appeared in the following publications:

Reimagining Irish Studies for the 21st Century edited by Eamon Maher and Eugene O'Brien (Oxford: Peter Lang, 2021).

Margins and Marginality edited by Catherine Maignant, Sylvain Tondeur and Deborah Vandewoude (Oxford: Peter Lang, 2021).

Patrimoine/Cultural Heritage in France and Ireland edited by Eamon Maher and Eugene O' Brien (Oxford: Peter Lang, 2019).

The Journal of Gastronomy and Tourism Volume 3, No.2 edited by Anne-Mette Hjalager (Cognizant Communication Corporation, New York, 2018).

Voyages between France and Ireland: Culture, Tourism and Sport edited by Frank Healy and Brigitte Bastiat (Oxford: Peter Lang, 2017).

Irish Communication Review: Vol. 15: Iss. 1, Article 7, 2016 [Online] Doi:10.21427/ D7F59C.

Notes and Narratives, edited by Una Hunt and Mary Pierce (Oxford: Peter Lang, 2015).

New Critical Perspectives on Franco-Irish Relations edited by Anne Goarzin (Oxford: Peter Lang, 2015).

A Socio-cultural Critique of the Celtic Tiger: Picking up the Pieces, edited by Eamon Maher and Eugene O' Brien (Manchester: Manchester University Press, 2014).

France and Ireland in the Public Imagination, edited by Benjamin Keating and Mary Pierce (Oxford: Peter Lang, 2014).

Index

Reimagining Ireland

Series Editor: Dr Eamon Maher, Technological
University Dublin

The concepts of Ireland and 'Irishness' are in constant flux in the wake of an ever-increasing reappraisal of the notion of cultural and national specificity in a world assailed from all angles by the forces of globalisation and uniformity. Reimagining Ireland interrogates Ireland's past and present and suggests possibilities for the future by looking at Ireland's literature, culture and history and subjecting them to the most up-to-date critical appraisals associated with sociology, literary theory, historiography, political science and theology.

Some of the pertinent issues include, but are not confined to, Irish writing in English and Irish, Nationalism, Unionism, the Northern 'Troubles', the Peace Process, economic development in Ireland, the impact and decline of the Celtic Tiger, Irish spirituality, the rise and fall of organised religion, the visual arts, popular cultures, sport, Irish music and dance, emigration and the Irish diaspora, immigration and multiculturalism, marginalisation, globalisation, modernity/postmodernity and postcolonialism. The series publishes monographs, comparative studies, interdisciplinary projects, conference proceedings and edited books. Proposals should be sent either to Dr Eamon Maher at eamon.maher@ittdublin.ie or to ireland@peterlang.com.

Vol. 1   Eugene O'Brien: 'Kicking Bishop Brennan up the Arse': Negotiating
              Texts and Contexts in Contemporary Irish Studies
              ISBN 978-3-03911-539-6. 219 pages. 2009.

Vol. 2   James P.Byrne, Padraig Kirwan and Michael O'Sullivan
              (eds): Affecting Irishness: Negotiating Cultural Identity Within and
              Beyond the Nation
              ISBN 978-3-03911-830-4. 334 pages. 2009.

Vol. 3   Irene Lucchitti: The Islandman: The Hidden Life of Tomás O'Crohan
              ISBN 978-3-03911-837-3. 232 pages. 2009.

Vol. 4   Paddy Lyons and Alison O'Malley-Younger (eds): No Country for Old
              Men: Fresh Perspectives on Irish Literature
              ISBN 978-3-03911-841-0. 289 pages. 2009.

Printed by
CPI books GmbH, Leck